BUS. CTR
658.827
?

W9-BFE-798

Branding
Demystified

THE FARMINGTON LIBRARY
6 MONTEITH DRIVE
FARMINGTON CT 06032

Branding Demystified

Plans to Payoffs

Harsh V. Verma

DISCARD

THE FARMINGTON LIBRARY
6 MONTEITH DRIVE
FARMINGTON CT 06032

Response
Business books from SAGE
Los Angeles ▪ London ▪ New Delhi ▪ Singapore ▪ Washington DC
www.sagepublications.com

Copyright © Harsh V. Verma, 2010

All rights reserved. No part of this book may be reproduced or utilised in any form or by any means, electronic or mechanical, including photocopying, recording or by any information storage or retrieval system, without permission in writing from the publisher.

First published in 2010 by

Response Books
Business books from SAGE
B1/I-1 Mohan Cooperative Industrial Area
Mathura Road, New Delhi 110 044, India

SAGE Publications Inc
2455 Teller Road
Thousand Oaks, California 91320, USA

SAGE Publications Ltd
1 Oliver's Yard, 55 City Road
London EC1Y 1SP, United Kingdom

SAGE Publications Asia-Pacific Pte Ltd
33 Pekin Street
#02-01 Far East Square
Singapore 048763

Published by Vivek Mehra for SAGE Publications India Pvt Ltd, typeset in 11/13 Californian FB by Star Compugraphics Private Limited, Delhi and printed at Chaman Enterprises, New Delhi.

Library of Congress Cataloging-in-Publication Data

Verma, Harsh.
   Branding demystified: plans to payoffs/Harsh V. Verma.
      p. cm.
   Includes bibliographical references.
   1. Branding (Marketing)—Management. 2. Communication in marketing. I. Title.

HF5415.1255.V47   658.8'27—dc22   2010   2009049001

ISBN: 978-81-321-0234-2 (PB)

The SAGE Team: Reema Singhal, Anupam Choudhury and Trinankur Banerjee

*To my grandparents, who helped me learn
the meaning of the Earth and the Sky.*

Contents

List of Figures

Preface

Success is alluring. Success also leaves footprints that often deceive the followers who blindly and mechanically chase the big dream of being successful. The phenomenal valuations that some brands enjoy fuel the aspirations of many who only end up as nonentities. In one of the recent surveys Coke, Microsoft, IBM and GE were valued at 67, 57, 56 and 49 billon US dollars respectively. Such magnificent monetary value attached to a name, sign or symbol is motivation enough for managers across all kinds of businesses to embark upon the so called 'branding brand wagon'. But the very definition of 'brand' and the practices that emanate therefrom often lay at the heart of brand failures that are so common that branding is viewed with either scepticism or called a divine intervention that God offers to a select few.

Brands come with all kinds of physical signs and symbols. The most ubiquitous of all symbols is the product or service that lies at the centre of the brand. And then comes marketing tools like advertising, sales efforts, distribution and sales promotions. The physical perceptiveness associated with these tools of brand building can confuse brand builders and make them trapped in the periphery, pre-empting them to reach and address the fundamentals of the brand. The foundations on which solid brands are built never catch the sight, but the tangential aspects that surround these become the insights for many brand builders. This myopic understanding of brand and brand building process floods the market with tens of 'me too' brands with every single brand trying to make it to the league of successful brands.

Great branding is not simply confined to the glamorous and exciting product categories like fashion or cars or jewellery. The possibility to powerful brand creation exists in virtually every sphere of consumer buying space. Branding marvels belong to diversified territories like tourism, services, business markets, commodities and not-so-liked businesses such as waste disposal. Brand building is also not a game that only big companies can afford to play. There are numerous small companies which operate in a limited market area but have strong brands. Brands like Ghari and Priya Gold, Shree Leathers, Khadims, Action, Symphony and MDH have evolved from being regional players to national prominence. At the heart of every brand success rests intersection points between the values embedded in the market-offering and the customer-need spaces. Brands are created when these intersections create values that are unparalleled in the competitive space. Brand name is only a visible sign of the currency of communication. The brand itself is what lies hidden below the tip of the iceberg.

The challenge for brand builders therefore is not to fall victim to the comfort that sight provides. Sight is mechanical. Thus mechanical observation of reality runs common across most of the people who take the mantle of brand creation. This book begins with the exploration as to why brands have come to assume such an important role in consumers' lives. Brands are valued for de-complicating human life. Brands act as short cuts or light posts that provide ease in negotiation through a complex maze of choices. For marketers brand and branding are important because these offer ways of achieving excellent performance on metrics that set the top performers apart from the also rans. The branding strategy in this context acts as a linking pin between the values sought by consumers on the one hand and the values defined and executed by the marketers on the other hand. The brand essentially germinates as an idea that seeks to uplift its potential prospects from a less-desired inferior state to a higher order state and finds expression in the product or service that is often mistaken as a brand. Brands involve transcendence beyond the functional utility embedded in the product or service component, thereby pushing the delivery to a higher value orbit.

Branding is a voyage into the discovery of the not-so-obvious value intersection points that defy logic and forge deeper connections of the brand to bond with its customers for which rational explanations are difficult to obtain. If one thinks Nike is worn on the feet and Rolex is a time-keeping device that can endure shocks, then one's analysis is entirely off the mark. This book precisely begins here and takes its reader on a tour of brand building in the context that most marketers face these days. In developing the idea of this book I have benefited from the rich discussions that I have had with my students who have taken my Brand Management course over the years. In many ways I have benefited from Professor V.K. Seth, my senior colleague at the Faculty of Management Studies, whose observations and suggestions kept me stimulated and encouraged. All of my intellectual and academic pursuits bear my sign, but the true forces behind making all these a reality are my wife Renu and daughter Ishita. Hidden behind every single word that I write, they are equal contributors.

Harsh V. Verma
harshfms@rediffmail.com
harshverma@fms.edu

Why Brands?

Brands are about navigation. Spend a day in the life of a customer or take a pause and recollect how you spent your last day. Was it peaceful and happy or did it bring you discomforting feelings? It was peaceful and happy because you managed and negotiated the maddening city traffic and reached office on time. You negotiated the product presentation made to new prospective buyers and handled their objections effectively. On your way back home you took a trip to the nearby market to pick up some essential items, especially broccoli, which your wife wanted for the next day's meal. It was not much of a problem locating a parking space and while pulling the car out of parking the way was not blocked by some awkwardly parked vehicles. Fortunately, the traffic was not bad except for the toll plaza, where vehicles generally pile up haphazardly instead of queuing up. However the meal at the restaurant turned out to be a bitter experience. First, its location in the shopping complex was not fully known and you had to bank upon others for guidance, some of whom guided properly and some who misguided. It would be better if those who are unsure of locations refrain from making suggestions when asked for directions.

In the above scenario a person negotiates his traffic, time, space, superiors, potential buyers, home requirements and shopping.

Take a closer look at each of these situations. The actor in such cases negotiates, wades through and makes way to reach his goals in the situations that are inherently challenging. It is all about developing formulae—some kind of coping mechanisms or heuristics that come to rescue in the navigation process. For negotiating on the roads one depends upon the signs and assistance from other people. Effective handling of social relationships requires thorough understanding of aspects like personality, motivation and styles of people involved in the situation. Shopping also presents its unique set of challenges. Making correct product choices and judging price–value payoffs is not an easy job.

With the dawning of complexities due to product and brand proliferation, excessive communication, attempts to create real and artificial differentiation and claiming and counter-claiming at the point of purchase leaves the buyer nothing but confused and frustrated. Negotiating this highly complex buying environment is a new emerging phenomenon of the post-industrialised world. The excess of supply over demand has made the life of the marketer miserable. The pressures to improve the bottom line and top line are causing the marketers to pull and deploy all kinds of ammunitions from their arsenals. In this context brands and branding have assumed new significance. In branding the marketer sees salvation. On the one hand brands are devices and new navigational tools for the marketers. On the other hand, brands have emerged as new trusted compasses that help consumers spot the correct way through the dense and dangerous marketing jungle. Brand is the consumer's formula to handle buying—an essential task or enjoyable task for survival. Brands are there because we want them. We may not expressly articulate the need for brands and even criticise them and call them 'manipulative' and in some cases 'exploitative'. But the fact is that we need them. That's what marketers know. Therefore, brands are created.

Brands draw their relevance from their ability to help consumers make effective and efficient choices. Brands equip customers to efficiently wade through congested goods racks, bewildering variety, confusing product displays and claims and counter-claims, product specification wars and pressure selling tactics of the sales people. The traffic in most of the major cities is complex and dangerous, and so is shopping, choosing and buying. Brands are the devices that marketers have invented to help customers go into maddening malls and departmental stores and come out of them without losing sanity. Buyers want to solve their problems of needs and wants by locating and acquiring appropriate solutions for their needs. Brands come to their rescue. Each brand signifies a bundle of unique utility and satisfaction.

Brands are also the ends for marketers, for their creation drives and for bottom-line and top-line performances. Branding is the most superior route to value creation and wealth generation. Recollect in your memory an instance when you wanted to reach a friend's house to meet him or her and the address did not have an identification number but the locality was mentioned. It is no great feat to find an unnumbered house in a colony of numbered houses. The feat is when you find an unnumbered house in a colony of similar unnumbered houses, especially when there is nobody to guide you and even if some did attempt to guide you, they could not be trusted. Brands in the modern marketing world come to customers like numbered houses—the solutions to specific needs and wants—which make life easy and simple.

BRANDLESS WORLD

You have a hen that is not different from other hens; yet it is extra-ordinary. On the outside it is a hen similar to others in the brood, but inside it is highly dissimilar. It actually lays golden eggs. Its one egg is worth more than thousands of those of the others. Yet on the face of it, it is just an ordinary hen. One day, as luck would have it, it crosses the fence and flies over to the adjacent farm. You approach the owner of the neighbouring farm and explain to him how one of your hens crossed over to his farm. For him it is just another hen flying over the fence into his farm, but for you, this hen is special, and you don't want to reveal the real truth. The neighbour counts his entire brood and finds one extra hen and asks you to pick one. For him the solution is easy, but for you the problem is difficult. All hens in the brood look alike from the outside, but from the inside one is unlike the others and unique when it comes to laying eggs. Now you wish this hen had a different mark, or colour, or shape, or size, or name, or could recognise you, or produce a different sound. But it precisely has no such distinctive characteristic. The problem is how to negotiate this complex situation.

The situation here is quite similar to what consumers face when they make their way through a commodity market. There are no short cuts available to figuring out the best product. All look similar and are apparently undifferentiated. In such situations the only alternatives are either to evaluate each and every available product for its merit and suitability for your chosen need, or go without such evaluation. The former option is difficult but safe and the latter is easy but risky. Normally a consumer would avoid risk and avert undesirable consequence by resorting to search and evaluation. But this kind of search and evaluation implies costs of various kinds such as time, energy and lost opportunity. Recall a childhood memory when you went along with your mother to buy vegetables at the nearby market. The shopping trip often left you frustrated and bored. She usually took a lot of time selecting individual pieces of fruits and vegetables from large heaps and often haggled for the price. The trip was not worth the compensation you got at the end when she treated you to an ice cream.

Unless shopping—search, evaluation and negotiation—in itself is an enjoyment, the preferred option would be to pick the tried and tested solution every time the need arose. The first and foremost consideration in buying usually is to pick the product or service that is the best suited for the given need. If a short cut to reach this goal is available then life for a consumer is easy and simple. One should be able to isolate the best among the plethora of products and services. The absence of such short cuts lays a huge demand on a customer. If one wants to safeguard his or her interest and avoid wrong purchases, the stakes in playing a buying game are quite high. Every wrong move in the buying battleground leaves the buyer worse off in several ways, and no one desires to be worse off, rather the end is how to be better off. A wrong purchase decision exposes a customer to a variety of costs, which include the following:

- Monetary cost — A wrong purchase makes some money go down the drain.
- Time cost — Time is a precious commodity. The time spent in one activity means time forgone for some other activity.
- Physical effort — Buying involves exertion of physical eloquence.
- Psychological cost — Psychologically some activities are rewarding and some are draining.
- Social cost — Most visible products have signalling power. A product may send inappropriate signals to the buyer and position him or her to make the wrong choice.

Suppose that one day, a monster from another planet removes all brands from the face of the Earth. Imagine how taxing, time consuming and difficult it would be to connect needs and wants with potential sources of their satisfaction. Each time a want would arise, one would have to run through a rigorous process of knowing, evaluating, selecting and buying the desired commodity. It would be reinventing the wheel again and again. No benefit of previous experience and learning would be available for future purchases. Buying would become a risk-laden process meant only for a few who would master the isolating skills and learn to distinguish in a sea of apparently similar products. Due to the paucity of consumer resources like time, money, efforts and psychological energy there is an acute need for the development of some kind of mechanism by which the buying process is shortened and simplified. The uncertainty surrounding the value contained and potential harm that a product may cause has to be contained and mitigated. Thus when one reaches out to a bottle of Kinley water in a remote location where water is problematic as it may be contaminated one is assured of purity. There is no uncertainty about the quality of water contained in a bottle marked with the Kinley brand. The risks are alleviated and the choice is simplified.

Which one of the perfumes in Figure 1.1 is the best for you to use? The answer will require the sampling of the contents of each of these similar bottles. But the efforts expended in the identification of the best perfume this time will not help in future occasions because there is no way the same perfume bottle could be identified in the future unless the same process is repeated. There is no short cut available to this problem's solution unless the perfume so identified could be isolated in the future by some kind of mechanism such as name, mark or symbol.

Figure 1.1: Which Is the Best Perfume for You?

EROSION OF TRUST

People are primarily seekers of certainty. A world filled with uncertainties is highly discomforting, scary and dissatisfying. Lack of certainty robs peace and poise. Constantly being in an alert and vigilant state is taxing on both the body and mind. People seek umbrellas of protection in most of their behaviours. The jungle is the epitome of uncertain present and future. There are no assurances of survival. Each day is a new day filled with challenges of defence and survival. The gazelle must learn to run faster and learn tricks to outmanoeuvre attacks by bigger animals. The lion must find ways to beat the gazelle in speed to out-compete the gazelle's moves in order to make a kill. There are no ration shops to meet daily needs.

Imagine being part of such a system where survival is not certain and risks come in all kinds of camouflaged forms.

People look to institutions for equity and fairness. Institutions of the civilised world are risk management devices. We trust the parliament for governance, the judiciary for justice, the police for protection of lives, defence for insulation against aggression, press for true and fair reporting and businesses for delivering products and services satisfying needs and wants. Our society can slip into anarchy if these institutions fail. Such failure would mark a return of *jungle raj*. The big and mighty would prevail and the weak and defenceless would suffer. Of late the trust in these institutions has taken a serious beating. One after another scams involving these institutions have seriously shaken our faith. Be it parliamentarians, the judiciary, religious institutions or business corporations, all have shown chinks in their conduct. Contamination crises hogged brands like Perrier, Exxon Valdez, Coca Cola and Tylenol. Sony had to recall batteries that were alleged prone to explode. Companies like Arthur Andersen, Enron and WorldCom exposed serious governance malaise. Their collapse led to the enactment of the Sarbanes–Oxley Act. Shoe brands have had their share of criticism surrounding the issue of sweat shops. Where does this erosion end?

There has been a general decline of trust within society especially of social institutions. A study by Washington, D.C.-based Pew Research Centre discovered that 45 per cent of Indians feel that their fellow countrymen are not trustworthy. Why is trust in society on a decline? One of the prime reasons for this mistrust is general lack of faith in administration. One study by Transparency International found that 76 per cent of the Indian public believe that politicians and lawmakers are 'extremely corrupt'. Police, which is another significant pillar of civilised society, is second to politicians in the corruption perception. Seventy-two per cent believe that the police system is corrupt. Even the judiciary, the third important pillar, those who are considered to be the guardians of law, do not escape this perception. Thirty-six per cent feel that the judiciary is corrupt. Overall the decline of the system is so much that India manages to score only 3.5/10 on the global integrity index (*The Week* 2008: 12).

At the fundamental level all of us feel more insecure and uncertain than our previous generations. When we reach out to pick a brand or seek employment in a company or check into a hotel or board a plane a lot of knocking happens in our brain. We wish that we could predict the future outcomes and navigate accordingly. Even in a country like India the family as an institution has undergone rapid transformation. The comfort and cushion that it provided to children, the elderly and other dependents seems to be vanishing. The discomforting news about abandoned parents, cheating partners and elimination of siblings appear on television channels and newspapers with certain regularity.

Edwards (1998) observes the transference of risk from state to individual and a steady decline in societal institutions. There is privatisation of risk. People are individually besieged to manage their risk. The choices are no longer simple and institutions that helped make choices are fast losing their credibility. One must find new mechanisms to cope with this emergent reality. Therefore one is on the lookout for new partners who will help manage risk. In this context, when people search for new partners, how do brands come into the picture? Can brands be partners in risk management for an individual? The answer is positively yes. Brands can be risk-neutralising devices in the world filled with risk in almost everything we do. Brands can be trust marks. Brands signify a promise that is infallible. Brands promise performance guarantee no matter what. Brands are not only about communicating what to expect and what not to, but also communicate a sure shot promise to deliver what falls within their purview.

The Reader's Digest (2008) conducted a survey of trusted brands. In this survey the respondents were asked to provide ratings of specified brands on six core parameters. These were trustworthiness, credible image, quality, value, understanding consumer needs and innovation. This 'trusted brand' rating helps consumers in seeking answers to questions like the following, which are essential in making an effective purchase decision:

1. Safety — Is the brand safe to use and does its delivery match with the promise it makes in its promotion campaigns?
2. Brand identity — Is it believable and appropriate?
3. Quality of make — Is the product or service of the brand well made and designed?
4. Value for money (VFM) — Does the brand offer good VFM?
5. Customer responsiveness — Does it respond to customer needs and satisfy them?
6. Innovation — Does it innovate new features or services?

What does trust exactly mean? Some of the common words that immediately get linked to the word 'trust' are:

- Reliance
- Confidence
- Dependability
- Assurance
- Faith
- Unfailing

All these constructs are important. They assume even greater significance because institutions in the spheres of both commerce and society are suspects on this dimension. Brands in a way guarantee peace of mind. A buyer typically entrusts himself or herself to the brand and feels secure and confident about the fulfilment of the promise.

Brands emerge as trust signs in all walks of life. When consumers reach out to a trusted brand like Colgate or Dettol or Tata it becomes a worry-free exchange. The consistency of performance as per the promise allows customers to have a tension-free relationship. The quantum of energy that is saved is freed for other difficult jobs. What else could a buyer look for if the mobile telephony service provider can be trusted and a hospital where heart surgery is performed is transparent in its dealings with its customers? When a brand consistently delivers promised performance customers reward it by trusting it—which means placing faith on a given name. It is an act of surrender. The brand implicitly says, 'Don't worry I am with you, you can bank upon me.' Trust is the reward a brand earns by consistency of performance.

Table 1.1: How Much Do You Trust the Following Brands?
(1–very highly untrustworthy, 2–highly untrustworthy,
3–untrustworthy, 4–indifferent, 5–trustworthy,
6–highly trustworthy, 7–very highly trustworthy)

Brands	
Cadilla Pharmaceuticals	☐
Godrej	☐
Tata	☐
TVS	☐
Bajaj	☐
Hindustan Lever	☐
Bombay Dyeing	☐
Cadbury	☐
ttk	☐
Kirloskar	☐
Hindustan Motors	☐
Indian Oil	☐
ITC	☐

SIMPLIFIED LIFE

Do customers need brands? Ask a customer and the answer is likely to be negative. It is not too difficult for anyone to develop a series of strong arguments against branding as a business practice. Many see it as a device of manipulation and deceit. Branding is cost added to an otherwise much cheaper product or commodity. Brands create confusion. However, the customers are probably not the right ones to approach in seeking an answer to this question. The merit of branding lies not only in what it does for the company or the marketer but what it accomplishes for the consumers. Something that is irrelevant to consumers but relevant to the company may have very little marketing significance. For instance a marketer may attach the highest importance to profit but profit is not relevant for customers or the market whereas satisfaction of their needs and wants is of the utmost importance. Therefore too much concentration on the pursuit of profit can lead a firm into doing things that are irrelevant from the customer's perspective. In such cases the results are quite dangerous. At the end a blind chase for profits can make the market irrelevant.

Marketing is a process by which a marketer gains by doing what is customer relevant. Justification of a strategy comes not from its merit for the manager but from its usefulness for consumers. Branding is a practice not because managers want it but for the role it plays in a consumer's life. Brands assume significance for the simplifying effect they have on an otherwise complex life.

The markets are oversupplied with products and services. There is virtually a product explosion. In every product category there is a plethora of brands that shout out at you. All clamour for attention. Our senses are assaulted endlessly by advertising messages. But the question is whether all this is simplifying the consumer's life or making it more complicated. Enter the world of oversupply and excessive choice and all this leaves us confused. With oversupply and brand multiplication the choice becomes difficult. All this overexposure and overcommunication is creating an overstimulation, bordering on invisible sensory assault. The pressure on the senses is far beyond the processing capacity. When the stimulation contained in any situation goes much beyond the optimum level it produces negative effects on consumers.

When too much pressure is exerted on the consumer's information processing system, the system develops coping mechanisms instead of breaking down. Accordingly, stimulating situations are avoided and incoming information is screened out. For instance when a brand highlights too many attributes, or a sales person is perceived to be highly aggressive or when a store displays too many brands, the consumer moves into a negative affective state instead of being in a positive state. Stimulation far in excess of the optimum level presents a Herculean cognitive challenge to the consumer. Consumers in such situations of overexposure get into withdrawal and avoidance modes (Streufert and Driver 1971). Customers usually look for simplification of life. Brand proliferation acts to compound customer problems instead of simplifying them but at the same time brands simplify life by routinising the purchase.

Brands make a consumer's life certain. Things around us hold different promises and risks. What outcomes would be anticipated in the future when we checked in on a flight, chose to spend a night in a hotel, or dined in a restaurant or bought a notebook; if these were not branded. Every consumer choice involves varying degrees of perceived risk and uncertainty. Choosing a wrong airline company may involve a great amount of actual physical risk. The airplane may not land safely and systems may develop snags causing heightened crash risk. A dinner at a restaurant may turn out to be a nightmare. Besides minor offences like slow services or unpleasant environment, the food served may become the cause of chronic stomach upset. A visit to a wrong hair salon can burden a customer with severe loss of self esteem. This way it is not very hard to learn that each choice that one makes since the time of waking up to the time of crawling into bed tends to be filled with dangers. In most buying decisions consumers have evolved some kind of coping mechanisms. With every purchase consumers learn to discriminate. But one of the preconditions to be able to discriminate is the availability of differences, be they physical or non-physical.

Make a visit to an electronics store and imagine if all available televisions did not have brand names on the face of their cabinets or refrigerators came without any name or monograms. The probability that most would appear almost the same is very high. And it would be extremely difficult to determine what to expect from which set and which one is better than the others. Brands simplify a consumer's life. For most consumers it is not very hard to find refrigerators with nutrition preservation systems, or ones which have four door cooling mechanisms or ones that can make ice faster. For these products with their unique properties have a definite name and symbol. Customers know what to expect from a brand like LG, Godrej and Whirlpool.

INTEREST SAFEGUARDED

Consumers are interested in guarding their interests. It is only in exceptional circumstances that a consumer would act to invite exposure to risk. Generally consumers use their intelligence or cognitive capabilities to make their way through life with a risk minimising mode. This involves making choices. Consumers use their cognitive skills or thinking system to manage monetary loss, performance loss when things don't work, physical harm or injury, loss of esteem in a social environment and preservation of self concept (Settle and Alreck 1989). Consumers who risk minimising attempts ultimately end up in identifying and narrowing down the total available alternatives to the one that fits the need structure the best. The world of brands makes the consumer's life easier. For instance in such a low interest product category like gasoline if a customer wants diesel with power one can easily narrow down the search to a petrol pump that sells Turbojet (it can turn your vehicle into a turbo charged raging bull) and if one is looking for acceleration and speed than the choice is Hi Speed diesel.

Life management requires making choices day in and day out. It is impossible to think about sustaining life without decisions. Every moment involves crafting a response that minimises exposure to risk, something undesirable. And some decision situations tend to be recurring. Which toothpaste to buy when the current tube gets exhausted? What shoes to pick when the ones on your feet wear off? Where do we go for entertaining guests? Similar challenges may be faced in buying products that are infrequently purchased like durables. Each of these situations presents a cognitive challenge for the customer. Ultimately what matters is that a decision outcome must not land the customer into some undesirable situation. The exposure to different kinds of risks should be minimised or altogether eliminated. How do brands help customers in simplifying life?

Making informed decisions is an essential condition for risk reduction. This requires that all available alternatives are properly identified and analysed. What each of the available brands promises for instance in toilet soaps or home generators has to be known. It is only then that these options could later be evaluated and compared with what is needed or expected by the consumer. Brands in this context act as information chunks. They represent in one word or a symbol what values, functionalities and benefits that a marketer has condensed in the offer. Brands draw boundaries as to what can legitimately be expected and what would be unfair to expect from a brand. For instance it is reasonable to expect safe travel from a no frill airline like Go Air or SpiceJet but it is unreasonable to expect these brands to provide their customers with high class cabin entertainment or service. In the economy hotel chain Ginger it is fair to expect a good night's sleep but it is unfair to expect services like food and beverages of the quality and variety available in five star hotels.

With such condensed information about what a brand stands for the buyer's choice process is facilitated and simplified. Buyers can make informed choices. This facilitates elimination of alternatives that seem inconsistent with what is looked for at a point in time. It is easier for buyer to know what brands to avoid and what brands to consider for buying. The brand information reveals the expected value delivery. If there is an economy traveller looking for an inexpensive travel solution it is easy for him or her not to consider full fare airlines like Jet Airways or Kingfisher or Air India. Imagine the difficulty level one would have faced if one was unsure of what these stand for. Brands are boundary defining mechanisms. They facilitate choices by accelerating information processing. Consider the toilet soaps market. Numerous brands crowd the supermarket shelves. Due to this congestion it is very difficult for a consumer to know what each of these brands stands for. A brand is information compressed into a sign or symbol or name. Consider the following brand names and their meanings in marketing language:

- Lux   —   Women, beauty, timeless, film stars.
- Pears   —   Child like skin, soft and glycerine.
- Dettol   —   Antiseptic, hygiene, effectiveness, germs free.
- Lifebuoy (earlier) red   —   Masculine, sports, health, economy, germicidal.
- Dove   —   Moisturising cream, women, cures dryness, expensive, class.
- Cinthol   —   Male, confidence, deodorant, freshness.
- Breeze   —   Floral fragrance, young, value for money.
- Liril   —   Young, girly, freshness, energy, vivacious, lime.
- Margo   —   Neem, green, herbal, medicinal.
- Nirma Beauty   —   Value for money, beauty.
- Fair Glow   —   Girly, fairness.
- Medimix   —   Herbal, fair prices, ayurvedic.

Brands act like names or symbols encrypted on files. And the brand file contains distinct meanings, symbols, images, benefits and attributes. Depending upon the contents sought by the user the files are referred to and used. A strong brand achieves great clarity and distinction about what should be linked and what should be avoided with its name. And these contents ultimately help consumers make correct choices. Consider the following questions and think of a brand that would be pressed into service:

- A cream for nicks and burns ....
- An ointment for backaches ....
- A fairness cream for men ....
- An antiseptic soap ....
- A toilet soap for infants ....

- A cream for protection against mosquito bites ....
- A liquid fabric whitener ....

ROUTINE

Customers are information processors. The active or passive encounters with buying situations cumulatively bring about changes in customers' cognitive systems. The learned information is used for the simplification of the buying task. This is called 'psychology of simplification' (Howard and Sheth 1961). Customers rely on previously stored information and learning to shorten the buying processes. The learning and past experiences with various brands help them use short cuts to get out of their buying modes. In this way a customer aims to optimise his or her cognitive resources efficiently. The cognitive processes involved in solving a buying problem are then replaced by habit or routine. This buying simplification is achieved by recalling previously stored buying decisions and/or choosing the brand that was purchased in a previous similar situation. This purchase simplification by habit formation or routine development is facilitated by the presence of brands.

With the passage of time life on planet Earth is becoming complex. The demands on available time are multiplying. Human beings are constantly embroiled in juggling among different activities. Material affluence is increasing but time availability is decreasing. One of the life simplifying mechanisms in such situations is habitual or inertia based buying. As marketplaces become grounds of brand proliferation and choices multiply the navigation through marketplaces with land mines becomes complex. Brand explosions in various product categories have created marketplaces of overstimulation. The nerve breaking communication and excessive choice has created far more pressures than can be coped with easily. Customers in such situations look for choice simplification. Ease of choice rather than complication is the order of the day.

Brands allow customers to develop preferences and fix choices. Preference development and selection of the best option from all the available alternatives demands that information about all these and the processes are known. What each of the options stands for needs to be known and then matched with the evaluation criteria. When the need arises customers want to be sure which brand to pick from a plethora of available alternatives. And once the degree of acceptability of options is arrived at to that extent the cognitive or information processing task is reduced. The consumer now knows exactly which alternative to settle for whenever the need or the problem faced are experienced. The development of a set of acceptable alternatives or a single option allows a customer to pull out of the information processing mode and economise on the cognitive energy spent. This permits the development of a routine or habit in solving specific consumption problems or needs. Consumers can then reach out to a chosen brand without much contemplation and thinking of its performance as the product's delivery of satisfaction is already known. Figure 1.2 shows how brands help develop routine.

Figure 1.2: Brands Help Develop Routine

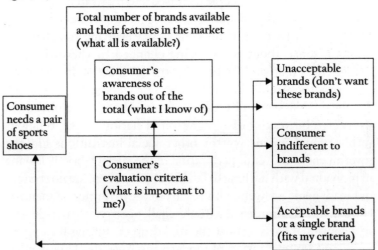

IDENTITY CONSTRUCTION

Brands assume importance for consumers as devices that help them in the expression and construction of their identities. From the philosophical perspective questions like 'Who am I?' and 'What would I like to be?' are important. The term 'identity' theoretically is conceptualised in many ways. The psychological perspective views identity as a mental model that someone has about himself or herself. The sociologists interpret identity in the context of social roles. Idendity is referred to as a person's capacity for self reflection and awareness of self in cognitive psychology. Essential to the concept of identity are characteristics that make a person unique. The idea about self as a distinct entity is shaped by ongoing interactions between an individual and the institutions that make up a society. Identity plays a critical role in how well an individual negotiates life challenges. A person with an ill conceived or diffused idea about the self is likely to steer through life challenges with a great difficulty. Identity is where most of our behaviours stem from.

Many thinkers have articulated on the effect that modernisation has had on identity in different ways. The clash between the old and the new is leaving people confused and frustrated as to what human existence is all about. 'The amalgam of once new ideas and tribal memory that constitutes our slowly evolving and changing common sense about self is being changed by these thinkers (Nietzsche, Freud and Richard Rorty)' (Pell 2001). In one of his addresses the Archbishop of Sydney, Dr George Pell discussed the 'meaninglessness' of today's culture. The waning of the old structures by way of disintegration of nation states, religious authority and untrustworthy other social institutions like the government and overall perforation of the social fabric is leaving an individual with nothing to fall back upon. There are no straight and readymade answers with regard to the definition of identity. The individual is burdened with the challenge to construct identity on a continual basis against the backdrop of shifting life experiences and fragmentation of modern institutions. This is what Giddens (1991) calls the 'looming threat of personal meaninglessness'. In this state of meaninglessness discovering a meaning for a person is a major challenge. The dismantling of the old structures has robbed individuals of an easy and convenient way to plug in defined meanings and identity structures. But now identity definition and construction has become a personal journey into discovering the answers to fundamental questions like 'who am I?' and 'what would I like to be?'

An individual's inner directed self—'who am I' or 'who I would like to become'; and the external self—how others view me or how I would like to be viewed by others are two dimensions where brands play a vital role. The consumption behaviour accords a person an opportunity to define and construct these identity dimensions. Brands at the core level carry meanings that are primarily functional or utility centric. Besides this brands are often imbued with symbolic meanings. These assume the role of signifiers. For instance a Rolls Royce is definitely a good car in terms of dimensions like comfort and engine performance. But more than its functionality this brand now has metamorphosed into a symbol. It is an expressional device that announces something about its owner without express communication and usage of words. It symbolises a class of super rich. Brands—with distinctive meaning invested in them—allow consumers to engage in an identity affirmation process. The adventurous concept is reinforced when a consumer buys a pair of Woodland shoes. On the other hand brands also act as compensating mechanism for the inadequacies felt by a person. A person not so confident in social situations may take refuge in a brand like Close-Up to make up for that inadequacy. In this regard the brand interfaces with customers not only as a toothpaste—utility or functionality aspect but also as an identity confirmation, construction and expression device. The multiplicity of meanings contained in a brand allows consumers a free choice to appropriate the meanings that are relevant to them. Valentine and Gordon (2000) use the expression of 'moments of identity' to refer to the process by which consumers participate in brand story and narrative to create identities for themselves.

EFFICIENCY AND EFFECTIVENESS

Brands are about efficiency and effectiveness. Efficiency in consumers' context implies reducing buying costs. Here the cost concept is not limited to monetary aspects alone. Besides monetary costs other sacrifices that a consumer may have to make are also considered as costs. These non-monetary sacrifices include time, energy, psychological and physical costs. Brands help consumers become both effective and efficient in seeking solutions to their buying problems. What does effectiveness and efficiency mean in this context?

- Effectiveness is about correctness or doing the right thing.
- Efficiency on the other hand implies doing better or with the least possible costs or sacrifices.

Brands from the customer's perspective play an important role in guiding buyers into making right choices and helping them in achieving this with economy of effort. Segregation of available options into various classes is a precondition for making an effective and efficient choice. In this context brands come as combinations of both quantitative and qualitative attributes. Each of these combinations can be distinguished with significant ease because of brands. For instance it is not very hard for a woman who is concerned about the health of the heart of her husband to know that Saffola is one brand of oil that can be considered. Similarly out of a number of chewing gum brands consumers know that Orbit White or Protex White are the brands that are beneficial for teeth whitening. This way a consumer is able to make an informed choice and steer effectively out of a clutter of available options. And once the solution is found to be satisfactory then the task is simplified for all future occasions. Problem resolution for all later occasions does not pose any daunting information processing challenge.. Buying now becomes not a matter of thinking but of simply buying.

**Box 1.1:   Marketer's Attempt to Educate Customers about What
Skoda Laura Car Has to Offer**

An advertisement of Skoda Laura (*Times of India*, 2 September 2008)
listed the following 50 features and attributes:

1. Electric stability programme
2. ABS and ASR
3. The tyre pressure monitoring
4. Xenon headlamps with dynamic adjustment
5. Projector headlamps
6. Curtain airbags
7. Slide airbags (front)
8. Dual front airbags with front seatbelt pretensioners
9. Three point rear seatbelts with pretensioners on side seats
10. Height adjustable front seatbelts
11. Front seats with active seat headrests
12. Front and rear foglamps
13. Two isofix child seat fittings on rear seats
14. Safety warning lights on front door panels
15. Rough road package
16. Driver side mirror with defogger
17. Rear windscreen defogger
18. Central locking remote control key
19. Engine immobilizer
20. Electric sunroof
21. Climatic dual zone AC
22. Mechanical rear window sunshade
23. CD/MP3 audio player
24. Integrated 6 CD changer
25. 12 front and rear speakers
26. Multifunction leather steering wheel
27. Auxiliary audio socket in jumbo box
28. Electronically adjustable driver seat
29. External mirror with memory function
30. Heated front seats
31. Adjustable front armrest with cooled storage space
32. Folding rear centre armrest
33. Height and reach adjustable steering wheel

(Box 1.1 Continued)

(*Box 1.1 Continued*)

34.	Height and adjustable front seats
35.	Adjustable lumbar support front seats
36.	Electrically adjustable external mirrors
37.	Auto dimming rear view mirror
38.	Small leather package
39.	Leather upholstery
40.	Front and rear parking sensors
41.	Cruise control
42.	Light assistant
43.	Rain sensor with automatic wipers
44.	Integrated pop out headlamp washers
45.	Boarding spots in external mirrors illuminating the door area
46.	Multifunction trip indicator
47.	Pump duse engine technology
48.	6-speed direct shift automatic gear box
49.	Tiptronic
50.	Unparalleled beauty

Source: The Times of India, 2 September 2008.

CONCLUDING REMARKS

Brands are created by the marketers as value beacons (Mitchell 2003: 39). In the maze of cluttered and confusing market reality brands stand for clearly defined, easily identified and trustable source of value. The clarity of meaning, ease of identification and something that one can easily bank upon creates enormous value for customers. For instance the brand 'Surf' stands for a distinct meaning among a plethora of detergent brands, it can be easily identified by its unique blue and white pack and there is very little reason to worry about its performance. The performance is guaranteed. When one is not sure of water quality, Bisleri is the brand that can be reached out to. Marketers help buyers to simplify choices, speed up navigation to finding the desired source of value and reduce verification cost and finally provide reassurance. In this context brands are valuable not only for the marketers but also to the buyers in facilitating buying.

2

What Is a Brand?

Understanding what brands stand for is important for managers. However the question as to what is the import of the term 'brand' is of less consequence for consumers. Brands are created and managed by managers. Brands are important because they are primary instruments of value creation. Brand is 'the' asset that makes the crucial difference between the sterling performing companies and the also ran ones. For the customers brands are valuable for the value addition that they bring to the market entity. With effective branding a product can be pushed into a higher value orbit by transforming its value content and connection with the prospects. On the one hand a branded product or service experience can provide higher satisfaction. On the other hand for marketers branding is important for it provides escape routes to all pervasive parity. Branding offers effective and forceful opportunity to achieve differentiation that is much less prone to perfect imitation.

WHAT DOES IT MEAN?

What is brand? The answer to this question depends on the perspective adopted by the respondent. For the uninitiated in marketing brand is a name or a symbol. The following are instances of brands:

- Reebok
- Ferrari
- Indica
- Bisleri
- Armani
- Rolex
- Mont Blanc
- Nirma
- Dettol
- Nike
- LIC
- Citibank
- Kerala
- Caterpillar
- Fair & Lovely

But what are these? These are all names or dictionary words or coined words. A brand is a name and the name is usually accompanied by a symbol or sign. Many of these brands have strong symbols associated with them. Mont Blanc has an ubiquitous flower shaped symbol (actually a representation of Mont Blanc peak), whereas Rolex is associated with a unique crown, Nike has a widely recognised 'swoosh' symbol and the three pointed star of Mercedes is well recognised.

In one of the early attempts, the American Marketing Association defined 'brand' as a name, term, sign, symbol or design, or a combination of them, intended to identify the goods or services of one seller or group of sellers and to differentiate them from those of competitors. This concept of brand takes branding in a physical sense. The external façade is highlighted in this context of a branded product or service. Brands it seems are created for the reasons of identification and differentiation:

- Identification – Where does this product come from or whose effort has gone in its creation? For instance the signature of a painter that appears on one corner of a painting allows people to know whether it is a work of art by Hussain or Amrita Shergil or somebody unknown. With the help of a clearly identifiable name or symbol strategically placed on the hood of different cars we know the company that produced it just by a glance. The propeller signifies BMW and five overlapping circles suggest it's an Audi.
- Differentiation – How is the product different from other similar appearing products in its category? Employment of different names or symbols makes signification about the nature and content of the product easy. Three names—City, Civic and Accord—used by Honda for its range of cars targeted towards different segments of customers with unique product functionality and imagery facilitate understanding of their differentiation.

From the above definition of 'brand' brand building seems incredibly simple and easy. And all this noise about brand building is undeserved. The coveted position enjoyed by brand builders appears unjustified. For those who read this definition as English prose branding is reduced to a simple process of finding or discovering unique words and symbols. The symbols and marks distinguish one car from others and one watch from others on the display window. Brand creation from this perspective becomes a play of imagination and creation. Branding also becomes a post production process of christening a nameless, indistinguishable and unidentifiable product. It boils down to an entirely creative endeavour in wordsmithery and artistic expression.

Brand names and symbols appear to be brands but a deeper understanding of the branding process reveals that these are actually the currency of communication that marketers use 'to talk' with the consumers or buyers. They are signifiers of what the brands stand for. Brands are actually hidden beneath these signs, names or symbols. For customers these names or symbols themselves are brands. Bata is a shoe brand, Taj Mahal is a tea brand, Zandu Balm is an ointment brand and Titan is a watch brand. The language involves use of symbols to convey a meaning. The words or symbols that we commonly use to 'talk' are carriers of meaning. These are not ends but means to establish a dialogue with others. The purpose is to use verbal or non-verbal symbols to execute meaning transfer as shown in Figure 2.1.

Figure 2.1:   Role of Symbol or Word in Meaning Transfer

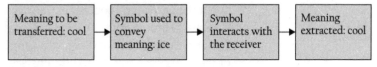

Source: Author.

Names are important. They are important because they both facilitate and obstruct meaning transfer. Improper names may create initial misconceptions but a good sounding name in itself cannot make a poor product a great brand. Similarly a good sounding name cannot make a man good. The logic operates the other way round. A good solid product despite a bad sounding name can gain the status of an iconic brand. Many of the exceptional achievers in various fields do not have good sounding names but they are rock solid brands. Consider names like 'Haldiram' or 'Tribhuvandas' or 'Usha' or 'Bajaj'. These names are very common and mean very little except to identify a person. In fact these names may sound odd and have very little appeal. Some of these may even fail to make it into the book of names for newborns. But these are power brands in their respective product categories. They enjoy phenomenal consumer trust and esteem. Many of the top global brands bear the names of their creators such as Kellogg's, Walker, Armani, Chanel and Mercedes. All these brands enjoy phenomenal equity. They can command their customers to take pains to reach out to them rather than buy a substitute. Brands like these are not reputed because of good sounding names but for what these names signify. Brand name is a medium of exchange. Names are currencies of present day markets. They facilitate transactions by helping marketers and customers have a dialogue.

BRAND NAMES OR SYMBOLS

Historically the origin of branding can be traced to the early 19th century. The names and signs were engraved on stones to identify roads and shops. Even the craftsmen like silversmiths and potters left distinctive marks on their wares to reveal their identity and differentiate them from hoards of others who also produced similar work. This process would surely help the artisan who was bestowed with better skills and imagination than others. People would go looking for a specific sign or a mark because it would deliver better value for their money. The word 'brand' as is used in present day language owes its origin probably to the Norse word *brandr. Brandr* is linked to the process of burning a mark on cattle to distinguish ownership of cattle in the herd. Prior to the industrial revolution or mass manufacturing the traded articles used to be produced by craftsmen who catered to local areas. Often the craft was patronised by the rich, noblemen and kings. Their signs on the products helped these craftsmen gain recognition and liking among the higher social classes. Branding in its early phase of development benefited those who excelled and distinguished in their sphere of activity. Many names that eventually became brands of reckoning were nothing more than names of craftsmen. Some of these names are even now in currency and enjoy phenomenal equity:

- Twinning (1706)
- Ballantine's (1809)
- Levis (1850)
- Burberry's (1856)
- Coca Cola (1886)
- Kodak (1887)
- Bata (1894)
- Harley Davidson (1903)
- Dunhill (1907)
- Adidas (1920)

A deeper understanding of the branding process reveals that brands are the tools used by the marketers to talk to consumers and buyers. What appears to customers as signs, symbols or names of brands, are actually signifiers of what brands stand for. What they convey is of greater significance than the symbol itself. Brand names are hence not ends but means to establish a dialogue with the audiences. The name is important, for, it can both facilitate and obstruct meaning transfer. Improper names may create initial misconceptions. But a good name in itself can not make a poor product a great brand. Brands like Kellogg's, Johnny Walker, Armani, Chanel and Mercedes enjoy phenomenal equity. They can command their customers to take pains to reach out to them rather than buy a substitute.

SUPERFICIAL APPROACH

In the year 2006 one brand name change exercise was carried in the Indian civil aviation industry. The national carrier Indian Airlines name was changed to 'Indian'. Indian Airlines has had more than half a century of existence. It came into existence in 1953 to cater to the travel needs of people within India and neighbouring countries. The brand name Indian Airlines stood as a synonym for air travel in India for over 40 years until other players were allowed to join the industry. From an entirely monopoly leadership situation with a market share of 100 per cent in the 1990s the carrier experienced drastic erosion in its share. Its share dropped nearly 30 per cent. This decline of the market share caused ripples in the management circles of a government run organisation. Often brands run in to rough weather involving the following critical situations:

- Drop in the market share
- Drop in profitability
- Drop in sales
- Erosion of consumer trust
- Some controversy involving the brand
- Competitive assault

The situation demands serious contemplation about the brand and its management in the light of descended reality. A brand cannot afford to stand static in shifting sands. It must move back and forth to maintain its position or else it would fall when the earth beneath has completely undergone change. The government carrier underwent an exercise involving the outward reality of the brand in late 1960s but the change involved was only that of name and logo. The first identity change was carried out way back in 1967 when its name was changed from Indian Airlines Corporation to Indian Airlines. The company's green winged logo was changed into a slanting IA painted in white colour against orange background. The idea was to communicate the new name and symbol adopted by the company. But now in the 21st century the issues were not superficial. The erosion of market share and declining consumer confidence was not a tangential consideration, rather it was too serious an issue to be ignored by a serious brand manager. The marketplace had undergone a sea of changes nothing short of a complete transformation. Private airlines like Kingfisher, Jet, Go, Indigo, Paramount and Spicejet arrived on the scene and had bitten a bite big enough leaving the incumbent Indian Airlines worried and concerned. And these new players' appetite for the market share does not seem to be ending. The cut in the pie had been growing year after year. It was not only competitors that were the cause of concern. Consumers had now tasted new service standards. Accordingly consumer expectation had been on the rise and the carrier's retaining its hold on its customers base was becoming increasing difficult.

The new logo was a mix of a sun and wheel like symbol painted against an orange background. The wheel/sun symbol was inspired from the wheel at the Konark temple and the background signifies continuity. But this change did not go well with its customers. The service touch points—stationery, the counters, inside aircraft ambience, cutlery, uniforms, service, and so on—hardly underwent any change. Instead it added to the confusion as to whether Indian and Indian Airlines were two different air services. The logo or name change without accompanying tangible and intangible changes reduces the entire exercise into a superfluous makeover game. When the substance beneath the surface remains the same but outward façade is changed the whole exercise boils down to image manipulation. This can stimulate prospects once but the discovery of old wine in new bottle can leave indelible marks in consumer memory. The foundation stone of branding—the trust—can get damaged beyond repair.

Branding is all about externalisation of the internal. The internal vacuum—values and vision—can hardly be compensated for by external glamour. The language is important but is secondary. Transactions can cut across language barriers. Communication can still be achieved in silence. In any social exchange if masking or makeup is an evolved art so is unmasking and peeling off layers. Marketers often go gung ho in deploying tools of manipulation to manage market response. But such strategy endeavours elicit quick behavioural response at the expense of long-term bonding and trust building. Safety and self preservation are powerful human drives. How long can consumers' senses and sensibilities be manipulated to achieve commercial advantage? The new empowered consumer's internal reality is far different from the early conceptualisation that viewed consumers as 'objects of manipulations'. Consumers of this century demand equity and transparency.

The iconic Indian car Ambassador is probably one living example of a marketing object that resisted change. If the people who went to their heavenly abodes in the 1970s and 1980s are reborn they would be shell shocked to observe the change that the Indian economy has undergone in the last 15 years or so. Change is all pervasive in both physical objects observable by the eyes and the invisibles like the attitude and values which could be deciphered only by human interactions. Cities' skylines and landscapes bear a drastically different look. Attitudes and values indirectly find expressions in consumption patterns and lifestyles. All of this may shock these departed souls. Change is of far too big a magnitude to be taken without awe. However one thing that would provide them the comfort of their previous lives and help them experience the continuity amidst change would be the Ambassador car.

The whirlwind of change has had very little influence on this iconic brand. The brand resisted evolution with time. Although the car market has underdone a radical change, the Ambassador is one symbol of stagnation amidst the change. Its companion brands like Premier Padmini and Standard have vanished from the scene. And in their place a whole lot of mechanically advanced and aesthetically appealing cars have hit the market including the top line Audi, Mercedes, BMW and Bentley, to the value for money players like Hyundai and Suzuki. So the car industry in India today does not bear much difference from any other country of the world. The brand Ambassador however did not undergo much change in terms of its engineering and physical appearance. What Dilip Kumar or Shashi Kapoor drove in their movies in the 1960s and 1970s in the name of Ambassador is not much different from the one that the company markets even now. However the brand does undergo periodic upgrading. Discovering the difference in its make and generation is difficult. The car's models are distinguished with what is called 'Mark'. Model differences can be found by physically checking the 'Mark' sign conveying whether a particular car is Mark one or two or three. It is extremely difficult for consumers to tell the difference among different models without having to search for the Mark sign. Brand stewardship is much more than carrying out cosmetic product or name changes.

Branding's conceptualisation may sometimes, as in the case of distinguishing Ambassador models with the Mark, be self-defeating and in a way indicate the absence of branding in the true sense. Branding is not about cosmetic changes and frivolous differentiation. For many branding is naming similar products to set them apart in different groups in order to appeal to different categories of buyers. Branding is also not simply upgrading the name or logo to signify development when there is actually none. For instance imagine the efforts that would be required to manipulate the ingredients of a product to make it different or packaging it differently or selling the same under various names. All of these acts require little efforts and even lower imagination. If this is branding then it is no secret skill and it does not deserve premium. For instance if a packaged bottled drinking water manufacturer creates three or four types of bottles and uses different brand names to market the same water in the name of branding then branding is reduced to an act or process of consumer manipulation. The physical aspects of brands like the product or name or symbols attached are indeed inextricably linked to branding but these are not brands. The name or symbol must signify the internal spirit or soul of a brand and its distinct mission. Different brands are needed when they embark upon a different journey to fulfil consumers' dreams. Each must have its own unique vision and mission. Brand is an idea that finds expression in a physical form. Without the distinctions in physical form brands may simply have different names for the same or similar concepts as in Figure 2.2.

Figure 2.2: Brands with Different Names but Similar Concepts (Parity)

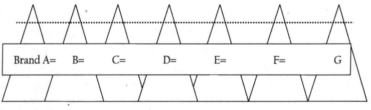

Source: Author.

The Economic Times reported that promoters of many companies have resorted to name change process in order to escape the downward pressure of the stock market. Ideally the trigger to a price rally at the stock market comes from factors like bumper profits, hefty dividends, liberal bonus or strategic moves like mergers and acquisitions. Some of the companies have resorted to executing a change in their name in order to beat the bear bug. Some of the lesser known companies have got on to the rechristening process in order to avoid capital loss. Name change is done to reflect the not so obvious strategic developments like diversification or business evolution. Some firms use 'in' business terms like 'infra-structure' or 'energy' or 'power' to mislead investors. Mere name change to influence public perception is nothing more than putting old wine in a new bottle. The internal and invisible part of the brand very much drives external reality. In the absence of a solid consumer idea or mission a brand is nothing more than a hollow entity with no specific direction and goal. The name plays an important role in conveyance of meaning but it is certainly not the brand.

BRAND THE PRODUCT

Temptation to adopt short cut to branding stems from the ease with which the products or services now can be made. The ad-vancement of engineering, reengineering, free flow of goods and ideas and dismantling of barriers has greatly facilitated fast diffu-sion of products. In one way this benefits customers by immensely increasing supply and product access; in another way this is at the root of the problem known to marketers as commoditisation. The problem of commoditisation has descended on most of the product and service categories. Coke faces competition from countless brands in the cola category. Xerox commercialised the photocopying process but was assaulted by various copier brands. Carrier invented air conditioning but its supremacy is chal-lenged by tens of brands today. Johnson & Johnson's (J&J's) Band Aid is severely contested by a number of players in its category. All these brands face serious challenges from the new contenders. Take a look at televisions, refrigerators, sports shoes, desktops and laptops, cars, fans, music systems, incandescent bulbs and paints; the brands come very close to each other to a point where the distinction appears merely in name and packaging. Although services because of their unique characteristics do not permit easy matching yet services in categories like travel and tourism, airlines, hotels, insurance, banking, credit cards and health care have begun to share space with providers that appear similar in terms of their offerings.

If the market forces on the one hand are unleashing the monster of commoditisation, yet on the other hand good managers have also been successful at resisting commoditisation. Despite serious competition from the new invaders, many of the pioneer brands managed to lead the product categories created by them. The pioneers that stay ahead cling to the very process that led to the brand's creation. Brands like Coke, Colgate, J&J, IBM, Citibank, Nike, Caterpillar, Xerox, Nokia, Apple, Harley Davidson, Disney and Toyota have been able to navigate successfully through the rough seas. Imitators are generally able to scratch the surface of a successful brand but end up as 'second' or 'me too' copy of the product without the genuine brand's DNA or core. And this is where the fundamental point of brand building is missed. The late entrants if they copy the established process without any genuine vision end up becoming just marginal players. Brand building is not a one shot process. It is a continuous exercise in visioning and doing. Brand starts with an idea whereas a 'me too' germinates in the product that somebody offers. Imitation is like sculpting the body by looking at an image. A sculpture without originality ends up as a copy of the original minus the soul.

The foundation of the market is mutually satisfying exchanges between the marketer and the consumer. Beneath the apparent trade or exchange of goods or services lie the utility or value that is transferred from one party to the other. A buyer may purchase a notebook for the utility it provides in terms of data and information processing. A hair saloon provides satisfaction of the grooming needs of the customers. A look at the historical evolution of the thought process or philosophical orientation governing the exchanges would reveal in an instant that brands and branding have been used as a tactical tool in eliciting favourable customer responses. Branding is often myopically used as a name giving exercise. First marketers would create products or services that they could create and then give them attractive names to woo customers. And many times this happened without any great idea or vision. Rather the product or service was created out of convenience. This is to some extent true when a baby is christened. People look for unique and appealing names. The assumption seems to be that good names create good babies.

Henry Ford once said, 'Any customer can have a car painted any color that he wants so long as it is black.' In India the chief executive of the largest scooter manufacturer and undisputed ruler of the two wheeler market said that we don't need a marketing department, all we need is a dispatch department. In this orientation of the production mindset confined company vision for producing internally defined quality products, production processes took precedence over anything else. But mere production of a product is no guarantee of its success in the marketplace. The failure rate of new products often goes upwards to 90 per cent. The belief that a good product will always find its market is untrue. Good products must satisfy needs or solve problems in order to be successful. In the earlier era, branding was nothing more than a 'giving a name' event. The object to be branded existed before and the brand was conceptualised later. The idea was to add gloss or attraction so that demand could easily be bended in favour of the marketer. In this era, marketers failed to realise that the branding process needs to be distinguished from brand naming exercise.

PRODUCT THE BRAND

Faced with the failure of the earlier approach, marketers looked for panacea in push. With time the supply eased and more and more firms began to participate in the markets. This resulted in difficulty in off loading the products on to the market. Marketers faced with customer resistance discovered solutions in use of pressure or push in achieving sales ends. The belief that customers resist buying or buying enough of what a marketer offers lead to the deployment of high pressure advertising and selling. Marketers had for a long time put forward the idea of selling or conversion of goods into cash in the forefront of strategy development. All the marketing tools were orchestrated into winning a favourable customer response without much regard to what would happen after the product changed hands. Later in the 1960s, Levitt (1960) challenged the then prevailing business mindset by clarifying the philosophical underpinnings of marketing and selling concepts. He proposed how these concepts rest on the opposite ends of the continuum. He argued that selling focused on the needs of the seller and marketing focused on the needs of the buyer. Selling seeks to convert goods into cash and marketing targets customer satisfaction. Selling begins with a product while marketing begins with the needs of the customer.

The production or sales paradigms reduce branding to a naming process. Myopically branding can be viewed as a process by which a name is given to a marketing entity be it a physical product or an intangible service. Brand does not appropriate a product. Rather it surmises the entire process that culminates in customer satisfying outcomes. In a way a brand is the signifier of the entire marketing machine and the process created to satisfying customers in the target market. Marketing begins much before the product; it starts with the customer's need identification, articulation, conceptualisation, creation, communication and delivery of value. This process starts with customers and ends with customers. Drucker (1973: 64–65) clarified that selling is not marketing. It is not even a big part of it. In reality true marketing makes selling superfluous. 'The aim of marketing is to know and understand the customer so well that the product or service fits him and sells itself.' When marketing is done in its right spirit then the outcome is the creation of brands that customers pull automatically without any need for pressure being exerted to overcome customer resistance. Power brands enjoy great customer pull. Brands like IBM, Intel, Pantene and Sony are labels that set apart one marketing system from another. Customers know they can be trusted.

Barista as a brand stands for? Does it stand for a finely brewed coffee or something much more? The brand may actually pull customers for providing a particular kind of relaxed sense-stimulating environment where coffee drinking is incidental to the entire experience. Thus the Barista brand at a deeper level appropriates distinct marketing competence and skills possessed by the marketer. Brand is like a floating piece of ice on water (Figure 2.3). It acts as an identification device. What appears visible is not the brand but the identifier of what is hidden. The brand itself is actually hidden. What is submerged is the true core of branding. Whether the piece of ice is on the surface of a submerged iceberg depends on discovery. True brands are much more than mere names. The hidden portion is what distinguishes the solid brand from the hollow brand. It is the hidden marketing component of branding that makes effective branding a rare feat that only a few are able to achieve. Nirma is a powerful brand in the value-for-money segment and there are hundreds of others that crowd the category. The same is the case for many other categories. The ones that crowd are never able to go beyond a generic product that they carry. Their name is just a name and nothing more for the buyer.

Figure 2.3: The Real Difference Lies in Submerged Portion

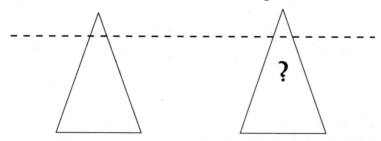

Source: Author.

CUSTOMER RETENTION

The greatest problem faced by marketers in different product categories is how to make customers keep coming back. Hindustan Unilever expects its Lux customers to keep coming back to its brand. Jet Airways would be happy if the market supports their brand with its continued patronage. In the car market Maruti Suzuki's challenge is no different. P&G gears its marketing machine to have its targeted customer stick to brands like Head

& Shoulders, Whisper and Pantene. The situation is no different in services and business-to-business marketing. Hotel chains like Taj or Oberoi do not want their customers to shift to rival chains in the hospitality business. Airtel and Vodafone battle to keep their customer bases intact. From the inside perspective the challenge is how to protect the customer base but for the aggressor or competing firms the issue is how to take a cut out of the market of the rival's share.

Customer attrition is probably one of the most important challenges faced by marketers of the 21st century. In the early phases of market evolution customer retention was not a major issue as the marketing function was locked in narrow confines to demand stimulation activities. For business managers the marketing function meant customer attraction. It is common in the economic development cycle for demand to far exceed the supply or presence of a huge demand potential. Prospects need to be converted into customers. Marketing therefore had been externally focused. What happened after a customer was attracted into the business fold mattered little. The entire focus was on matching the count at the beginning and at the end. It did not really matter as to how many customers were lost at the end of a marketing cycle. The markets ensured perpetual supply of fresh customers. The marketing efforts focused on customer attraction. Demand generation guided marketing efforts for long until market saturation set in. As long as customers could be created with ease there was no motivation to look at what happens after they are scooped in from the market. But when the marginal rate of return of resources spent on customer attraction began to seriously decline with dwindling catch rate the attention shifted from attraction to retention.

Why does customer retention make sense? It does not make sense for any emotional reasons but for the economics related to lifetime customer value. A customer retained for a longer term can fetch much higher value for the firm. With retention the marketing costs decline, the sales volume increases, premium can be commanded and good word of mouth is spread. A study by Bain & Co. concluded that customer retention has a positive dramatic impact on profits. A reduction in customer defection can boost profits from 25 per cent to 85 per cent (Reichheld and Sasser 1990). The key to keeping customers is to develop long-term relationships with them. Some of the thinkers believe that marketing has entered in the fourth era which emerged in the last decade of 20th century. Business systems have to cultivate long-term customer relationships as a crucial driver of performance. This relationship building approach need not be limited to consumers. Rather firms must evolve like a network of partners who collectively come together to satisfy particular customer needs. The most visible sign of companies seeking to build long-term alliances with customers is the use of membership cards. New retail chains like Shoppers Stop, Reliance Fresh and Big Bazaar attempt to get valued customers into their relationship building programme by offering them privileged membership cards.

Relationship marketing emerged as a strategy only when marketers discovered that customers cannot be taken for granted. Customer satisfaction was seen as a route to business survival in the 1960s and 1970s. Stability in market share could be achieved if a firm differentiated itself from the block in terms of provision of customer satisfaction. When a firm satisfies while other competitors do not, customers can be retained. Switching may invite risk and leave customers worse off. By developing a relationship with marketers customers also improve their position. Consumers in India have developed trust in brands like Godrej, Birla, Tata and Dalmia in the regulated era for they meant better value delivery than others. But when the production of a satisfied customer as a strategy is not limited to a few but many customers then switching is encouraged. Earlier if a satisfied customer switched brands he or she could end up getting hurt. But now when everyone more or less guarantees satisfaction, switching may not hurt but instead one may gain if not in any material way then at least in the manner of a novel stimulation. When production of customer satisfaction becomes the common denominator new ways to enchant customers have to be discovered if the goal of retention is to be achieved.

Studies by Jones and Sasser (1995) of the relationship between satisfaction and loyalty threw up startling findings. The study found that the often assumed direct linear relationship between customer satisfaction and loyalty does not hold true as might have been expected. Mere customer satisfaction cannot guarantee customer loyalty. The generally held belief, that it is sufficient to merely satisfy a customer and the investment required to move a customer from satisfied to completely satisfied status does not provide an attractive financial return, was challenged. It was found that complete customer satisfaction is the key to achieving loyalty and generating superior financial performance in the long run. Moving a customer from satisfaction status to a higher status of complete satisfaction is a serious challenge in value generation. The marketer must rate complete satisfaction much ratings above mere satisfaction ratings.

Customer loyalty can be defined in many ways. Overall brand loyal customers provide stability in the market share and growth. Generally marketers with large market share have had a high proportion of loyal customers (Dick and Basu 1994). The big advertising budgets of the firms are directed to making consumers learn that their brand is the best buy and others are inferior. The idea is to achieve reduction in consumers' consideration sets to the extent that only one brand monopolises them. Branding in this way is a choice reduction exercise. Brand achieves monopoly when for a particular problem only one brand becomes the destination and the rest are perceived to be inferior alternatives. The 'Incredible India' campaign directed at foreign countries to woo travellers to India aims to position India as an ultimate travel destination. The same holds true for other marketers.

PATRONAGE AND LOYALTY

Repeated patronage and loyalty is not the same thing. For instance when a customer is seen to be buying a brand again and again in every consumption cycle the observed reality may not signal the inner invisible reality. A customer may stick to a brand behaviourally but internally may have no commitment and attachment to the brand. Repeated buying may be caused by easy availability. For instance in a family the husband and wife live together but actually they may have no love between them. Living together is a poor predictor of internal bonding. This situation could be pretty misleading. With a slight provocation this so called relationship would break down. The house here is brittle and fragile. Similarly some consumers simply cohabitate with brands, they live together without any ties and bond. Others truly marry the brands which they buy and consume. These intersections go much deeper than apparent physicality.

The true test of loyalty lies in discovering the inner feeling. The really loyal customers tend to be brand faithful. They not only favour the brand for its superior functionality but also because of their attachment and affection. Loyalty must be seen as an attitudinal construct. A brand must forge ties with a customer's higher order needs besides performing utilitarian functions. Which brand interactions with customers are the most crucial considerations in defining and designing the brand identity structure? How do these interactions take place? After all, loyalty and patronage cannot be constructed in a vacuum. Dick and Basu (1994) distinguish among four types of loyalty based on relative attitudes and repeat patronage. Relative attitude is made of two dimensions—strength of attitude and degree of attitudinal differentiation among competing brands. The four loyalty types are:

1. High loyalty (high attitude and high repeat buying).
2. Spurious loyalty (low relative attitude and high repeat buying).
3. Latent loyalty (high relative attitude and low repeat buying).
4. No loyalty (low relative attitude and low repeat buying).

These four situations could be illustrated by four consumer buying situations:

1. Maruti Suzuki repeatedly buys tyres from Goodyear and prefers its supplier for its support, trust and partnership. A homemaker gives her child Bournvita because the child likes its taste and nutrition and it is her mother's trusted brand and she herself grew on it.

2. A household buys monthly groceries from a nearby store but finds its services to be just acceptable but the location is convenient. It would have no qualms about shifting its business to another store if it opens nearby. A customer may buy Tata salt regularly but if the stated brand is not available any other brand is substituted without any thought and deliberation.

3. A child has strong liking for Add Gel pens because these pens write without any breaks and come with smooth writing mechanisms. But unfortunately the child uses very few of these because of their lack of availability. Buyers of electrical switches are often hunting for Anchor brand for its heritage and quality but end up not buying it for its distribution flaws.

4. Many brands that lack personal significance and differentiation fall into the category of no loyalty. A consumer of incandescent bulbs, socks and battery cells may exhibit an 'any brand will do' attitude and have little inclination to stick to a particular brand.

The salvation in the present day marketing environment lies in cultivation of loyal customers. Loyal customers make sense for their insulation from competitive pressures and higher returns on marketing investment. Strategy must not only get the customers to buy the product or services it must also get customers to develop attachment and affection. High performance brands consistently outperform their rivals by becoming incontestable entities. The ability of a brand to keep competition at bay may stem from a variety of factors. For some brands it is outstanding performance and service. Caterpillar, Siemens, IBM and Accenture are trusted for their performance. These brands evoke feelings of trust. These brands signify consistency of performance. They mean promise kept. They bring certainty amidst uncertainty and chaos. Great brands escape parity by breaking free from the commodity spiral. With branding marketers can transform a physical entity into an icon which can be blindly relied upon. Brands in a way are mechanisms to take worries off consumers' heads. The greater is the faith engendered by a brand the higher is the likelihood of consumer patronage. After all trust and faith are foundations on which relationships are built.

TRUST MARK

The gems and jewellery market in India is fragmented. People buy their gold, gems and jewellery from their very private time tested jewellers. These are like family jewellers who have catered to their needs for generations. Despite all kinds of criticism about the impurity of gold in the ornaments made by these so called local jewellers, people continue to repose trust in them. These outlets enjoy phenomenal faith and loyalty. This is one set of players. Many sceptics may believe that these are not gold orna-ment brands as Tanishq or Gili or D'damas. But they are also brands in their own right for the customer groups they target and inter-face with. To equate visibility with branding is to miss the essential core of branding and brand building. Awareness is required for brand building but is just the first step toward brand creation. Local jewellers may not enjoy restricted awareness unlike their organised counterparts. But the fact remains that these brands do not target larger national or regional markets, rather they aim for a limited customer set with whom they not only enjoy high awareness but also trust.

The true measure of branding success is customer trust. All these are brands in their own right. Their name creates bonding based on trust with select clientele. For their target customers these are brands on which customers put their faith. On the other hand some big jewellers have created the Gems and Jewellery Trade Federation. The federation has created a trust mark as a mark of purity. The purpose here again is to win the trust of customers. The mark signifies that in whichever showroom this sign is dis-played there the customer can be sure of getting pure hallmarked jewellery. The idea behind this trust mark is to win customer confidence and business. Unlike many other product categories which involve comparatively lesser risk gold being precious is considered a high risk buy. And a buyer is likely to respond to only those brands that enjoy customer confidence. In both of these cases branding is about trust. In the case of local jewellers the trust is cultivated as an outcome of years of interactions. However in the later case the trust is attempted to be bought with advertising and symbols. For any sign or symbol to evolve into a trust mark a tangible support to its claims is required in some way or the other. Trust is not a commodity that could be bought over the counter. It is a time consuming long drawn process. Japanese cars when they first arrived on the American shore were met with great doubt and suspicion. It took a while for Toyota and Honda to build customer confidence in their cars as safe and reliable. Now Japanese brands of cars not only enjoy customer trust but have moved up a step further and have become love marks.

Brands begin their journey with the idea that seeks to make customers' lot better and ultimately manifest in the product. Brand is a label, name or sign that subsumes under itself the entire marketing process. A brand is an unwritten contract between the marketer and customer where the marketer undertakes to deliver a specific value or performance. How well the brand actually lives up to its promise determines its equity. Every brand interaction with a customer goes into making some kind of deposits in the customer's mind. And the deposits so made create brand equity. Customers maintain a mental score card of the brand's performance. It must be realised that performance indicators registered thereon are not determined by the name of the brand but rather by the value delivery at every touch point during the customer and brand interface.

The name just acts as a number or sign of the image vault. What is contained therein is what matters. For instance a new brand begins with an empty chest but only a name that is disseminated by mass media. Nano by Tata has just managed to open a chest in the prospects' cognitive space. The real contents of the chest would be determined later once the customer and Nano interface would begin as the car is delivered. Established names do enjoy an initial advantage at the account opening stage compared to an altogether new name. Brands like Ujala, Ghari detergent, Nirma and Color

Plus had to really work hard initially to win customer favour. Now all of these brands are powerful players in their own right.

CONDENSED VALUE

Branding is conceptualised in a number of ways. But the essence of brand building is to somehow neutralise the forces of competition by reducing substitution among alternatives. Solid brands create value by making the elasticity of demand asymmetric in their favour. A brand benefits the consumer when its demand is made inelastic at the cost of rivals whose demand has turned elastic. In this way price competition is avoided. This obviously requires development of customer pulling factors. The brand must successfully set itself apart or differentiate itself from others in the pack and create intense customer motivation. In modern day marketing it is difficult to create and maintain differentiation solely based on the product and that is where branding comes in handy.

Jones (1998) defines 'brand' as 'a product that provides functional benefits plus added values that some consumers value enough to buy'. The strongest brands have two important characteristics. First, they are highly distinctive. This distinction is built on a balanced combination of two benefits:

- Motivating benefits   –   that prompt consumers to chose a product category (usually product-centric functionality).
- Discriminating benefits   –   that make consumers choose one brand over the other.

No brand can ever be successful by giving poor performance on motivating benefits. Motivating benefits are fundamental building blocks of a strong brand. For instance a laptop brand would fail to gain any favour from its customers if its information processing capability is suspect. Getting into customer consideration requires that the brand must meet the minimum customer expectations criteria. It must qualify as a laptop computer in terms of its features and attributes like the processing technology (processor, cache, speed), operating system (DVD drive, VRM, DDR, Serial ATA, Windows, HDD protection), screen, security system, weight, thinness, battery life, robustness and warranty. A purified water brand in a similar vein must achieve a certain level of purity by eliminating harmful bacteria and other impurities in order to be considered as a pure aqua brand.

Discriminating benefits can pull consumers only when enough motivation exists to choose the product category. The second level consideration in branding revolves around the challenge of winning customers' favour over the other brands in the consideration set. Unless a brand develops some discriminating consumer benefits it may not move beyond consideration. For instance, in the laptop category, Sony Vaio brings in customers with its small size and colours, Lenovo focuses on the performance of the machine while Apple attempts to knock off competition in terms of its looks and user interface.

No brand can find favour with all customers. The attempt to establish relevance among all customers is a ready recipe for disaster. Markets are no more large chunks of similar customers. Presently markets are highly evolved and customers tend to be fragmented. Prima facie in the men's apparel market all shirt customers buy shirts to wrap their bodies. Therefore for a novice a shirt is a shirt is a shirt. Therefore the shirt market is made up of one big segment of customers who buy shirts. But actually the motivations to buy a shirt differ radically from one customer set to the other. Consider the case of Madura Coats. It has four shirt brands in its portfolio instead of one, each aimed at a different segment with uniquely defined value propositions:

- Louis Philippe   –   Luxury
- Van Heusen   –   Power dressing
- Allen Solly   –   Friday dressing
- Peter England   –   Value for money

It would be nearly impossible to combine all the attributes and benefits desired by different customers under a single brand. When one tries to be everything for everybody the danger is one may end up becoming nothing. Combining two benefits within the ambit of a brand may make great intuitive sense. This is akin to killing two birds with one arrow. Consider a toothpaste that seeks to combine the benefits of cavity protection with breath freshness. How successful is this brand going to be? The answer is that it would end up becoming a dud. The reasoning is elaborated here:

- Cavity protection is coveted by mothers who want their kids not to develop cavities in their teeth.
- Fresh breath is demanded by socially conscious young customers who want to seek acceptance and avoid rejection in proximate situations.

A brand that seeks to combine both the benefits may end up appealing to neither of the customer groups. Combining one proposition with the other has an effect of dilution of the brand's core essence. Mothers looking for cavity protection are likely to prefer a brand with exclusive cavity protecting rather than the one seeking to combine one benefit with the other. For this segment the other benefit, freshness, is an outsider in their consideration. The same would hold true for the youth segment. However this strategy would be feasible when there is a third segment of customers present in the market that seeks cavity protection along with fresh breath.

A brand therefore has to limit its target to a chosen consumer segment. A brand's added values stem from the following:

- Brand experience   – Consumer's brand experience resulting in familiarity, known reliability and reduced risk.
- User profile   – Value added by the kind of people who use the brand (user profile as glamorous, well-heeled), like Armani wearers or Harley riders.

- Brand effectiveness — Development of beliefs by consumers about a brand's effectiveness, for instance, in medicines and cosmetics brands act like ingredients and thereby create the perception of superior performance. Customers may find Crocin as a better pain reliever than an unbranded tablet with the same salt combination.
- Brand appearance — Value addition from the way a brand is packaged and made to appear to its audience.

PRODUCT AND BRAND

Product is a narrow conceptualisation of what a marketer offers to customers. It is production centric perspective of value. The outcome of a production process is usually a physical entity in the shape of a car or a computer or a watch. For instance advertisements of Intel usually show robots working on the assembly line to produce different micro processors like Centrino or Intel Core 2 Duo. 'Assembly line' is the term that refers to a place where different parts or components are assembled which end up as a finished product. However when a product is made to pass through a reverse process of production, that is, deconstruction, it ends up in a number of parts or components. A product is a physical entity which is produced or manufactured in the factories. In the context of services where nothing physical is produced but a service is created the logic of a service product is no different from a goods product except that the outcome in the case of services is an intangible product. For instance banking operations performed anywhere on earth produce banking services and courier service operations produce similar consumer overnight delivery benefits. Deconstruction of a service product would lead to the identification of activities and operations performed somewhere in the back end of the service operations system.

Brand on the other hand is a wider conceptualisation of what a marketer offers to its market. Although brands are pervasive and ubiquitous their conceptualisation as products is tantamount to catching water with the fish net. Fishing net can only catch fish not water. Catching water requires a different apparatus. Consider the following:

- There is a watch that is engineered to keep time with high accuracy and is officially certified. The parts of the watch are carefully mounted in the case with uncompromising quality checks and are put through rigorous performance tests. It is durable and made of high precious metals. It is programmed automatically to adjust days and dates.
- A company markets a liquid germicide. Its chemical formulation is tested and proven to have high effectiveness in the application areas where germ fighting is the concern. The antiseptic liquid has a clinical smell which some people find offensive while others like it.
- There is a company which pioneered making of trousers designed for very rough and hard wear. Heavy-duty blue-dyed cotton fabric is used for their construction. The trousers are given double seams with rivets to provide extra strength. Big pockets are patched-on that can hold good weight.
- Performance in sports is influenced by the shoes. The comfort, traction, weight, fit, flexibility and air circulation are all important for sporting performance. Therefore like cars sports shoes need to be engineered. A company keeping all these considerations in mind designs high performance sports shoes. A lot of money is spent on research and development in shoe design to facilitate high performance in the sports arena.

Consider customer reactions to aforementioned products in terms of price perceptions, quality perceptions and willingness to be loyal to the given entity. The customer responses in these cases are likely to trigger left brain activity—purely rational, analytic and product centric. However, when the brands Rolex, Dettol, Levis and Adidas are mentioned along with the above descriptions the buyer response would take an altogether different turn. Now the perception becomes much richer and more meaningful striking a deeper connection with customers. Now gauge the perceptions of customer price, quality and willingness to be loyal. Mention of brand names has transformational influence. The physical entity is transformed into a perceptual one.

Products are physical entities and they reside in the physical world like a Peter England shirt. Brand on the other hand is an intangible concept constructed in the perceptual or mental world. Brands reside in the perceptual space of the prospects. Unlike physical products that can be seen and touched through our senses brands are non-physical and do not permit access by senses. Their existence manifests at the point of purchase through consumer behaviour. The approach and avoidance behaviours are caused by branding activities. Brands differ from products in the following ways:

- Product is a physical entity; brand is a perceptual entity.
- Product is made up of physical parts, components and materials; brands are made up of perceptions.
- Product is amenable to easy copying; brand does not lend to easy copying.
- Product is an outcome of production; brand is created by communication.
- Product usually follows a life cycle; brand can achieve immortality.

MENTAL ENTITY

One observation in the context of the world's top brands is particularly revealing. A manager once observed that if Coca Cola were to lose all its production-related assets in a disaster, the company would survive, whereas if all its consumers were to have a sudden lapse of memory and forget everything related to Coca Cola, the company would go out of business. The implication of this statement is far reaching. The ownership and possession of brands unlike other conventional assets like the plant or land tends to divided between the marketer and the consumer. Although the Coke brand is owned by Coca Cola Company it is not possessed by it. The brand Coke resides in the minds of the consumers.

Brand building efforts unlike creation of something physical are directed at consumers' minds aimed to create, maintain and nurture a concept. Marketers with their brand building efforts make investments in peoples' minds by linking a name with associations, images and emotions to enhance the perceived value of an entity. Brands are transformational in nature. For instance the value perceptions greatly differ when 'Coke' is imprinted on a cola bottle rather than 'RC' even though in reality the contents may just be the same.

Products are entities of the real physical world. Brands on the other hand are entities of the perceived subjective mental world. The product component is essential for brand building. Products draw their justification from their functions. Brands create transformational influence. The brand Coke transforms a cola into a higher satisfying drink not because of better thirst quenching or better tingling in the mouth or superior taste. Rather the drinker psychologically feels better for choosing Coke, which is the number one brand. It is ubiquitous, it represents what America stands for—leadership, originality and heritage. This instantly allows you to get clubbed with a class of people. The non-product pull has become so strong that in many cases brand names have become badges. Brand names and symbols have come out in the open and consumers are happy to flaunt them. For instance brands like FCUK, Nike, Adidas, Louis Vuitton, Bulgari and Chanel. The draw here lays a brand's ability to make its customer feel better. Brand is a perceptual entity that resides in the mental space of consumers.

A technical perspective adopted by experts which combines diverse fields is a psychological view of the working of the brain and brand as a 'totality of stored synaptic connections… a web of connecting neurons that "fire" together in different patterns' (Gordon and Ford-Hutchinson 2002). Brands exist in consumers' minds as complex neural networks. A set of associations are pulled together in the form of a web of nodes and connections when a brand name hits the consumers' minds. Marketers like a spider weave this web of related concepts around brand names using a verity of tools. All these signals stemming from marketing programmes are received by prospects and stored under a banner or a computer like a folder called 'brand'. McCracken (2005) further clarifies that brands are like bundles of meanings. It is because of these meanings that it is possible to talk about brand image, brand personality and brand position. When marketers craft brand experiences, it is done to communicate brand meanings.

As products become similar, the justification to exhibit preference may stand diminished on rational basis. But brands thrive by inducing a psychological discomfort for not choosing them. In product categories where psychological guilt is difficult to induce, the brand building rests on the cultivation of superior product functionality to connect with customers and achieve differentiation. Brands in such cases have to thrive on superior product functionality in order to create valued differentiation (in automotive tyres Goodyear brings new technology to enhance road safety benefits, Orient fans talks of PSPO for superior air delivery and Head & Shoulders once boasted of micro ZPTO).

Even in product categories which appear totally cold and rational brands acquire power by adding non-product dimensions in the consumer's perception. For instance anti skid technology may give Goodyear a powerful way to differentiate its tyres from the others in a real sense, yet unless these benefits are translated into the personal consumer context the brand is likely to struggle as a commodity. Brand is a devise to fix a dispassionate product in the consumer's very personal life which also comprises of psycho-social dimensions. Goodyear gains consumer confidence not entirely from its technology but by how technology makes life secure and tension free on roads. Security and peace are feelings cherished by consumers and that is where brands hit to gain strength. The perceptions of a confidence and tension free ride besides other things are the contents contained in the brand Goodyear.

CONTAINER AND CONTAINED

Products are physical and therefore they are contained in the real world. The real world is their container. Brands are perceptual entities and they are contained in consumers' minds. A consumer's mind is an information processing system. It stores, processes and reproduces informational output. Like any other storing system marketers create brands as containers in which they deposit emotions, values, promises, images and associations. The combination of product and non-product-related associations determine the type of brand created by the marketer. Brand choice is dictated by a gamut of considerations including customers and competitors. Consider for example the repertoire of associations contained by the following brands:

- Colgate Dental Cream – Family, traditional, conservative, old fashioned, not outgoing, practical, price conscious, dependable, logical, ring of confidence, white paste and cavity protection.
- Close-Up – Youth, freshness, confidence, new, mouthwash, red, gel, tangy, enthusiastic, ambitious, upper class, smile, energetic, carefree, youthful, romantic, excitement and happening.

Depending upon the deposits made in the container, brand acquires meaning. The above list of associations can be divided into three groups: product and functionality related (such as red, mouthwash, cavity protection); non-product-related like feelings engendered (romantic, excitement) and user related (youthful, ambitious, practical, confident). Upon seeing the brand these contents of brands are activated to create the pull. Which of the consumer motivational forces a brand seeks to activate, defines the nature of the brand. In the aforementioned example, Colgate comes closer to a functionality orientation whereas Close-Up is a more sensory and expression oriented brand. Often in some cases category constraint forces a brand to rely upon the functionality route. However if there are no restrictions imposed by the category brands create value addition and differentiation by adding sensory or experiential and self expressive dimensions. BMW is a fine piece of mechanical engineering, but its brand is created out of experiential inputs (driving pleasure) and user imagery (achiever, success, rich, refined taste and statement).

CONCLUDING REMARKS

Branding does not provide a shortcut way into winning consumers. Brands have acquired their relevance from equipping marketers with paths to add value beyond functionality embedded in the product component. Brands are not about names and symbols although these are used to signify the brands. Brands are not about communication although communication is an essential part of brand building. Often the manifested part of a brand is mistakenly taken as the brand whereas it is not so. It is important to dig below the surface to discover how a brand intersects with consumers and creates value. Simplistically, a brand is a sign, symbol, a name or a combination thereof; but actually, building a brand is much more than a quest for an appealing sign, symbol or a name. Brand begins with an idea or concept which often is rooted in an extraordinary vision. Every successful brand name is built on a consumer-relevant idea that makes the life of the customer better. And it is this idea that manifests into a product or service.

Brand Transformation

The ivy league of brands on earth is headed by Coca Cola followed by Microsoft and IBM. According to *Business Week*/Interbrand survey of top brands (2005) these brands are valued at 67.5 billion, 60 billion and 53.5 billion US dollars. In India Colgate tops the list of the *The Economic Times* (2006) listing of top Indian brands followed by Lux and Dettol. Why have these brand listings become important in the recent past? Many managers often lose their jobs when their brand slips down in the ranking. Some managers are rewarded handsomely for their brand's upward movement. Business firms are rarely ranked on the basis of their conventional assets. The assets as disclosed in the financial statements seem to be pushed to the background. The market valuation of business enterprises is governed by brands more than anything else. This growing fascination for brand building and ownership is a manifestation of deeper level changes that the business system has undergone in the last three decades. To a simple eye business continues to operate as it used to in the past. It would take a probing eye to reach beyond the surface to appreciate how the concept of value and value creation process has drastically changed over time. That is, brands have acquired their coveted superior value creation capacities, which were once invested in tangible assets that get reported in conventional financial statements.

ASSETS AND THE ASSET

In the new system of business brands are more coveted than anything else. How important a brand actually is for a manager can be gauged from a statement made by John Stuart, the then CEO of Quaker Oats. He remarked, 'If this company were split up I would give you property, plants and equipments and I would take the brands—and I would fare better than you' (Chiaravalle and Schenck 2006: 259). And the value that companies attach to brands in their acquisitions tells the same story. Philip Morris paid more than four times the book value of Kart in 1988. Nestle paid more than five times the book value of Rowntree. Ford once coughed up 2.5 billion US dollars for the Jaguar brand. One of the most talked about brand acquisition stories in India has been that of Tata acquiring two legendary British brands—Land Rover and Jaguar—from Ford. The brands have changed hands at a whopping 2.3 billion US dollars. Tata clinched the deal at an attractive price. Ford had acquired these brands for 6 billion US dollars. Ford bought Jaguar for 2.5 billion in 1989 and Land Rover for 2.75 billion in 2000.

It is not uneasy to understand that there is something about brands that makes firms clamour for them. Following deductive logic in its simplest way the rise of brands as coveted assets and branding as among the most important business functions signify some change that the business environment has undergone. The balance sheet of a firm was typically constructed to depict the financial state that revealed the liabilities on the one side and the assets on the other. The statement about the assets that a firm held allowed the analyst to make judgments on the strengths and weaknesses of the company. A balance sheet is typically a navigational tool used by both internal managers and the outside public to judge how well the business has been performing.

The Oxford Dictionary of Finance and Banking (1997) defines assets as 'any object, tangible, that is of value to its possessor'. Assets drive the value of businesses for their capacity to create wealth by generating revenue streams. Historically some assets like the plant and machinery, land, buildings and equipments were most coveted for they were used to manufacture products. This method of reporting originated to cater to the needs and compulsions imposed on firms by the environment that prevailed then. The concept of value and value creation process in the industrialisation wave hovered around the physical product and the tangible assets. The value creation capacity of a firm was invested in the assets assortment owned by the firm. For instance Ford achieved remarkable success in the automobile market in its early years on the strength of the plants it owned and assembly processes it mastered. Companies like General Electric, Gillette, Chrysler, Sony, Marconi, IBM and Motorola went on to become great players in their respective industries on the strengths of their products' uniquenesses often based on proprietary design and technology. At the end the success of business was determined by two things: the value and the value creation process.

- Value   – Customer satisfying capacity, embedded in a product.
- Value creation process – The manufacturing or production embedded in a plant or factory.

The focus in the early part of industrialisation had been on 'manufacture' and 'manufactured products'. Firms used conventional assets as prime weapons to compete in the market place. In both of these conceptualisations tangibility played a dominant role. Accordingly product innovation and differentiation assumed a critical role in the competitive strategy of business. But with the onset of new business environments the concept of value as being embedded in a physical entity has been seriously challenged. Products in various markets are closely matched in terms of specifications. These offer similar functionality. At the same time it is becoming nearly impossible to create a unique manufacturing system.

NEW PARADIGM

As the previous century came to a close the critical factors that organisations relied upon to succeed have also undergone a radical shift (Ashkenas et al. 1998). The advent of microprocessors, information processing speed, speed of communication and emergence of global economy has shifted the basis of competition and competitive success. The shifting paradigm of success has made the old factors of success such as the size, role clarity, specialisation and control obsolete. These factors in the new context are more of liabilities rather than assets. The new factors for organisational success are speed, flexibility, integration and innovation.

Marketers in the earlier times controlled and excelled in the twin tasks of manufacturing and marketing under one banner. The old system of value creation had been based on the concept of bundling of activities as a tendency to domesticate the value adding processes and activities. But this paradigm is giving way to fragmentation. Firms that are closer to process than to technology are better positioned to perform manufacturing efficiently and the firms closer to the market or customers are better positioned to understand their problems and develop solutions (Achrol 1997: 9).

The new world without boundaries has unleashed a new order wherein the entire value-creation process need not be domesticated. The value chains have become fragmented. The divorce has been propelled by pressured search for higher efficiency. The twin set of manufacturing and marketing competencies are emerging to be somewhat incompatible. The resulting effect is seen in the emergence of a new order of firms that own and specialise in marketing and manufacturing competencies. The organisational format is networked systems. Managers of modern enterprise must learn to give up control over assets and people and rely instead on partners and outsourcers to run their assets. The managers need to become dexterous in managing relationships instead of assets (Sawhney 2006: 10).

The firms close to the market with competencies in brand building, marketing research and intelligence, response flexibility and speed act as conduits between the back and front ends of the entire marketing system. Table 3.1 lists some of the front end firms that own brand power and enjoy the marketing edge and the back end suppliers of products. The firms that enjoy marketing connect at the front end and are brand builders and at the back end are the firms that play the manufacturing game. Top sports shoes marketer

Table 3.1:   Brand Makers and Product Makers

Product/brand	Manufacturer	Marketer
Dalda	Pyramid Lamba	Bunge
Sweekar	AP Organics	Marico
Britannia Milkman	Modern Dairy	Britannia
Nature Fresh	Parekh Food	Cargill
Fa Talc	Avalon Pvt. Ltd	Henkel
Spinz	Avalon Cosmetics	Cavin Care
Vanish Washing Powder	Trisis Corp	Reckitt Benckiser
Kitchens of India	Innovision Foods	ITC
Robin Dazzling	Modern Whiteners	Reckitt Benckiser
Parachute	Amit Ayurvedic	Marico
Palmolive	Accra Pack	Colgate
Lakme	Jas Cosmetics	Hindustan Lever
Denim	Sonia Industries	Hindustan Lever
Old Spice	Rubicon Formulations	Meneze Cosmetics
Savlon	Vita Soaps & Specialties	J&J
Cinthol Talc	Ishwar Mfg Co.	Godrej
Park Avenue Perfume	J K Helene Curtis	Raymonds

Source: Compiled by the author.

Nike invests heavily in brand building. It concentrates on shoe design and not on shoe manufacturing to propel its business into huge success. Leader in the mobile communication field, Airtel also follows a similar approach. Airtel concentrates on brand building while the greater part of its mobile telephony operations are sourced to suppliers' networks management firms.

One of the top companies that have been performing extremely well is McDonald's. What does it owe its success to? Is it the burger that it manufactures? Is it something else? In fact McDonald's does not manufacture the burgers it sells, rather its outlets are assembly factories and the manufacturing of the ingredients required to assemble a burger is done by collaborators. McDonald's strength lies in sensing and marketing while its manufacturing is outsourced to other players. For instance, a vegetable burger sold in India is made in parts by companies that include EBI Cremica (butter and breading), Kitran Foods (vegetable patty), Trikaya Agriculture and Ooty Farms (fresh iceberg lettuce), Dynamix Dairy (Cheddar cheese), Shah Bector (buns) and Quaker Cremica (special vegetarian sauce).

In this new paradigm of value creation, Tata has been able to make a very successful foray into the passenger car market with Indica. Telco, instead of focusing on the manufacturing of a complete car, concentrates on the core, and the rest is procured from outside suppliers. The company makes only the critical parts like cylinder head, block and transmission. The other units like piston parts are manufactured by Goetze, India Pistons and IP Rings; electrical parts are sourced from Lucas-TVS; Lucas supplies the fuel injection system and head and tail lamps; brakes are supplied by Kalyani and Brakes India; Gabriel makes shock absorbers; sheet metal parts are provided by Jay Bharat and wheels are sourced from Wheels India (Shridharan 1999). This new emergent model of manufacturing is disintegrating the conventional value chains and yet casting the marketers into a new role of integrators of value, to sense and respond to the speed of market needs with greater flexibility.

This trend of limiting the business focus on to a few core activities and developing high competencies is also illustrated by the computer industry. It is rare to come across a firm that manufactures the entire computer by itself. This is discernable from a built unit. When a computer is disassembled than the reality of the computer comes out in the open. Various parts like monitor, keyboard, mouse, printer, scanner; CPU, motherboard, casing, software, and so on, are sourced from vendors like Samsung, LG, Logitech, Sony, Mercury, AMD and Intel. Earlier the products used to be identified by the manufacturer's name with lines like 'Manufactured by ...' but now such lines are replaced by new lines where 'by' is replaced by 'for'. For instance the cell phones of the market leader Nokia now have the marking 'Made for Nokia'.

RATIONALISTIC PERSPECTIVE

In the industrialisation wave the firms invested all the want fulfilling capacities in the physical product that they manufactured. For instance Gillette's empire was built on the patented safety razor design and Ford's Model T revolutionised personal transportation. The incandescent light bulb for General Electric and Jeep for Chrysler were the bases of connection with the market. The firms manufactured and marketed the complete built units of their products. The unique design or technology permitted the firms to build barriers for customer switching and repeat buying. The firms could hold on to their technology and prevent it from getting diffused in the market for long durations. Some of the product pioneers include:

- Carrier   – Air conditioners
- Kellogg's   – Cereal breakfast
- Apple   – Personal computers
- Parker   – Ink pens
- Sony   – Walkman/portable cassette players
- Panasonic   – VHS/video recording

The product used to be the focal point of all marketing and manufacturing endeavours of the firm. The customers drove utility from product performance. In the early stages of the evolution of market and business brands were driven by features and benefits. The features-benefits marketing were the product of industrialisation (Schmitt 1999). This approach focused on functional features and assumed that customers' behaviours are rational and they use analytical, verbal and quantitative approaches to buying. Marketing in the early stages of development indeed had tended to address the fundamental concerns of human existence. Previously when goods tended to mean essentials of food, clothing and shelter, practical matters were important. The consumer concept was that of the economic man concerned with more judicious spending. Accordingly concrete value embedded in the products mattered to him or her (Levy 1959).

The excessive focus on product and its rational aspects that managers seem to have been concerned with stems from the fact that managers are scarcely trained to look beyond. Consequently the other side of the product is not explored to create value.

Typically managers by training and background come from so called rational disciplines like management and engineering. The excessive rationalistic or left brain perspective often causes the marketing approach to be marred by a tunnel vision. And the value definition is locked in the narrow confines of functionality. A person who is exclusively trained in the field of electronics engineering may have a vision of a television that does not transcend the circuits and technology complications. The vision of an ideal car of an automobile engineer may be at radical variance from the vision of a customer. The specialist orientations of these technicians get them to pay excessive attention to that part of the product which customers may be less concerned about. Attention to technical details may be prompted by in the situation of default when products fail to function as anticipated. In India, the Onida brand of televisions was first to lay stress on product aesthetics when it launched a range of television christened 'Candy' to promote the concept of a second television in a home.

Excessive rationalistic perspective is also visible in marketing strategy development. As a result the aesthetic aspects do not factor in their decision processes and excessive attention is consumed by known and beaten aspects of marketing strategy such as segmentation, targeting and positioning (Anderson 1980). Consequently firms find it difficult to achieve breakthrough gains in strategy development. Big and visible segments are excessively chased and segments hidden beneath scarcely discovered and penetrated. Managers are oriented to view innovation as something applicable to the field of product. Accordingly product features, ingredients and attributes are taken to ultimate heights to develop into buyer rallying points. This rationalistic orientation is also visible in theories explaining buying behaviour. Excessive focus has been given to information processing models (Bettman 1979). These models of choice are built on the assumption of rationality and view consumers as users of logic in solving buying problems. Consumers are observed as information processing systems who deploy cognitive capacities to negotiate buying problems.

COMMODITISATION

In virtually every market leading firms are seriously challenged by the competitors. And this competition is fuelled by the fact that leaders have difficulty in maintaining the lead in the marketed product. Sustaining product differentiation in terms of unique features or functionality is near impossible. The product pioneers are challenged with very little time gap as the technology gets shared and diffused. The diffusion of the value creation process and the parity in value creating assets is unleashing the forces of mass cloning of products and services in various industries. Consider the following players in different product categories and examine whether the products offered under different names are different in significant manners:

- Coke and Pepsi cola drinks.
- Xerox and Canon photocopiers.
- Lenovo and HP computers.
- Adidas and Nike shoes.
- Ford Endeavor and Mitsubishi Pajero sports utility vehicles.
- Rolex and Omega watches.
- Canon and Nikon cameras.
- Tata and SAIL steel.
- Carl Zeiss and Essilor optics.
- Philips and Surya CFL lamps.
- Sony and LG LCD TVs.
- Whirlpool and Samsung refrigerators.
- Kingston and Transcend pen drives.
- Parryware and Hindware sanitary ware.
- Lizol and Domex household cleaners.
- ACC and Gujarat Ambuja cements.
- Indian Oil and BP petroleum products.
- Aquafina and Kinley packaged drinking water.
- Orient and Usha fans.

A technical product analysis of various brands is likely to reveal a discomforting reality. The products have narrow points of differentiation between each other. The barriers to imitation stand so diminished that product parity is a big and nasty reality for the marketers. The technical side of the products is increasingly becoming a commodity. The inability to hold on to real product differences is a depressing reality of modern day marketplace. The products can be disassembled easily in order to learn about their construction and uniqueness. The developments in the fields of engineering and re-engineering allow others to create similar products. Increasing the technical parity of products in no way suggests that the product functionality embedded in technical products is becoming less relevant. On the contrary customers seem less tolerant of technically deficient offering by a marketer.

Consider the automobile car market. Most of the cars in different segments have come close to each other to the extent that they fail to offer any real product differentiation. Various brands fall short on offering any real hooks for customers to base their preferences on. Take for example Maruti Esteem, which competes in the 'C' segment. This offering of Maruti competes with other players like Ford Fiesta Exi, Chevrolet Aveo 1.4 (base), Hyundai Accent GLE and Honda Citi Exi. One of the advertisements of the Esteem follows the cognitive route to persuade the potential customer by establishing its credentials. The dimensions of the vehicle are used to compare Esteem with other brands to draw the inference that this car is the 'best in its class' as shown in Table 3.2. Promotional effort notwithstanding the comparison appears to be an attempt to enlarge the perceptual gap between the car brands that in actuality is not so much. Most brands come dangerously close to each other and create a parity perception. But despite this perception of parity Honda City leads the pack. The reason for this accomplishment probably does not lie in the car but elsewhere.

BRANDS COME CLOSE TO EACH OTHER

In various categories, specification parity is one of the important headaches of the marketers. The new emergent business environment allows the competition to replicate offerings point by point easily and quickly. One of the important and noteworthy

Table 3.2: Brands Come Closer to Each Other

Dimension	Esteem	Ford Fiesta	Chevrolet Aveo	Hyundai Accent	Honda City
Performance to weight ratio (BHP/tonne)	97.2	73.8	85.8	92.7	73.9
Acceleration (0–100 in seconds)	11.49	13.18	13.42	13.12	13.11
Mileage (in kmpl)	16.7	15.3	14.9	13.8	16.6
Driver seat height adjust	Yes	No	No	No	No
Rear seat armrest	Yes	No	No	No	Yes
CD cum MP3 Player	Yes	No	No	No	No
Power antenna	Yes	No	Yes	No	Yes
Rear spoiler	Yes	No	No	No	No

Source: *The Times of India*, 24 August 2006, p. 9.

developments in the last century has been in the field of tech-nology. Nothing seemed to have escaped from the impact of technology (Davis and Meyers 1998). The products' availability has dramatically increased in the last century. And various industries suffer from the menace of excess capacity. In the beginning of the 20th century most industries had an easy going because of demand far exceeding the industry capacity. But when the century came to a close the situation reversed into that of excess supply. Another important change has been the standardisation of quality. The competition forced firms to invest in production systems and achieve certain standards in product quality. The quest for quality has eliminated shoddy products. Concepts like Six Sigma, Total Quality Management, Quality Circle, Poka Yoke and a host of Japanese practices are now widely spread throughout the world. This has had an effect of product quality standardisation.

If on the one hand product quality has been improved dramat-ically on the other hand the simultaneous effect of this has been narrowed differentiation in product functionality. The quality of products and services does not differ much from each other. This has relegated the role to the product to achieve market success. Markets are pushed into the parity game and buying shifts to becoming price driven. The biggest of all fears for a marketer is to witness its product getting sucked into a commodity spiral. Even an iconic brand like Marlboro is not saved from the commoditisation peril. Philip Morris experienced this about two decades ago when the brand began to lose its share to unheard of brands. And reasons for this decline were attributed to apparent lack of distinction (*The Economist* 1993). The concerns on this one sided method of pulling customers led early advertising thinker Martineau (1957: 4) to write 'insistence on product claims, economic benefits has turned far too much advertising in to dull, uninvolving chant of mechanica....' The rise of sales promotions and incentives in most categories to move the market response is the manifestation of this malaise that marketing suffers from.

THE MISERY UNLEASHED

The technical value parity has definite consequence for businesses. All aspects of business strategy are condensed in the value that is offered to customers. The ultimate deliverable sought from marketing strategy is a blueprint to murder competition in the prospect's mind. And this is achieved when the prospect's choice set is reduced to only one brand. This is the one single most legitimate method of elimination of competition and creating monopoly. The parity created in the technical aspects of the product, enabled by the new business environment, diminishes the appeal to customers, to some extent, to stay loyal to a particular marketer. It creates conditions for inclusion of offerings of other marketers in the choice set.

The first level of brand building starts with matching 'what a product does'. The functionality embedded in a product category imposes the first barrier that has to be crossed in order to participate in the marketing game. Market leaders in competitive frames have to always be on their toes and make value additions to keep ensuing competition at bay. Failure in this regard aversely affects the marketing bottom line. Parity induces market sharing. As more players join the market the pressures to retain and defend market shares increase. Technical product parity influences the marketing performance by adversely impacting both the cost and the revenue side of the marketing equation. On the cost side the pressures mount as investments in the defensive strategies have to be made. Defections to rivals have to be minimised or else the leadership position would get seriously challenged. Some of the market leaders like the following have undergone similar challenges in various product categories:

- Colgate   –   Toothpaste
- Maruti   –   Passenger cars
- Iodex   –   Pain-relieving ointment
- Bata   –   Shoes
- HMT   –   Wrist watches
- Bajaj   –   Scooters
- Hero Honda   –   Motorcycles
- Philips   –   Lighting equipments
- Godrej   –   Refrigerators
- Bisleri   –   Bottled water
- Brooke Bond   –   Tea
- Atlas   –   Bicycles
- Escorts   –   Farm tractors
- Raymonds   –   Men's wear
- Surf   –   Detergent

Given these developments the challenge for the marketer is to unearth new ways to kill the parity unleashed by the forces of the new marketing environment. The exhaustion of supply-side drivers—plant and technology—in building competitive superiority is creating pressures on marketers to look elsewhere for breaking product parity and creating differentiation. The ultimate challenge for a brand manager is to find ways to achieve brand discrimination in consumers' minds. Marketing strategy succeeds when it builds and promotes discrimination. Branding fails if the marketer is unable to discover ways to transcend product functionality and add something more that kills the dawning customer indifference towards the brand. This requires a shift in the thinking and mindset of managers who look and plug into traditional assets to build customer pull.

Now that the supply side drivers of value creation have ceased in their efficacy to add value it may be better to look outside in the market for discovering such sources. The quest for the cultivation of brand superiority calls for a transcendence of the product centric vision. Perhaps the value drivers are located outside in consumers' minds. The issue is how to endear a brand with customers when the product element of the brand is on the threshold of commoditisation. Often brands are contextualised narrowly as products or services with embedded performance capabilities. However the same product when it enters into a consumer's consumption system may assume a greater psychosocial–spiritual meaning. Discovering conceptualisations that are beyond functionality may hold significant promise in brand building.

BRAND FOR VALUE TRANSFORMATION

Branding offers marketers escape mechanisms from the commodity spiral. It offers paths to transform the nature of value delivery by pulling the product out of its narrow functionality capsule. It aims to push the marketing entity on a higher value orbit by transforming a physical object into something greater than merely an assembly of ingredients or components or parts. When the product as the driver of customer value begins to get marginalised by the availability of look-alikes, branding can come to its rescue. It can achieve significant value transformation by adding new value drivers to the basic product available for consumption. Value dimensions so added can successfully create consumer discrimination and beat commoditisation. The question is how can this be achieved? Where would the value adding dimensions come from?

At the very fundamental level a product or service seeks to lift a customer from a less desired state to a more desired one. The product and services assume roles of tension reducing mechanisms. The human drive at the most basic level is to get out of negative sates of existence. First the dissatisfaction has to be weeded out of life. But what could be the dimensions of these negative states? The state or condition implies the world of customers. This includes the internal and external world, the physical and non-physical world, the functional and non-functional world and the physiological and psychological world. The clues to value adding dimensions are found in understanding the world of customers. The utility or rationalistic consumer perspective narrowly locks the customer as a utility maximiser. This may be true for people surviving at the bottom of the survival continuum. But economic prosperity allows people to 'move up' on this continuum of existence. Once a person achieves satisfaction of needs essential for survival, consumption tends to assume a bigger socio-cultural–psychological orientation. The utilities embedded in products become essential for brand creation but what these are 'topped up' with become true motivators. The solutions to the branding riddle may just lay hidden in this movement. However they may not always be explicit. They don't always manifest on the surface. They are seldom articulated and communicated. Instead they lay hidden, masked, submerged and implied. It is for the marketer to revisit the concepts of value and value creation process.

What can be done when a washing powder or detergent has done enough shouting about its technical excellence but still continues to be perceived as a mundane concoction of chemicals used to getting dirt out of clothes? How can the marketer respond to forces of parity when the rivals match the chemical formulation point by point? An inward marketer would typically 'move in' the organisation to look for ammunition. This mentality leads to the degeneration of marketing into attributes war, formulation war, advertising war, specifications war and price war. The smart strategy on the contrary should work in the opposite direction. It must rise and push the brand into a 'beyond the reach' zone. The product part of a brand is physical and amenable to engineering and reengineering. However brands provide an opportunity to transform physical entities into something perceptual with their genetic core that are much less amenable to imitation.

Hindustan Lever's premium detergent 'Surf' got stuck in this slow earth when its rival P&G matched its efficiency with Ariel detergent. The company instead of the 'move in' approach adopted the opposite. It turned to customers for possible ways to develop rallying points of value that reside outside the narrow product features and benefits domain. The product–customer interface was seen in a larger context to include social, psychological and emotional dimensions. With this deeper understanding the brand Surf Excel successfully made attempts to burst the narrow boundaries imposed by its product and went beyond. Now the Surf brand has little to do with washing powder and dirt removal and has more to do with allowing mothers to be good mothers in their role of allowing children to reach to their true potential. The brand facilitates mothers in their true role of making children 'grow up'. The growth here does not imply physical growth but mental growth. Their brand allows children to go through life's learning process without being bothered all the time about clothes getting dirty because now Surf is there to take care of that. It is a device to eliminate obstructions that come in the way of the real growth of children. To the naïve Surf Excel is a detergent but in the mental world of targeted customers (the mothers with growing children) it is 'much more'. It is this 'much more' that holds promise in elevating the product to a higher altar of value and escape the imposition of product parity.

The transformation of the 'Surf' brand from a lowly detergent or surfactant used to clean clothes to something of higher value for the targeted customer clearly demonstrates how newer brand missions or meanings could be created. This essentially involves asking fundamental questions about the 'business' the brand is currently seen to be in and where it strategically wants to 'move up' to. Getting the dirt out of clothes is a menial mission and that runs common across all brands in the category but the mission of allowing children to grow is rare and much higher on the value ladder.

The product part of the brand represents the entry ticket to a marketing game. It is essential but not sufficient for success. Product signifies delivery on the reason side of the customer but it leaves a lot to be achieved. A customers must be visualised in her or his totality. It is this exploration of the customer's totality that unveils the hidden opportunities to extend the product and catapult it into a higher value orbit. With astute branding the marketer is able to shift the marketing contest to an entirely different value space. Most strong brands like Caterpillar, Rolex, IBM, Nike, Mercedes and Mont Blanc have managed to break boundaries imposed by the products that these brands carry.

BRAND NEGOTIATION

Marketing for long has been too much driven by the 'matter', that is, the human body. Accordingly it is visualised more as a discipline related to materialism or the material aspects of human existence. The customer is often seen as matter driven by material concerns rooted in the body. Typically managers approach strategy development process with a fully conscious state using cognitive thinking procedures and routines with the assumptions of the customer being a conscious entity. But this may not be a complete understanding to base strategy on. There is much to be learnt about how customers think and act (Day 2002). There is an extreme necessity to understand customers' unconscious thinking. The challenge for the marketer is to overhaul the basic thinking about persuasion and product meaning and the place of logical, highly rational appeals versus emotional appeals (Martineau 1957).

The new consumer profiles do not match with the conceptualisation formed during the periods of economic deprivation and scarcity. The notion of value and the dimensions thereof have undergone a change. The issue is not whether a new consumer is the same as the old one or not, but rather it is how much is she different. In different places the shades of grey may differ. For new consumers time is a precious commodity, life is complex; she is informed and marketing literate. The new consumer looks for brand 'experiences' over and above bundles of product features and benefits (Baker and Bass 2003).

The great Indian philosopher Sri Aurobindo proposed the concept of evolution and involution (Maitra 2001). He states that there is descent of Spirit even into Matter. It for this reason Matter seeks to evolve into something higher than Matter, namely, Life. There is descent of the Spirit into Life that is why it seeks to rise into something higher than itself, namely, Mind. And the

Mind must move towards its source, that is, Supermind. And the ascendance continues till Absolute Spirit is reached. This process of evolution signifies the transformation and move towards something higher. Two facts must be recognised: the facts of being and becoming. The context of these processes is spirituality and higher order existence.

Marketing has been obsessed too much with one side of consumption. The resultant frameworks that have evolved to guide strategy look narrowly at the consumer as one who is concerned with the materialistic side of consumption or consumption for existence. This happens to the peril of ignoring the other side that involves consumption for meaning. The process of progression and evolution of a living being often takes a trajectory where quest for something beyond 'existence' is triggered. This marks the beginning of meanings in consumption. Great existentialists like Sartre and Camus have attempted to explore the purpose of existence and concluded that existence (the physical life) precedes essence (the meaning) (Gascoigne 1967). Humans are born and given a meaningless existence. The entire life turns into a struggle to give some meaning to a meaningless existence. For Sartre it is the exercise of 'free will' or 'choices' that we make, that give meaning to our lives. This interpretation of life accords a marketer an opportunity to assume the role of a provider of meaningful consumption. Here in this context beyond the role of the product as attendant of existence related concerns, brand can assume the role of serving the higher order values concerning existentialist issues.

With the rise in incomes as the bottom level sustenance is assured the tendency to move up and seek higher order values is imminent. Brands can be developed to engage customers at a higher value level. This necessitates viewing customers in a new light beyond the body to include emotions, intellect and spirit. Branding strategy is by and large created out of a conscious process relying upon data and insights. Conscious reflections may not adequately provide insights into what exactly motivates customers' actions and decisions. The outward façade needs to be penetrated into the deeper recesses of the subconscious to fully understand what motivates consumer actions and decisions.

Various parts combine to create the customer's world. The customer's mind, brain, body and external world influence one another in fluid and dynamic ways. Learning how these parts interact and influence each other is crucial for understanding the customer. Marketing research is often conducted on product features and attributes and their immediate consequences. This pays attention to psychological benefits at the cost of emotional ones. Product functionality is important but it represents only a small part of what motivates the customer (Zaltman 2003). Consumption in post modern society encompasses various nonrational aspects that have been ignored in the practice of marketing because of the dominance of the rational perspective in consumer behaviour theories. Consumption includes aspects like leisure, sensory pleasures, daydreams, aesthetics, emotions and fun. This consumption view falls within the purview of experiential consumption (Holbrook and Hirchman 1982).

VALUE TRANSCENDENCE

Powerful brands transcend the narrow boundaries of the product that they carry. They burst the hedge by transforming the marketing entity into something of greater importance by negotiating customers on vectors of coveted value. What are these vectors of value that a brand can use to climb up the value hierarchy? The value vectors would emanate existence and existentialist concerns—what life experiences the customer looks for and what life experience the customer now has. A brand must choose its value vector to deliver the expected value with one caution that most market entries now seem to reach parity on the functionality vector. That is where the logic of discovering the other value vectors begins.

Consider a brand like Tag Heuer. The brand achieves its exceptional cult-like status not as much from the character of a time keeping device that it apparently sells. In fact the watch function is not what pulls the customers, commands price premium and provides extreme joy from the ownership of a Tag Heuer watch. The brand draws its strength from its strong connection with the prospect's identity and the desire to express this identity. The brand Tag Heuer is not about time keeping which is only by the way. It is more about its ability to connect with the self-concept of the buyer ('What are you made of?' 'Don't crack under pressure'). The brand negotiates with the customer at a vector different from lower order product functionality. Rather it throws the time keeping object into an altogether different personal realm of self-realisation (an inward movement) and expression of a character (an outward movement). Almost a similar path is followed by another powerful watch brand, Rolex. The brand commands an almost fanatic following. The watch quality and excellence should not be mistaken for what the brand sands for. The pulls lie elsewhere, in its connotations—the stature, cut above and achievement.

For the brand manager an important and probably the most crucial issue is to obtain insights about the value vectors. Where should the journey begin? It must start from the value space. The value space implies the spectrum of values that offer the potential to satisfy customers. Brands represent condensations of entire efforts that a marketer undertakes to elevate customers from the lower end of existence to a higher one—from an imbalanced state of existence to a balanced one. The marketer has to analyse customer concerns regarding existence to discover the paths to be followed for value creation. In this regard customer insights play an important role. Where does the customer's concern lie? Any superficial scratching of the surface would lead to common discoveries about the riddles of customer satisfaction. A deeper and more penetrating search would allow a marketer to take an unbeaten path of more relevant and precious value delivery.

VALUE DIMENSIONS

From where should the journey to find the value adding dimensions start? The answer to this question cannot and must not start with the available assets and competencies vested in a business.

If it does then the chances that the branding process is likely to be reduced to a demand manipulation process become very high. The voyage for the discovery of brand mission or meaning must start with taking a deep plunge into the world of consumers. Existence from a customer's perspective is all about body, mind and soul. The value vectors emanate from what the customer perceives his or her existence to be all about. At the most mundane and primitive level human existence is all bodily survival and existence. This primary concern in the conceptualisation of need hierarchy is stacked at the bottom (Maslow 1970). In many societies and market pockets the customers may be stuck at the bottom level of existence. In such cases the brand building based on product—attributes and functionality—still holds the key. The value stems from product performance. It is about defending existence against the forces that endanger survival. At the bodily or basic-level human concerns allow brands to take on the utilitarian route to develop customer satisfying intersection points. Consider the following:

- Defensive existence concerns emanating from biological, physiological needs: water, food, health, physical fitness, procreation, sex, safety both physical and financial, thirst, hunger and sleep. Colgate attends to the fundamental need for oral hygiene and LIC promises financial security. Household cleaner brands like Domex and Lysol cater to the concern of safety against germs.

Progression or moving up implies that as needs regarding basic existence are satisfied people move up to higher order needs. In many parts of the world consumer society has crossed the survival threshold. Accordingly brand building must look beyond the product to encompass other sources of satisfaction. The possible paths to achieving this goal do not lie in the product, or product factory or technology. Within the human body is housed the brain and mind. This is home to cognitions and emotions. The cognitive part is driven by rationality and objectivity. Emotions on the other hand are subjective and non-rational. The consumer's consumption now takes on a beyond utility centric orientation. The other needs such as acceptance and belonging identification now assume the steering role. Accordingly brands must be invested with meanings that render them relevant in the consumer's consumption context. The psychological, cultural and sociological orientation of products becomes necessary. Consider the following:

- Offensive existence concerns stem from the desire to satisfy sense stimulation, acceptance and belonging to a group, identity construction and expression and emotional satisfaction like love, friendship, control, power and achievement. Brands in this realm have to cross over from the functionality–utility perspective to symbolic orientation. For instance the Apple brand is much more than customer friendly interface. It is about being individualistic and nonconformist. The brand is more about the user and relatively less about the product that it markets.

The forces of liberalisation and globalisation have been working to bring about a strategic shift in the lifestyle of millions of Indian consumers. The consumption paradigm is shifting from basic necessity to something beyond necessity. The economy is no longer operating in the 'need based' mode where people tended to buy only necessities of life with some 'indulgent' purchases thrown in. Now we operate in 'consumption based' economy, where indulgence is an accepted form of lifestyle. Austerity and necessity are appearing to be ceasing from our lifestyle (Confederation of Indian Industry 2006: 4). The marketers for long have relied on substance over style in their efforts to connect with customers. But now style is seated next to substance and the language of commerce is shifting to images and perceptions from nuts and bolts (Drawbaugh 2001: 2).

Emotional space accords opportunity to transform a product into a brand by making it a source affective experience. One of the typologies of emotions classifies the emotions as interest, joy, surprise, anger, distress, disgust, contempt, fear, shame and guilt (Izard 1977). One of the top selling brands in the perfume category is Calvin Klein's Obsession. This brand is not about the liquid that is contained in the bottle or its odour neutralising or creating effect. The brand very smartly stirs the desired emotions. In its early promotions men and women were shown the proximity of all consuming situations ('Ahh...the smell of it') involving lust (Sloan 1985: 104). Japanese car maker Toyota followed the initial strategy of building cars that appealed to thinking and reason. Toyota adopted a strategy of winning the customers on the basis of product appeal. The company's competitive advantage was based on cheap inexpensive labour. But this route was soon copied both within Japan and outside leading to the erosion of Toyota's uniqueness. It is then that the company took the next leap forward by evolving processes and technology to add quality, features and capabilities to its products to elevate them to the high value of the so called 'luxury' market.

As societies gravitate towards higher levels of economic affluence the social context of which the buyers are a part of begins to assume importance. The loss of self creates hankering for establishing identity. In this context possessions assume importance. There is a perceived loss of identity in vast oceans of humanity where everyone seems to be a faceless part of the crowd. The assembly line civilisation creates deficiency not at the level of basic survival but at the higher level of existence. The loss is made up by brands that help define and express the self that is otherwise hidden from the view. Brands become both creators and communicators of identity.

The self is very fragile and it needs support. Products provide the support to the delicate self that we possess. To a large extent we are what we have and possess (Tuan 1980). 'A man's Self is the sum total of all that he CAN call his, not only his body and his psychic powers, but his clothes and his house,....his lands, yacht and bank-account' (James 1890). The shift from the body to 'self' allows marketers to discover newer paths to serve customers by offering compensating mechanisms.

In this role brands become silent talking devices for many customers to 'speak up' without using conversational language. The hidden side is made public in a polished manner. Pepsi is an icon for 'youth and what convention is not all about'. Armani stands for sophistication and class. Brands in this respect both help customers belong and 'unbelong' to different classes that matter and do not matter. In the mobile phone market Motorola eased into a niche that Nokia left unoccupied. Their strategy was to lift the mundane communicating device into something of an instrument of style. The ultra thin Motorazr line of models is identified with a range of slim phones aimed to define the personality of the buyer. While Nokia phones were dedicated to functionality the likes of Samsung and LG moved on to create brands on the dimensions unfilled by the leader. But Nokia sensing the role of design has created 'Vertu'. The company has patented many of Vertu's design elements to prevent any dilution (Kukday and Mahajan 2006: 17).

Further beyond the body, brain and mind some people have an element of spirituality embedded in their value space. The existentialist concerns sometimes descend on people who act as both value creators and consumers thereof. Consumer's needs may extend way beyond the physiological, social and self expressive space to embrace 'beyond self' concerns like oneness with God, ecology, freedom, peace, salvation of the poor and service of the needy. In this journey of a human being, akin to the transcendence of a brand beyond the product element, here a person seeks transcendence beyond the self and self aggrandisement. This implies a search for a meaning. It is a path of self realisation when life is seen as a journey towards a cosmic link with the higher force. Progression on the path of need satisfaction in a hierarchical fashion sometimes leads to a confrontation with questions that relate with frictions and dissonance at the spiritual level. This level is akin to self actualisation where one tries to be what inherently one can be:

- Satisfaction is the all consuming concerns related to body and mind. Desire for power, achievement, belonging, hedonism or sense satisfaction and security make up a major motivational force up to a limit. Then one is expected to graduate to a higher order of being and becoming. For some people it is much more and it creates a craving for something beyond what is within the scope of physical to metaphysical reality. In this context brands may go on to attend the existentialist concerns and forge a cosmic link. Body Shop's basis of bonding with customers extended way beyond cosmetics made from natural ingredients to resisting painful animal testing. The Whisper brand attempts to make sense to customers at a higher order of concerns by contributing a part of its revenue towards girl education. Infosys stands tall among other software companies in terms of its ethics and value centricity.

What made the IBM brand different for the people working for the company? It was a set of values that included respect for the individual. This 'sacred cow' of the brand or brand essence made IBM a great place to work and perform. Brand meaning that transcended typical business like strategy, resources, cost, technology, and so on, charged the outstanding performance of IBM. The core values struck a spiritual connection with the people working for the company (Watson 1963). In a similar vein, British Airways championed people through its brand's central idea of putting the people first. It was designed to address concerns extending the business boundaries to connect with people at a higher level of existence. Putting the people first not only appealed to commercial logic but also to a spiritual sense. That is, life can be made much better for everybody on the planet if one takes little more care of each other (Campbell et al. 1990).

CONCLUDING REMARKS

Branding begins with the product element. There was a time that the product provided the basis for building successful brands. But now in the new emerging business environment product commoditisation is a dark marketing reality. In most product categories the product component is harder to differentiate. The parts, ingredients, components and technology are increasingly shared among various players in the market leading to a descending commonality factor. It is in this context that managers are faced with a challenge to transform value delivery over and above what is embedded in the product part of the offering. In this regard brand managers are charged to explore ways to achieve value transformation. Unlike the past when marketers turned to manufacturing and operations to create differentiated products now marketers have to turn to consumers for exploring possible value drivers which may be embedded in their value space consisting of body, mind and soul. As societies make a progression to higher economic development, as basic needs of customers are taken care of, the ascendance to higher order needs provides possible value dimensions to transform brand as a product to brand as a symbol capable of delivering psychological, social and spiritual satisfaction as seen in Figure 3.1.

Figure 3.1: Branding and Value Vectors

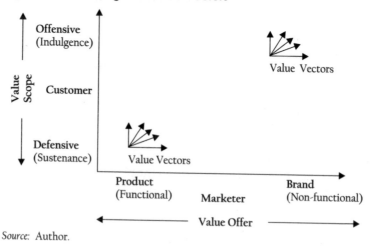

Source: Author.

Brand Vision: Concepts and Creation

Take any product category and seek answers to the following questions: how many brands make up the category in question and how much is the market share owned by the top three brands? To begin with let us start with the following product categories:

- Toothpaste
- Televisions
- Personal computers
- Refrigerators
- Shoes
- Detergents
- Biscuits
- Jeans

As in the above categories, the number of participants in most product categories has witnessed a big explosion but this does not imply that markets have become democratised. The market shares continue to be skewed in favour of a very few brands who enjoy a dominant share of the pie. The story is just about the same across all categories. There are 'the' brands that enjoy a share of the leadership as much as 80 per cent of the total market. And then there are hundreds of brands which have to be content with sharing a space as low as 20 per cent. Implicit in a branding exercise is category dominance. Branding is about reductionism. It involves the elimination of rivals from the marketing race in the consumer's mind. But what may be intriguing is the results that the top brands manage to achieve despite the all pervasive similar arsenal deployed by each one of the players in the category.

SIGHT AND VISION

Collect a sample of any five brands in a product category—let it be televisions or toilet soaps—and break these down to their smallest level. And now look for what that unique part or ingredient is that produces enormous discrimination at the consumer buying level. At the end the entire exercise may turn out to be futile. Nothing may actually be different among these brands. The inside of brands in many categories may reveal a very discomforting reality—a fairly high degree of sameness of suppliers. A high common denominator across brands is one of the factors causing enormous brand proliferation. Product creation is considerably facilitated by easy access to factors of production. But this ease does not translate into the creation of power brands.

The single most important contributor to a brand's superlative performance is a vision or an idea that cannot be captured by the deconstruction or reversing of the engineering process. The physics of product analysis may allow for sound technical product analysis. In product testing and construction labs the instruments of analysis permit breaking the product into its parts and components but the brand's soul or idea cannot be captured by the instruments used in physical analysis. Developing an exact replica of Kellogg's corn flakes is hardly a difficult challenge given the advancements in production technologies but translating these into a successful brand such as Kellogg's is. It is enormously difficult to create what Kellogg's is in a customer's mind.

Brand creation is much more than an exercise in production. Production is a mechanical process within the bounds of many. Branding on the other hand is about what happens prior to its physical manifestation in the form of a product or service. Super brands like Nike and Lacoste have some hidden reality beyond the physical sporting shoe or shirt and that is where it all begins—something that is within the bounds of eyes and something that is not.

The *Random House Unabridged Dictionary* (2006) defines 'see' and 'vision' as follows:

See:

> To perceive by eye; knowledge of the existence and apparent qualities of by the organ of sight.

Vision:

> The act or power of anticipating that which will or may come to be (prophetic vision or vision of an entrepreneur).

Merriam-Webster Dictionary (2009) defines 'vision' as:

> Something seen in a dream, trance, or ecstasy: a supernatural appearance that conveys a revelation; a thought concept formed by the imagination'; 'the act or power of imagination'; 'unusual discernment or foresight.

Selfknowledge.com (2009) defines 'sight' as:

> The act or power of sensing with eyes.

What do these words and their meanings have to do with branding? For some these may have or very little or no connection with branding. But for the creators of brands like Sir Watson, Dr Kellogg, J.R.D. Tata, N.R. Narayana Murthy, Shahnaz Husain, Henry Ford and Karsanbhai Patel—these words actually capture the essence of branding. Consider the following names and their extraordinary ideas:

- Richard W. Sears: catalogue shopping (product could be bought without having to go to a store).
- Henry Ford: Model T (a car could actually be affordable so that everyone could buy one, thanks to assembly-line operations).
- Elisha Graves Otis: elevators (besides horizontal movement that people always do there is also vertical travel).
- Robert Wood Johnson and James Johnson: Band-Aid (dressing for wounds and cuts to prevent infection and provide healing).
- King Camp Gillette: safety razor (device that makes shaving a simple and easy process for mankind).
- Isaac Merritt Singer: sewing machine (machine that allowed women to dress up stylishly).
- Levi Strauss: blue riveted jeans (rugged bottom wear made from tent material, American icon).
- William Colgate: dental cream (cleanliness and hygiene as a path to Godliness).

The mass onslaught of me-too brands proliferating supermarket shelves are caused by something that can be called the 'ease of sight'. Many brands of this kind are fast to arrive but they are also fast to vanish into oblivion. These are simply products assembled or outsourced from an external supplier and then christened by a brand name for the purpose of differentiation and identification. Brands so launched by taking an easy path end up crowing the shelf space but often do not go beyond that. These are soulless copies of the brands that bring categories into life. With essentially the same composition, components and ingredients a product can be copied because a product is a physical concept but brands cannot be copied.

Every brand is a product but all products may not be brands. A brand is much more. The product is an essential platform to intersect with customers but it is not all. Brand is an idea, belief, soul, a vision that is difficult to decode and even more difficult to copy. What sets a power brand apart from hundreds of similar product copies is the brand idea or soul or concept. All these constructs take the brand development process to the realm of the vision. Me-too copies hugely bank upon the sight, the process of perception based on the organ eye. Real brands begin with the idea and a sense of vision. The pioneer brands are usually created by the process of entrepreneurial vision. There is somebody somewhere who has a capacity to look beyond the apparent prevalent structures and is able to visualise the gaps. Brands are not given birth as a result of seeing things as others are able to. Rather the roots of brands are sown in visioning and imagination. Brands provide alternative conceptualisation of the world. Structured thinking is easy. But it is not so great a thing. Linearity of thoughts and tunnel vision can create only copies and nothing more.

For instance the fabric whitener market in India was once dominated by Reckitt's Robin Blue. And it is not that Robin was the only player in the market then. On the contrary there were hundreds of local brands which shared the fabric whitener space with Robin. But none had an existence of significance. All were more or less products of sight owing their existence to sense perception developed by the eye. The eye could capture the product and so called entrepreneurs developed more or less identical copies of brand Robin. None could copy the DNA or brand idea. In branding the product is the manifestation of the idea or concept and that was appropriated by Robin in the prospects' minds. Rivals could physically copy the product but not the brand idea.

Copying a product is a physical process that takes place in the material physical world of manufacturing in factories. However the brand idea or concept is non-physical and it exists in the prospect's mind. A concept once appropriated by a brand in perception is difficult to evacuate for it is not a physical evacuation but a perceptual one. It is a result of perception and learning. Encroaching on the brand idea is a Herculean task because the prospect has to undergo a process of unlearning and relearning. In this situation, M.P. Ramachandran envisioned fabric care from the side of demand and not from the side of supply. He could sense the hidden dissatisfaction with powder based fabric whiteners hence he created an alternative in the name of Ujala. So instead of taking the easy route to brand development wherein one could create a similar product, the brand broke the mould in a bid to push the embedded value on to a higher value orbit.

Ujala changed the product from being powder-based to being liquid-based. Instead of blue it created an ultraviolet purple liquid (it was called 'safedi ka naya rang' [the new colour of whiteness]). Keeping the target customer in mind the brand promised to deliver economical benefit by focusing on the adequacy of just four drops of the liquid ('chaar boondon wala' [of four drops]) for the process of cleaning. The brand's crucial valued differentiation from its rival Robin was based on spotless whitening. The blue powders usually did not mix evenly in water and created blue spots on the clothes which often became cause of embarrassment ('neeley dhabby wale'). The brand claimed that the Insta Whitening System promised customers spotless white and thereby provided defence of their egos. The brand permitted easy and affordable access of its product to its targeted average lower middle and middle class customer by innovative small packing starting with 30 ml to 250 ml. Ujala was launched in late 1997 and it went on to become the leader in the fabric whitener market by cornering over 65 per cent of the market by early 2001.

As is generally the case, the pioneers are followed by an army of similar products with different brand names. So was the case with the liquid blue fabric whitener market pioneered by Ujala. The competition law does not allow creation of monopolies by way of erection of physical entry barriers or monopolistic trade practices. Rather competition laws encourage competition. When an army of similar product brands arrives in the market true branding comes to the rescue of the pioneer brand. The product is copied but the brand is not because a true brand defies copying. Brand throws a physical entity into the realm of the non-physical. Like the human body provides casing to the spirit. Though cloning may make it possible to develop an exact replica of a human being, it may not be possible to replicate the spirit or soul. This has been the case in the liquid fabric whitener market. Ujala leads the market and hundreds of other brands continue to lead a faceless existence.

PRODUCING THE BRAND

What is the genesis of a product or brand? A product originates in the factory. But brand does not originate in the factory rather it originates in the imagination and thinking of somebody. Product and brand operate on different platforms:

- Product is physical, brand is intangible.
- Product is the sum of physical parts, brand is more than the sum of the parts.
- Product is about function, brand is about meaning.
- Product is about cold statistics, brand is about emotion and expression.
- Product is factory manufactured, brand is mentally processed.

A brand is about spirit, soul and vision. A product is an assembly of ingredients, parts or components. A brand is about values, meaning and human existence. A product is how a production manager looks at things but a brand is how a true marketer looks at prospects. A product is designed to meet a brand's specifications whereas a brand is about helping customers meet their life challenges. Brands have come to play a very important role in customers' lives. Brand is about transforming consumer life from its present inferior state to a better superior state. Brand is a marketer's vision about how life of customers can be made better so that they are able to make most out of their existence. Brand success stems from the relevance of the company's mission from the customer's perspective.

One of the greatest brands of cereal food is none other than Kellogg's. This brand rules the breakfast cereal market in many countries. Despite being such an old product it continues to achieve blind market following. It is not that the cereal food market is not crowded. Hundreds of brands chase for customer's trust and purchase vote but Kellogg's commanding position remains unassailable. The product element that a Kellogg's carton carries is not very hard for rivals to copy and match. But this is where most of the brands miss the point. A brand is much more than the product. The tools of engineering that heavily bank upon physical elements may help achieve fairly high degree of product similarity but these fall miserably short on capturing the essence. Branding is not about branding the product as many with short-sighted vision believe. Nor is it giving a name to a product but it is about producing the brand—the core idea or vision.

Kellogg's cereal as a product form was born accidentally when Kellogg left a pot boiled wheat to stand and became tempered. The rolling process of these wheat grains created thin large flakes. However the context of this accidental discovery was John Harvey Kellogg, chief physician, whose intent was to discover an improved vegetarian diet for patients. He was looking for a breakfast that was easy to digest and an alternative to bread. His brother Will Kellogg made this discovery of corn flakes which become a hot favourite with the patients. It did not take much time for the news about this easy to digest breakfast to spread and soon hundreds of orders were placed by mail. Soon the Kellogg cereal business expanded. The brand in this case was germinated in an idea which culminated into a product although accidentally. The brand as intent and idea expressed itself into a physical form not the other way around.

What is the brand that dominates the children entertainment industry? There is very little reason for confusion and the name that strikes is obvious—Walt Disney. The Disney experience that every child on the face of the earth craves for cannot be attributed to the ad hoc assembly of people, cartoon characters, rides, shows and exhibitions. All these that are typically associated with Disney do not make the brand in a sense that the assembly of different organs would not create a human being and make him or her come alive. The assembly of these elements is powered by the vision of Walt Disney, who designed Disney as a delivery vehicle of wholesome family entertainment. A strong sense of direction prevails about what fits within the concept or vision espoused by Disney as the driving force behind the brand.

In the recently held Auto Expo 2008 at New Delhi, Ratan Tata unveiled the much talked about car for everyone and said,

'A promise is a promise and I have delivered on my promise to present the world the rupees one lakh car.' Nano in many ways embodies a departure from the way cars are manufactured. It has a luggage compartment in the front that holds windshield water bottle, battery, spare wheel and room for a suitcase. It has rear mounted twin cylinder petrol 624 cc, 33 bhp engine. To achieve the cost target it has no radio, power windows, remote locks, air-conditioning or air bags. It employs a manually actuated four-speed transaxle with rear-wheel drive. The weight savings have been achieved via design and choice of materials used for manufacturing. Instead of two windscreen wipers Nano has one and its roof is ribbed to provide structural stiffness. What prompted Ratan Tata to embark upon such an ambitious project which many sceptics believed to be impossible? The idea or vision behind the fructification of Nano has been Tata's observation of families riding on two wheelers—father driving the scooter, his young kid standing on the little space in front and wife seated at the back holding another little baby (Das 2008: 1). Tata Motors engineers devoted about four years to create a car for such families. The solution created in the form of Nano is a safer form of transportation for any weather for these families.

In the similar entrepreneurial imagination, Ratan Tata now envisions creating a low-cost solution to purify water. He dreams of coming up with a 'low-cost water purification system'. It is his vision for millions of people in India who do not have access to safe drinking water. The current water purification products cost anywhere between Rs 6,000 and Rs 15,000 in a country where the average per month earning of a person is less than Rs 3,500. Tata intends to build a budget water purification system that would allow access to pure drinking water to millions of people. The process of having such visions and bringing them to fruition is depicted in Figure 4.1.

In the travel market it is obvious that there are people who fly and there are people who drive between cities. It is case of a rare imagination when someone comes up with an idea to provide the car driving public an opportunity to fly minus the negatives associated with full service air travel that conventional airlines

Figure 4.1:   How Vision Uplifts the State of Existence

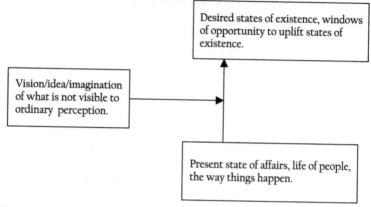

Source: Author.

provide. Herb Kelleher created a brand in the name of Southwest Airlines precisely to break though this hidden market opportunity. The result was the birth of the no frill airline model that challenged most of the accepted rules of running an airline. The hallmarks of these operations were short trips, no frills, low cost and simple fare structure. Now Southwest is the largest airlines by the number of passengers carried domestically within the US and it has the distinction of consistently posting profit for the last 35 years.

The accolade that the airline has earned has not come without imaginative and non-linear conceptualisation of the business. The brand vision was actualised by a series of operational and marketing practices innovations. These include:

- Quick turn around of aircrafts (10 minute turn).
- Short hops.
- Not using hub and spoke model, rather using a point to point system.
- Focus on local passengers.
- Use of secondary airports (low cost).
- More flying hours per aircraft per day (approximately 12.30 hours).

- Tickets sold directly by airline (not conventional agents).
- No assigned seating.
- Reservation change without cost.
- No video entertainment.
- Packed snack packs.
- Single aircraft type (Boeing) for easy maintenance.

Southwest Airlines started with a mission to make travel between two points in the US less expensive than driving. All systems and structures that were developed to actualise this mission now have come to be known as the 'Southwest effect' or no frill model. Many airlines in different countries have aped this low fare model. Here the brand began its journey as mission (an invisible force or belief) which was actualised into reality by assembling all brand elements (both physical and symbolic) with a conviction. Strong brand building often calls for departures from the norm. It invites criticism and scepticism. But if the vision is real and the idea is compelling all it takes is to develop structure and systems around it. Nirma took detergents to a customer group not considered right; McDonald's created a consistent all assuring burger; FedEx made overnight parcel delivery possible. The absence of conviction is often the root cause of the creation of hollow brands which have managed to assemble all visible elements of a successful brand but lack the inner force or mission.

All the consuming pressures to meet and surpass the immediate target leave very little time for most top mangers to engage in visioning. But vision is what is needed in the present day environment. In a survey (Taylor 2006) of managers about the importance of various growth drivers the following factors were rated: consumer promotions, advertising in new media, advertising in mainstream media, training in best practice in marketing, brand supportive structure, trade partner relations, new product development, pricing, consumer insight, aligning organisation and clear inspiring vision. The most important driver was found to be clear inspiring vision. Vision for the organisation and brand vision have great potential in inspiring and guiding the members of the organisation in achieving their end goals.

BUSINESS OF BUSINESS ORGANISATION

Take a look at the following names and consider developing a perspective on these names:

- Nestle
- Hindustan Unilever (HUL)
- Bank of Baroda
- Tata Steel
- MDH (Mahashian Di Hatti)
- Help Age
- Doordarshan
- India Post
- Group 4 Securitas
- North Delhi Power Limited
- Videocon
- Thermax
- Biocon

All of the above are the names of business organisations if the term business is expanded to include non-profit operations as well. These are collections of resources and competencies brought together with a specific purpose. They are business vehicles made to reach a destination. And the destination here is to achieve fruitful exchanges in the marketplace or market space. This assembly of resources and competencies is not an end in itself. The logic and rationale driving the creation of a business system resides outside in the external world of which it is a part. The justification for HUL to be there on this list stems from the role it plays in the lives of the target customers. Often strong and successful enterprises vanish from the scene when they cease to be relevant from the customers' perspective. There cannot be a business system unless it enjoys patronage of its customers. Globally the challenge for business systems to maintain their relevance and salvation lies in defining the role that their products and services would play in their target customers' lives.

Although business organisations differ in terms of their product portfolio yet they perform essentially similar functions. If a generic list of functions performed by business systems is developed these functions would be to a great extent similar. For instance the activities performed by rival companies like Vodafone and Airtel are not different in any significant manner. The activities and processes involved in marketing of Surf by HUL and Ariel by P&G may not significantly differ from each other. The business activities of companies like Tata Sky, Big TV and Dish TV are similar. The core processes tend to be similar of companies in a common business space. And all these activities forming the core are not performed for self consumption but are done for an entity external to the organisation—the customer. At the generic level the value creation process essentially involves similar activities.

In the very early period when marketing thought was getting crystallised, Culliton (1948) described the business executive as 'mixer of ingredients'. The marketer is seen as a 'decider' or an 'artist' who mixes the ingredients either by following a recipe developed by others or a self developed recipe. The mixer sometimes uses the ingredients readily available or sometimes he invents these. The ultimate purpose of all this mixing is to produce profitable operations. For instance HUL's Surf brand is a sign that represents a unique set of mixed ingredients and P&G's Ariel brand is also in a similar vein a symbol of an assembly of ingredients. Depending upon how these mixed ingredients match and measure up to the expectations of the target customer they achieve success in the marketplace. At the enterprise level each business system mixes ingredients often referred to as business functions. The elements of these functions tend to converge on to some common set for the firms that operate in a given market space.

Borden (1964) extended the concept of mixer of ingredients. If the business executive was a mixer of ingredients then what he would produce at the end of this process is the marketing mix. His list of marketing mix elements of manufacturers consisted of 12 broad heads. These were:

- Policies and procedures related to product lines, markets to sell new products.
- Pricing policies related to price levels, specific prices, margins and price issues on price policy.
- Branding policies related to trademarks, brands, private or unbranded sales.
- Channels of distribution concerning channels between plant and consumer, selection of wholesalers and retailers and eliciting cooperation.
- Personal selling polices related to reliance on personal selling and methods to be employed.
- Policies related to advertising, that is, amount to be spent, copy, image, corporate image.
- Promotion policies regarding the use of special selling plans, forms of consumption and trade promotions.
- Policies related to packaging and labelling.
- Display polices, that is, burden on displays and method to secure displays.
- Servicing policies regarding service needed.
- Physical handling policies about warehousing, transportation and inventories.
- Fact finding and analysis of marketing operations.

The above list of elements was later refined by McCarthy (1996). In his conceptualisation of mix he reclassified the mix elements that a marketer employs to pursue marketing objectives into four groups: product, price, place and promotion. The product element includes decisions like product variety, quality, design, features, brand name and warranties. The price component encompasses decisions regarding the list price, discounts, allowances and credit terms. The promotion aspect of mix refers to an assortment of tools like sales promotion, advertising, sales force and public relations. And finally the place part of the marketing mix includes issues regarding channels, coverage, assortment, location and inventory management.

Figure 4.2 depicts the precedence of brand idea over every-thing. Ideally the brand idea must be clearly articulated which

Figure 4.2: Brand Idea, Business Organisation, Business Activities

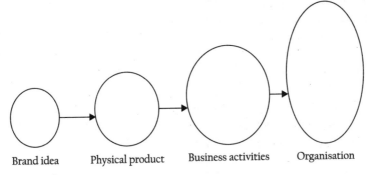

Brand idea   Physical product   Business activities   Organisation

Source: Author.

envisions how the potential customers could be lifted from their present inferior existence to a higher level of existence. The idea must manifest in a physical form in a product or service. The business activities come later and must be inspired from the brand idea. A good service product is actualised by value creation activities often called the 'mix'. And all this is subsumed under the overall banner of the business organisation.

The value creation potential lies in all the mix elements. Each of the marketing activities is performed because it produces a result for the end customer. For instance should the product be distributed directly or indirectly using the indirect channels? The answer to the question sought by the marketer has to be based on the value effect that each of the alternatives has on the target customer's value perceptions. Should the price be kept as an odd one like the one followed by Bata (ending with 95 paise) or should it be rounded off? Again the answer to the puzzle resides in the prospect customer's mind. So depending upon customer behaviour, competition faced and other macro environmental variables the business executive has to develop a mix to balance marketing objectives and the available resources.

Viewed from a macro angle most firms juggle the marketing mix elements to produce value for the target market. Sony mixes elements so does Samsung and the same is true for Nokia and LG in the mobile phone market. Business system is a device for producing a mix. But a mix is of little use unless the purpose of the mix is specified. The specific role and objective of each element has to be decided. In the absence of such meditation the business system is reduced to a commodity making device. Brands that have become legends in their categories draw their market power not from the products but from the brands that they have created around the products.

Lux as a bathing bar may not be greatly different from other bathing bars in the category but it leaves others way behind the reckoning. The bath bar making activities run common across most manufacturers but they do not culminate into the making of a Lux like brand for a simple reason. There is not much distinction in the job the bathing bars perform but there is the all meaningful distinction in the brand of the bathing bar that is Lux. Manufacturing activities create a manufactured output in the form of a good product which offers functionality (the functions performed). But all manufacturers that compete in a product domain offer similar functionality. This leads to a situation where products of the competitors of the pack hit parity. Here the product requires transcendence beyond functionality. Failure to transcend sticks the offering to something that buyers take for granted.

BUSINESS OF PRODUCT AND BUSINESS OF BRAND

As people do jobs so do products? Teacher does teaching, driver does driving and a sports coach does coaching. And teacher, driver and coach are valued for their inherent excellence but their performances are also valued by somebody or the other. If the market ceases to attach importance to their activities they would go out of business. In a similar vein, products are prized for their value—the performance capacity vested in them. Consider the following products and find the business that they are in:

- Pressure cooker
- Safety razor

- Mobile instrument
- Toothpaste
- Watch
- Deodorant

Is it really hard to find the business of the above-mentioned products? Probably not, even a small child can list what these are supposed to do. These terms, which refer to different product classes, activate recall of the functions that they perform as distinct from others, such as:

- Cooking device that reduces cooking time.
- Device used for shaving.
- Communication instrument.
- Paste used in brushing teeth.
- Time-keeping instrument.
- Something that neutralises body odour.

Product is about functionality—the functions that it performs that provide utility to customers. It embodies the rationalistic justification for buying. Inside the organisation product is the technical side of the brand. Often a highly technical perspective is shared by experts within an organisation. For instance the technical conceptualisation of cosmetics is nothing more than some kind of chemical formulation which buyers use for 'make up' purposes. A laptop technically is nothing more than an assembly of micro processor, a casing, RAM and screen. And it is about data processing. This is a dangerous perspective to adopt. If a brand manager is locked in this kind of myopic vision, in that situation the brand is likely to rot in production centric conceptualisation. A camera for instance in this scheme of things is going to be:

- 10.1 megapixels, 7 × optical zoom, 2.7″ LCD monitor, dual IS, face detection, shadow adjustment, in camera panorama, in camera help guide and true pic.

Or a car marketer may describe his brand as:

- Height 1660, front legroom 1250 mm, rear legroom 880 mm, front headroom 1000 mm, rear headroom 980 mm, rear shoulder room 1070 mm, split rear seat, boot space (rear seat unfolded) 312 liters, full flat reclining front seats and reclining rear seats, 16 bit computer, 16 valves 4 valves per cylinder, dual distributor less digital ignition, on board engine check, electric power steering, max speed 151 kmh, acceleration 1–40 km/h 2.89 secs, 0–60 km/h 5.59 secs, 0–100 km/h 14.5 secs, acceleration through gears (secs) 20–40 km/h in 3rd gear 13.5 and 40–100 km/h in 4th gear 21.8.

The above kinds of perspectives tend to be narrow and inward oriented. They best describe the product and often embedded functionality is suggested. Otherwise in both of the earlier descriptions a camera and car brand are no more than confusing product specifications that hold meaning for a highly technical mind but for customers they are perfect recipes for turnoff. In a crowded marketplace like what is prevalent now there is a deluge of products in most categories. Technical specifications make sense for people inside the business but they may appear to be an unknown language for customers. And that is where deciphering meaning is difficult. Inability to find relevant meaning leaves customers confused and baffled. And the coping mechanism in such cases is to 'pull out' of the confusion by avoiding such brands. What business the brand is in beyond the product was once truly stated by Charles Revlon about the cosmetic industry when he said, 'In the factory we make cosmetics. In the store we sell hope' (http://www.answers.com/topic/charles-revson, accessed on 30 September 2009).

MEANING FOR CUSTOMER

The first task therefore is to translate these product specification measures into functionality statements. Many marketers wrongly take customer expertise for granted. For instance the concept of megapixels is quite well understood within companies like Nikon, Canon, Olympus, Kodak and Sony. But if you ask a man on the street it would really be wonderful to get a correct interpretation of the term. What is a 16 bit computer in a car specification? It is nothing more than a cold piece of statistic. And customers may not really know whether more bits are better than less bits. So first of all in the branding process it is essential that the product breaks free from its mother department, the manufacturing or production. The language of production and the language of the market tend to be different. After all brands are meant for customers who buy it. The technical specifications need to be translated into consumer behaviour terms that trigger energy, pull and bonding. To make a brand out of a product it must be invested with meaning that rhymes and resonates with its customers.

So at the first level of the meaning investment process, the product specifications need to be interpreted in consumer behaviour terms. Interpret these product features '10.1 megapixels, 7 × optical zoom, 2.7" LCD monitor, dual IS, face detection, shadow adjustment, in camera panorama, in camera help guide and true pic'. The outcome in this case is going to be a paragraph describing the product's functionalities. Megapixels give better picture resolution; zoom allows taking pictures from a distance; bigger LCD monitor helps better view of the shooting object; and image stabilisation adjusts lens to avoid blurring of image.

Branding in this fashion brings the product functionality to the centre in order to develop pull. Here product features allow customers to do or perform a task better. The brand makes a pitch for why this brand of camera allows a person to click pictures better in certain ways. Products draw their utility from their functionality. These allow customers to do something desirable or necessary. A product is valued for its function. So long as a product's function is desired or satisfies customer needs or wants it would enjoy the market. For instance:

- Pen allows writing.
- Mobile phone allows communicating.
- Car provides transportation.
- Spectacles correct sight.
- Computers permit computing or word processing.

- Detergent does cleaning/dirt and stain removal.
- Watch keeps time.
- Tooth paste cleans teeth.

Products in various categories now come very close to each other in terms of specifications and thereby deliver similar functionality. It is becoming near impossible for marketers to sustain differentiation based on product specifications. The functionality route to branding is a good idea if it allows sustenance of differentiation and thereby allows a brand to elicit discriminative response from the market.

Product functionality intersects with customers on a 'reason why' platform. Why must you favour LG Viewty? Because besides being a mobile instrument it now allows clicking pictures with 5 megapixels clarity. Why must you buy Orient fans? Because it is the only fan with PSPO (Peak Speed Performance Output), which allows better air-delivery? Why must you buy a Van Heusen shirt? Because it is a non-iron shirt. The edge so created on the basis of functionality leaves the brand open to competition for two reasons:

- The source of distinction/edge is rooted in the product or production system.
- The customer looks at the brand through logical/reason lenses.

First, the product or production-centric differentiation is easily neutralised by competitors who are quick to achieve parity. Second, the patronage based on logic does not elicit commitment based on emotion. Reason can be challenged by superior reason. Figure 4.3 displays the relationship between product attributes and reasons inferred from the attributes by the customers.

Effective brands are those that manage the transcendence from product functionality and acquire more significant meaning that is less open to arguments and competitive challenges. For instance a scribble on a piece of paper whether it has been done with

Figure 4.3: Product Attributes Appeal to Reason

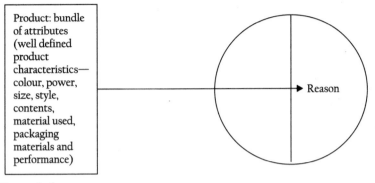

Product: bundle of attributes (well defined product characteristics— colour, power, size, style, contents, material used, packaging materials and performance)

Reason

Source: Author.

a Mont Blanc or an unbranded pen could hardly be deciphered but Mont Blanc commands a phenomenal price and following for not what it does (it writes more or less the same as others) but for what it means to customers. The brand has managed its evolution from being an excellent writing instrument to something more. Its pull lies in its ability to push the right hot buttons in customers so that reason takes the back seat and customers in a way become 'mad about' (less concerned with logic) the brand.

BRAND IDENTITY

Branding is all about value transformation. The value embedded in the physical commodity sometimes turns out to be of limited significance considering the consumer's psycho–social–spiritual space. With branding the brander seeks to add value newer intersection points to create value in the perceptual space of customers. It is in this sense that brand and branding has been defined in a number of ways. Consider the following:

- 'Brand is a sum total of all perceived and emotional aspects of a product or service'—Alan Bergstorm (http://www. allaboutbranding.com/index.lasso?article=191, accessed on 30 September 2009)

- 'Brand: a product or service which has symbolic significance beyond functional value ...'— Roddy Glen (quoted in Edward and Day 2005: 41)
- 'It is complex symbol that represents a variety of ideas and attributes. It tells the consumer many things, not only by the way it sounds (and its literal meaning if it has one) but more important, via the body of associations it has built up and acquired as a public object over a period of time' —B.B. Gardner and S.J. Levy (Gardner and Levy 1955: 55)

Brand in a way is a connecting link between the external physical product world and the internal perceptual world of the customer. Brand exists in perceptual space and allows for investment of meaning that adds value and achieves value transformation beyond functionality. For instance toilet soap brand Lux's meaning as a bar of soap and as promise of beauty in the internal world operate on different planes. The essence of branding is the belief that the branded commodity holds greater value than the naked product. Stephen King (1973) once in the context of marketplace success wrote: 'What makes companies succeed is not products but brands.' Brands assume importance both for the companies and the customers because of value addition. Over time however branding has evolved from being an act of achieving differentiation by the provision of features and augmentation.

Branding in its present day avatar comes as 'brand' as an idea or concept. This is a transformation from the traditional product centric approach to the market centric approach. What a brand now stands for is excessively governed by the product element. Rather it is rooted in the consumer it seeks to serve. It is a customer centric belief or idea rooted in customer concern related to his or her state of being and becoming. For instance, to view brands like Nike, Swatch and Body Shop as sports shoe, watch and cosmetics respectively, is to completely miss the essence of these brands (Riezebos et al. 2003). These brands represent a compelling concept valued by a certain group of customers. And for this idea to be visible the brand elements have to be 'laddered up' to reach the core proposition that created powerful pull in favour of these brands despite of a plethora of competitors. Brands in this scheme of things find favours with customers for becoming instrumental in helping them reach the end states' existence—the terminal goals that customers seek to achieve. However it must be noted that value in this conceptualisation is not defined as the economic or utility value of a commodity.

What does my brand stand for? Or what is the intent of this brand? These questions are apparently simple and have simple answers. But the depth and richness in their answers comes from how deeply the brander takes a peek into the world of consumers. The obvious answers would revolve around product functions, attributes, benefits and value for money considerations. But here the brand identity is tied to the narrow shackles of the product. For a brand to find deeper resonance with its prospects its meaning or identity must be broadened to encompass the role it is intended or designed to play in consumers' lives. For discovering ways to develop a deeper connection with customers it is important to understand how brands find meaning both at the conscious and subconscious levels. For a brand to be able to develop a holistic appeal its physical and non-physical elements must be woven together for a seamless value delivery. The hemispheric theory points to the two sides of the human brain: the left and the right brain. The rational and emotional sides of the brain are devoted to differencing specific aspect types of processing:

- Right hemisphere: non-verbal, emotive, feelings, sensations, instincts.
- Left hemisphere: language, cognitive, analytical, thinking.

The two hemispheres of the brain perform two different types of processing, but they do not work completely independently. Their functioning is not compartmentalised. A person's response to a stimulus activates both hemispheres but one side may outweigh the other in some situations. It is therefore difficult to have a response that is either completely rational or completely emotional. The overt reaction may be so overwhelming that the covert reaction may appear to be absent. Neuroscientists now take the traditional separation of left and right brain with a pinch of salt. Damasio (1994) flatly says that 'reason without emotion is neurologically impossible'. Even when decisions appear to be rational they may bear the influence of the non-rational part of the brain. Reason rubs shoulders with emotions and feelings which my however operate below the level of our consciousness.

Consider a print advertisement for a watch brand. The left brain activity pushes towards the analytical side of the watch in terms of its price, attributes, metal, movement, reliability and functions. The right brain on the other hand activates the emotional subconscious reactions triggered by colour, looks, signs, style, imagery, emotions and personality. Every brand must begin with a journey in the quest of meaning that must be endowed in it in order to achieve customer approval. The big question is:

- What is the business of my brand?

It is important to find out how a product or brand is abstracted in the personal individual world of the customer. The sociocultural-psychological interaction between the commodities and customers must be explored to get an insight into the meaning held in the consumer's mind. Developing a richer perspective on customer–brand interactions requires a probe into a deeper, more primitive and non-conscious working of the brain. What promises does a brand hold for a customer that makes it the preferred brand which lays hidden beneath the apparent functionality that the commodity delivers? Brands have to strike a deeper connection with their customers in order to be relevant and valued. Consider the following communications done by two brands of anti dandruff shampoos:

- Brand A—A girl is not able to go on a date for the fear that her date would reject her upon seeing dandruff flakes on her shoulders. And then she washes her hair with this brand of shampoo with a specific ingredient called ZPTO which kills germs that cause dandruff and make the scalp itchy.

Now she has hair without dandruff which accentuates her looks. This makes her the centre of attraction and confident enough to handle a social interaction well. She is able to win admiration of people around her especially the opposite sex. This way she manages to win a good boyfriend which makes her happy.

- Brand B—A man is not able to think because dandruff in his hair does not allow him to concentrate on anything. Dandruff is shown as a big distraction which hampers focus and thus leads to failure. Now this young man washes his hair with this brand of shampoo with micro ZPTO which not only removes dandruff but also prevents it from coming back. Now with a tension free head he is able to perform his job well which gives him a sense of accomplishment and satisfaction.

The above brand communications reveal the path as to how brands are translated into the subjective personal world of customers. Both brands though considerably similar in their contents and functionality take different paths to find meaning from the customer's perspective. At the product level both brands remove dandruff but at deeper levels each take a different route to establish relevance. The first brand's business of brand is to make its target customers happy by enhancing social confidence. The second brand aims to help its customers to perform better with undivided attention and thereby achieve targets. The path to satisfaction and happiness here is accomplishment in a field of activity. The brands in the two cases take different routes to developing customer relevant meaning. The actual physical product or commodity is laddered up by way of a means–end chain in order to deliver values held important by the target customers (Gutman 1982). The brand has to define its business in terms of end states of existence that its target customer seeks to achieve. All behaviours including the buying are contextual to the values that customers strive to achieve as shown in Figure 4.4 with regards to the example of the anti dandruff shampoo brands.

Figure 4.4: Contextuality of Customer Values of Brands and Customer Behaviour towards Brands

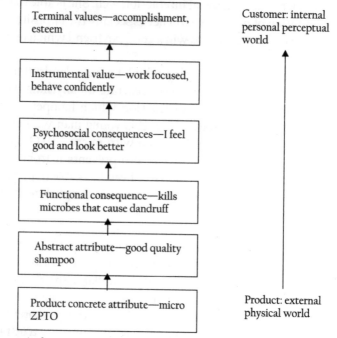

Source: Author.

Clearly, in the light of the means–end hierarchy model brand buying cannot be an end in itself. Rather brands are means to reaching a higher level of existence which may involve rational-emotional, conscious–subconscious, physical–metaphysical, psycho—social aspects of consumers. Finding the business of brand is about discovering the role brands are expected to play in customers' lives. In this scheme of things brand may be given—functional role (Anacin, Tata Salt, Pril dishwashing liquid), emotional role (Cadbury, Gilli and Calvin Klein—romance), psychological (self definition and construction) role (Van Heusen—confident, Armani—sophisticated) and social self expression role (Woodland—adventurous and outdoorsy, Peter England—down to earth and free from pretensions). In the process of assigning a brand a mission it is extremely important to discover the internal personal world of customers and how things interact therein. The value or utility hooks are rarely within a given product or commodity. They are outside the product and inside the consumer. A deep and profound peek into the consumer's inner world should mark the articulation of a brand's charter.

CONCLUDING REMARKS

Product categories have witnessed a big explosion in the number of brands that inhabit them. Despite the large number however few brands rule the category and others are just confined to a token presence. One thing that is a differentiating factor among the leaders and also rans is the process that precedes their conceptualisation and creation. Solid brands are products of vision whereas 'me-too' brands that crowd the category are creations of the sight. It is the ability of the brand creator to go beyond the obvious and uncover the latent consumer concerns that finds manifestation in the form of a product or service. Great brands originate as ideas which find expression in a product. Vision generally precedes brand and when the process is reversed only copies are created. In this context answers to two important questions need articulation—what business my product is in and what business my brand is in. The product element of a brand usually attends to the reason which may fall short of what the customer expects a brand to deliver. The holistic approach demands that the business of brand is articulated to encompass those value aspects which lay hidden but tend to be instrumental in driving consumption behaviour. Therefore a peek into consumers' personal worlds is necessary for giving the brand the mission that it is assigned to play. In this regard the concrete product aspects need to be laddered up to figure out the ends that are sought by consumers.

Pushing the Brand to Higher Orbits

In a recent interview, James Stengel, P&G's global marketing officer highlighted the importance of energising brands (Colvin 2007). P&G sits on many brands that are over 50 years old. Tide was first introduced in 1946, Crest arrived in the market in 1955 and Pampers created the first wardrobe for babies in 1961. These iconic brands could easily have been pushed into oblivion had they resisted evolution and fine tuning the embedded value with changing times. This requires energising brands. The new Tide besides offering great wash does its bit to conserve environment by saving energy. It allows customers to achieve the same great dirt removal and wash even in cold water and thereby does away with the need for warm water. Cold water means energy conserved that otherwise would have been used to heat water. Often brands are conceptualised in terms of functional benefits that they provide to customers which may be limiting both for the customers and the employees of the brand. The equity of great brands has to be something that is inspiring and organisations find it inspirational. Pampers has now evolved from being about benefit of dryness to helping mothers with baby development. Olay is no longer about a moisture providing pink fluid but it is about helping women look and feel better as they age (Colvin 2007). All these examples suggest that there is more to branding than making a product. Brands in order to rise above the others in the category have to develop intersections with customers that extend beyond what is contained in the physical reality of the brand. Branding is a journey into discovering consumer reality and incorporating higher order values.

MUNDANE DETERGENT AND DIRTY WASHING

What kind of images conjure up in your mind when the words 'laundry detergent' is tossed? The chemical engineering mind would gallop in the direction of chemistry and look for the composition of this compound and the formula that captures it. For a chemist or chemical engineer that concept is unlikely to cross over the chemicals that go into making a detergent. A person who fits in the stereotype of a 'typical' man would find a detergent as nothing more than a pack of laundry powder that one buys every month for daily wash. A typical consumer usually is uninvolved and attaches very little significance to the detergent category as such. The perception of this typical person is likely to be limited to powder and various dimensions like the form, fragrance, function, colour and packaging. For a non-involved person the imagery and associations may be highly limited. For non-buyers both the awareness and richness of associations are likely to be minimal. Detergent is hardly a category that one is going to be interested in. There are better things in life which are more deserving of both our time and attention.

But for women who are considered to be the typical buyers and users of this product category the responses are likely to be many, rich and emotionally strong. The term detergent is likely to trigger associations of dirt, stains, foul smell, a chore, frustrating, disgusting, unrewarding. Very few people may see reward, meaning and stimulation in this product category and its application. Detergents are often seen as a necessary evil. Washing of dirty clothes is required. It is necessary. One has to get the dirt out of clothes to prepare them for reuse. The process of washing and cleaning is culturally and symbolically constituted to be menial and lowly. Unlike many other activities which enjoy higher status washing is hardly rewarding for body, mind and soul. It is not unsurprising that women do not win accolades both inside and outside the home for that great beating of clothes that they do in the confines of the bathroom.

Is there a connection between good parenting and washing? Many may find it hard to correlate the two concepts. Parenting apparently does not have any relationship between such a low order often abhorred activity. These two are separate sets of activities with no apparent connection. The linking pin between being good parents and washing clothes is that good parents generally do not allow their kids to wear dirty clothes. Broadly, the reasons are two:

1. Hygiene   – Dirty clothes may contain harmful germs and bacteria which may expose the child to health risk.
2. Expression – Dirty clothes on a child would project the family in a poor light. Socially this is not acceptable to many parents.

It is in this context that washing and detergents assume importance. These are two paths that most brands of detergents apparently use to acquire importance from the customer's perspective. Most brands attempt to acquire importance by harping on their functional superiority in terms of wash quality and thereby allow customers to have clean clothes minus the dirt and stain. But no matter how hard the brands attempt to persuade customers to be serious about washing laundry continues to be an insignificant issue of life in the modern day context. The detergent technology has become so standardised that almost all detergent brands in a category look and work similarly. No one pays attention to washing as long as nothing goes wrong. It catches attention by default. It takes a stain or patch of dirt to draw attention to washing. One only looks for an acceptable solution. People tend to be in the problem prevention mode. The idea is to get rid of dirt and grime. For customers detergents, detergent buying and its usage are highly insignificant activities. This is where marketing of such products becomes both complex and challenging. The customer wears an 'I don't care attitude' and the marketer precisely has to achieve the opposite.

The salvation of the brand manager lies in how the customer can be made not only to care about the brand but to develop 'I can't live without you' commitment. Lack of preference and commitment to a specific brand are manifestations of missing hooks. Consumers do not care when something does not matter. This signals a brand's inability to do something that is unique and of higher significance. Customers are usually willing to be loyal and committed provided brands provide them with right reasons. A brand has to develop indispensability by becoming a provider of a value that no other participant in the industry delivers. The question then is what are the paths available to a brand to promise an inimitable value delivery? The value embedded in the brand should make customers behaviourally and emotionally loyal and committed.

In this regard a brand has to make a transition from being only a product or bundle of utilities to acquiring higher order meaning. When a brand continues to get trapped in the inner domain of what it carries, a product or services, it remains open to contest and competition. For instance an air conditioner marketer may not be able to visualise its brand beyond the air-cooling electrical gadget. The vision of a tea marketer may not get something beyond CTC process. A television may be nothing more than a gadget that receives signals and reproduces sounds and images. A mobile service provider is nothing more than a network of cell towers used for receiving and transmitting signals. This marks the defeat of branding as marketing process. Branding is all about value transformation which is not as much about physical aspects as about mental transformation.

I DON'T CARE

The biggest bane for any brand manager is when its customers develop an 'I don't care attitude'. This is the bankruptcy of marketing. Of what significance is the branding process if at the end of it the customers exhibit indifference to the brand? In such a situation the marketer treads on a very slippery patch. There is no certainty of a pay check coming in next time. No brand ever survives because it is backed by a talented marketing or branding team. Outcome is what matters. The acid test for each brand that wants to prove its worth in salt is certainty of customers who keep coming back to it. It is the solidity of customer base that makes the brand. Commitment and loyalty defines the strength of a brand. If a customer gives into temptations or lures of rival brands there is reason to revisit branding strategy. Brands should not only be trusted for their performance but be loved.

Customer indifference is a natural outcome of diminished importance attached to either product category or brand or both. Look round make a conscious note: do we attach importance to everything around us? The answer is likely to be negative. Things have to be prioritised. Discrimination resides at the heart of consumer behaviour. With intellectual and cognitive maturity comes the ability to adopt discriminating responses to things around us. Things are accorded importance according to the importance that these hold in our lives. Those things that play a significant role are likely to be paid attention to. How things fit in our state of being and becoming determine their appeal and importance. Are socks more important than trousers? How important is salt compared to a piece of jewellery? How important is a wedding dress in comparison to everyday wear? Some things are held special and some are not so special. In a similar vein our relationship with people is defined. Absence of some people who are close to us not only has an upsetting effect but can also lead to depression. However, absence of many who are not close to us does not even get registered.

Why do things vary in their importance? The answer lies in the role that they play in anybody's life. The more significant the role is the more likely is to be the importance attached to a person or a thing. The mother of a child draws importance not entirely from the feed she provides. It is the invisible intersections between the baby and mother that form the true foundation of bonding. She is not as much about physiology as she is about psychology.

She is not the source of physical nourishment alone. Her inter-sections go much beyond the physiological level and encompass emotional and spiritual dimensions as well. A baby can procure its feed from a number of sources but the mother–child relation-ship has a much deeper meaning. The mother acquires significance for the child not only for physiological satisfaction but also for a bonding that extends deeper, touching emotions, senses and spirituality. Many of these intersections between a child and mother are so unique and special that there tends to be no avail-able substitute for them. Brands escape the product tunnel by developing customer intersection points that extend far beyond the bare products contained within them. With time a child evolves in terms of food and food habits. The physical nourishment space is shared with other stomach filling things. But the motherly space is always held sacred and unequalled. When a brand moves up to an unrivalled and irreplaceable position the branding has done its job right.

RISK

The importance attached to a product category or brand stems from the concept of risk. Risk is the exposure to undesirable con-sequences or ways in which a customer may get hurt. A cus-tomer negotiates environment cautiously if there is probability of exposure to physical, financial, social and psychological harm. When a product scores low on these dimensions of risks the nat-ural importance attached to it stands diminished. The capacity of a product or service or brand to send a customer to a diminished state determines how unimportant it becomes. Products assume importance when they can positively make an impact in one's life. Answer the following:

- How do you respond to brands when they deliver similar product performance (function alike)?
- How do you respond to products that do not involve sig-nificant monetary values?

- How do you respond to a product category that is perceived to be psychologically irrelevant (not related to the idea of self or self concept)?
- How do you relate to a product category that does not hold a badge value (incapable of making a social statement)?

These product categories are likely to be relegated to a perceived lower level of importance. Customers in such situations are likely to behave in an uninvolved fashion. When things don't matter the behavioural coping mantra boils down to 'anything will do'. This is a state of degenerated marketing. When the product category itself holds less significance like shoe polish, salt, toilet cleaners, and so on, the marketer faces a tougher challenge of creating a brand in an unimportant category. When the category is itself unimportant how can the brand therein achieve the status of importance? There is no way a marketer can be sure of his brand's bottom line if customers don't care. It is not hard to imagine the presence of umpteen numbers of brands in the customer's consideration set. All enjoying similar status and hence none is able to command the customer's consistent patronage let alone loyalty and commitment.

What will happen if all prospective candidates for marriage both boys and girls one day become clones in their respective categories? The entire marriage industry may become extinct. Partner choice would not require any contemplation and thinking. The decision component in the decision process would cease to be of relevance. Any boy would be good enough for a girl and vice versa. There would be no chance of an inferior partner getting selected and a better one getting rejected or a better getting selected and an inferior one getting rejected. Use of thinking and decision making in such situations of perceived similarity leaves very little scope for evaluation and decision making. It just adds up to cost with no corresponding benefit of effective decision making.

The competitive angle of marketing acts to unleash a cloning effect in the market. Free markets engender similarity and parity when competitors copy products, distribution, advertising and other aspects of marketing. Breaking out of this degenerative cycle necessitates branding in the real sense. Coming back to the case of detergents, the category on the one hand is low involvement on the part of the consumers and on the other hand products offered by the marketers are not differentiated. This is a typical case where the market is likely to be sucked into a commodity spiral. In this kind of situation brand managers find it difficult to create and sustain real product differentiation. Accordingly brands in such markets find it difficult to break away from the cloning syndrome by way of various product related improvements. Giving in to commoditisation and playing a commodity game is no great feat. The real feat is when a brand is able to swim against the tide of commoditisation and forge bonding with customers by adding higher order value vectors. The Surf brand by Hindustan Unilever was once locked in the same battle with other brands which offered almost similar functionality. The pressures were mounting on sales promotions and price. But Surf subtly transformed something of low value and a mundane product into the realm of higher significance for customers by evolving the essence of what the brand stood for.

SHIFTING THE BATTLE SPACE

Surf pioneered the detergent powder market when it hit the market in 1959. This brand introduced the concept of bucket wash in India. Prior to Surf washing was done by using laundry bars. So powerful has been the category dominance by Surf that it came close to becoming generic for detergent powder. How long can a marketer exploit its pioneering advantage? It is almost impossible to stall competition forever. At the heart of competition is the race to stay ahead and constantly setting new targets for the competitors to cross. Differentiation is a moving target. Failures to differentiate can easily plunge a brand into a meaningless commodity spiral. Surf successfully managed to keep its competitors at bay. These included Det, Magic, Swastik, Key and Sixer.

Brand leadership is not about advertising. Great brands are not created by great symbolism alone. An advertising hyperbole initially can create excitement and arouse interest but later at the delivery level it is the brand's actual performance that forms the basic building block of trust and affinity. Omega is not a good brand just because James Bond sports this brand on his wrist. Historically Omega has created various landmark developments in the art and science of time keeping. Omega first created Calibre 19 and NASA approved it for its space program and the watch has been to the moon. The Mercedes brand evolved into its present day iconic status not by the power of communication but by serious investments in car engineering leading to superb motoring performance. The brand itself became reputation and customer equity as a marvel of mechanical engineering which later evolved into an ultimate symbol of luxury and safety.

Surf as a brand has been through constant creation and destruction process. How can a brand be a constant in the midst of change? Constancy is a sure shot recipe of failure. But that does not mean change without any anchor. Such change can make a brand drift into different directions. In this context the brand identity assumes importance. The fundamental essence of the brand has to be encoded and preserved. In the absence of an identity a brand is likely to be a mistress to any one who happens to have an opportunity to flirt with it.

Surf has constantly renewed its product in order to effectively cater to the changing washing needs of Indian consumers. The brand's evolution can be deciphered from the tag line or signoffs that it used from time to time:

- 1950s – From bar wash to bucket wash
    - Significant saving in elbow efforts (better clean with lesser efforts).
    - Surf washes whitest.
- 1970s – Competition from economy detergents
    - 'Aadha kilo Surf ek kilo sadharan powder ke barabar hai' (Half a kilo of Surf is equivalent to a kilo of ordinary washing powder. Value consciousness, sensible value-for-money buy).

⊙ '*Surf ki kharidari me hi samajhdari hai*' (There is wisdom only in the purchase of Surf).
- 1980s – Performance era
  ⊙ Whiteness and stain removal.
  ⊙ '*Daag dhoondte reh jaoge*' (You will keep searching for stains).
- 1990s – Surf Easy Wash (low-lather variant) and Surf with wash boosters to provide best clean even in hard waters.
- 2000s – Surf Excel Quick Wash
  ⊙ Eco-friendly detergent that needed considerably less water.
  ⊙ '*Surf Excel hai na!*' (Don't worry Surf Excel is there!).

The brand kept pace with the detergent technology that it carried in its carton. For instance Surf appealed to senses by suggesting that only half a kilogram of Surf provides wash equivalent to a kilogram of an ordinary powder (famed Lalitaji campaign). The idea was to ward off economy washing powders from nibbling its market share. Surf Quick Wash again demonstrated incorporation of path breaking development. This product reduces water consumption and time consumed in washing to about half. Obviously the appeal of the product is high for both time and water shortage consumers. The product evolution did not stop there. Then came improvement in the detergent formula investing the product with exceptional dirt removal ability (*Daag dhoondte reh jaoge*, Surf Excel *hai na*). The smart sensors of the detergent can differentiate colour from stains and hence give better stain removal benefit without damaging the fabric colour.

Figure 5.1 shows that the product-centric approach to brand building seeks to enhance consumer benefits in the originally conceived functional domain by tinkering with the product formulation. Surf as a brand has been through its own product development process by which its ingredients have seen continuous improvement—washes white, washes whitest, fights dirt and stains, removes tough stains, fights stains even on colour clothes,

Figure 5.1:   Product-centric Brand Development

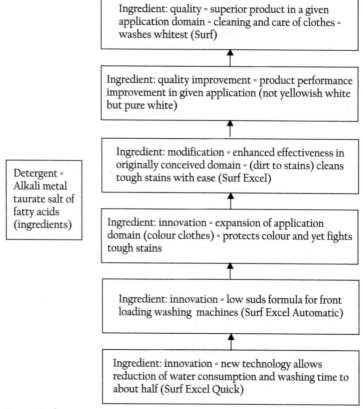

Source: Author.

saves time and water and low suds for washing machines. This kind of product evolution surely does enhance consumer benefits in the form of better cleanliness, versatile wash, fabric care, fragrance and freshness. Solid product performance is an essential foundation for strong brand building. Without solid product functionality the brand is destined to be a failure at the very first value delivery encounter. The core of any brand is the product component which makes up its functionality. Product functionality attends to the 'logic' or 'reason' of buying. A solid product is an essential condition for brand building. What would one do with a car that does not drive well or a computer that fails in processing of information or a watch that keeps incorrect time? Figure 5.2 displays the upward movement of the evolution of a product as its product functionality goes from low to high.

Although the brand continued to evolve as product and managed to keep its competition at bay however the brand's intersection with the customer continued to be locked in a lower order value game. The brand continues to fight a glorious battle in its originally conceived battlefield—the washing or dirt removal. The brand's meaning does not expand. Though it does manage to become the choice in its chosen field of application but it continues to operate in a lower value orbit. Unless the brand raises its role in the consumer's life it has to be on a continuous run to beat the competition on product specification. The competition would generally catch up with the technology aspects and achieve near parity on product specifications. Commoditisation is a great challenge in such a situation. A detergent brand if it is envisioned like a chemical formulation to get rid of grime and dirt would never be able to get out the shadow of its product.

Figure 5.2: Brand's Evolution: Perfecting the Product Functionality

Product more evolved: high functional delivery

Product less evolved: low functional devivery

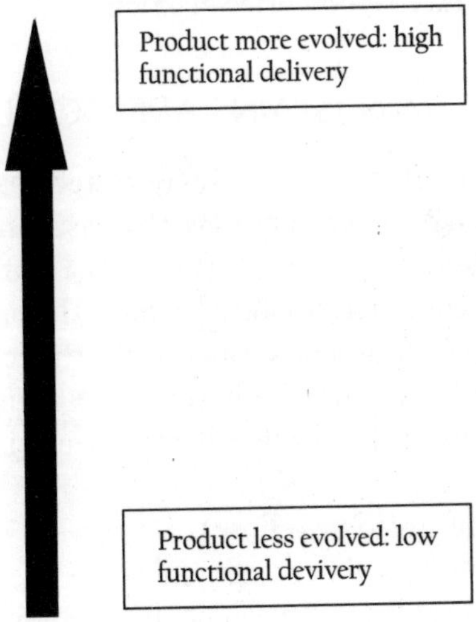

Source: Author.

And when consumers see nothing beyond the product in your brand it is a case of acute vision deficiency syndrome. Commodities are no one's love, they are bought for a price and consumers hardly given a damn about them. There is no love lock for a commodity. One has to rise above a commodity status to entice a customer.

In the year 2004 P&G launched a major assault on the fabric wash market by reducing the prices of its Tide and Ariel brands by 20–50 per cent. This was triggered by its experience in the price reduction of its sachets. The company could multiply its volume in sachet market by price reduction. The price of one kilo pack of Ariel was reduced from Rs 135 to Rs 99 and Tide's price went down from Rs 85 to Rs 46 for a one kg pack (*The Business Line* 2004). This kind of price or promotion oriented moves are effective strategic weapons only in those circumstances when the brands do not go beyond its functional utility platform. Parity in ingredients exposes the brand to the dangers of brand switching. Brands intersection beyond functionality allows it to forge non-functional linkages and thereby secure its position for reasons that transcend logic. After all loyalty, commitment, trust and love are emotions. It is this glue that produces stability in market share and allows a brand to enjoy price elasticity.

DAAG ACHE HAIN (STAINS ARE GOOD)

The fabric wash market is a severely contested space. A huge number of brands seek to strike a chord with consumers. These include Tide, Ariel, Henko, Surf, Wheel, Nirma, Sasa, Ghari, Mr White, Rin and Fena besides hundreds of local brands. Although these brands broadly target three different segments like the economy, the mid-priced range and compacts. Whatever the segment the brands come dangerously close to each other in terms of:

- colour (blue, green or yellow)
- touch and feel (powder or granules)
- brand message (better wash or stain removal)

- smell
- visual imagery (women, bucket, clothesline, dirt getting off the clothes)
- price (proximate in a range)
- packaging (carton or poly pack yellow, green, blue)
- user stereotype (homemaker)
- distribution (modern formats or grocery stores)
- benefit (detergency—dirt and stain removal)

What is a detergent or a washing powder all about? The obvious answer to this question is that it is all about getting clothes clean. It is about cleanliness, wash and dirt and stain removal. When a branding team is locked in an 'obvious' tunnel vision then it is difficult for a brand to jump over the existing marketing paradigm. This is what ails many industries. A product is nothing more than an inanimate formulation or assembly of its components or parts. A product is what body is to a human being. A body is essentially not sufficient. Human existence is all about evolution. Many people choose to exist like a living animal possessed only by survival. But many evolve. They discover the soul. An existence without 'realisation' is incomplete. Similarly when brand managers fail to see beyond the product the brand's potential is killed prematurely. It is left to operate like a commodity.

What is Surf? The answer is it is absolutely a chemical cleaning agent? What is a Whirlpool refrigerator? The answer could be that it is a steel box divided into compartments cooled by a compressor that runs on electricity. What is Tata Tea? Well obviously it is a mix of CTC tea leaves. The brand conceptualisation in this fashion is technically correct but limited marketing wise. Branding is about transformation. A brand starts its life as a product to evolve and acquire greater meaning. A brand must forge links with its target customers and transcend its product domain to acquire higher order meaning that potentially holds greater satisfaction. Brand is not what marketer wants it to be but what its customers expect it to be. It is customer centric conceptualisation of value. So the following questions remain:

- Do customers want a detergent?
- Do customers want a refrigerator?
- Do customers want tea leaves?

For the uninitiated in the field of marketing, the answers may be positive. But actually this opens the gate to consumers' individual private worlds. The role and significance of products in consumers' lives has to be explored and envisioned. It is where the seeds of branding are sown. It is where a product begins its journey of value transformation. It is where the brand is born. In the absence of this uncanny vision and visualisation brands often fall prey to commoditisation especially where copying the product does not pose any significant encumbrances. Kellogg's is much more than corn flakes; IBM is much more than a network of computers; Apple is much more than a computing device and Rolex is much more than a time keeping device. What is important is a brand's intersection with consumers as shown in Figure 5.3.

Figure 5.3: Brand's Intersection with the Customer

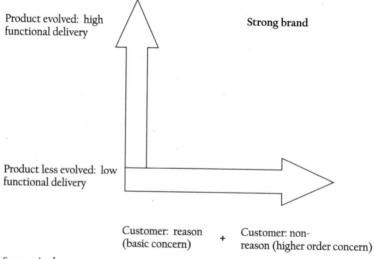

Product evolved: high functional delivery

Strong brand

Product less evolved: low functional delivery

Customer: reason (basic concern) + Customer: non-reason (higher order concern)

Source: Author.

Unilever's vision of brand Surf is much more than is deciphered. When most brands are engaged in slogan shouting matches about dirt, stains and detergency, the brand has connected its proposition to good parenting. Its slogan '*daag ache hain*' turns the conventional detergent marketing logic upside down. The sceptics who take a conscious and rationalistic approach to understand the brand's core may be at a loss. And this campaign for them becomes an easy case of vampire creativity. A good product may not evolve into a good brand but a good brand is not possible without a rock-solid product. Surf as a product has an advanced formulation to take care of stains effectively. But it is here that a brand hankers for building a higher order connection with its target audience. And the audience expects the brand to deliver much more than what runs across other brands in the category. Surf with its current proposition 'stains are good' managed to lift the brand from the mundane cleaning agents' category to something highly important like good parenting.

The brand seeks to establish a bond between their detergent and good parenting with the campaign wherein kids are shown to forego a great life learning experience if they are not allowed to live the way they are naturally inclined to—carefree, naughty, experimenting, exploring and playful. The mother's concern of spotless clean clothes often causes kids to abstain from doing many things that could provide great life learning experiences. Things are best learnt when they are experienced directly. A child who is scared to go home with dirty clothes for the fear that he or she may be admonished cannot play a natural game, climb a tree, play in a water puddle, run carefree in the rain or use a paint brush freely. Every stain on a child's clothing has a story behind it. Every stain is a mark of a lesson learnt. Stains are like a report card indicating how many lessons a child has learnt and how well she or he is prepared for taking on the challenges of life.

The Surf brand has taken the ghost of stains off the mothers' heads. Its promise has evolved from being an effective cleaning agent to good parenting. It allows a child to go though learning experiences without any botheration. Is the good mother the one whose children wear spotless clothes or the one whose children have been through life learning experiences? Is good parenting about clean clothes or smart children? Clean clothes on children have a hidden cost with mighty implications. Such concern for cleanliness can be the root cause of a child not going though the great learning experience that happens in childhood and thereby prevent him or her from becoming competent to take on life challenges later in life. The branding process here seeks to liberate the brand from the mundane washing powder category to place it into a very high concern category of parenting. Surf now seeks to connect with higher order needs of mothers. It allows them to get out of the menial game of washing to donning a role of a good mother. The brand now allows mothers in their quest for helping their children grow to their full potential.

CELLULAR NETWORK TO TRANSCENDING BOUNDARIES

The Airtel brand has grown leaps and bounds over time to emerge as the leader in the mobile communication service market. S.B. Mittal started the Bharti Group in the 1970s with a small bicycle-parts operation in New Delhi and later in 1985 he branched into the telecom business and Bharti Telecom Limited was born as a manufacturer of telephonic equipment. Bharti evolved as telephone equipment manufacturer by expanding its portfolio into push-button telephones and answering machines. A real turn of events took place when it entered into the telecommunication industry in the early 1990s. It was 1992 when Bharti entered the cellular services by launching mobile services in Delhi. And over the years it expanded business by various telecom circles in different states. Initially there were only two players in the mobile telecommunication market—Bharti and Essar and both offered mostly post paid services. However in the late 1990s prepaid services were added to target customers from the lower end of the market. For Bharti's prepaid services brand 'Magic' was created.

A service brand like Airtel which provides mobile communication services is technically nothing more than a network of cell towers which receive and disseminate low frequency signals to mobile instruments owned by people. The product centric myopic orientation of managing a brand like this would lock vision to the tower network and switching equipments. And with this vision an effort to seek customer relevance and competitive superiority would lead to a heavy concentration of efforts on the technology dynamics of the brand. But every brand has to fight the first battle embedding the brand with winning functionality. Accordingly the brand's first milestone in value creation was that of laying a communication network that allowed widest coverage, clarity of voice, congestion free network, service availability, product plans, complaint handling and customer care. Airtel first established its brand equity by focusing on technology and infrastructural requirements to be in position to provide seamless communication service. At the most basic level a mobile communication brand allows people to talk and communicate even on the go. And this functionality and superiority of network cannot remain unchallenged and unique in an evolving market. Brand superiority rooted in product functionality becomes common across brands causing serious erosion in brand preference. Therefore a brand has to discover newer intersection points to create value and bonding.

Awareness and Resonance

In the brand building process the first challenge is often to establish brand awareness. Awareness is the first necessary condition for brand building. Accordingly in the first wave Airtel relied heavily on the celebrity endorsement route to create awareness. Airtel Magic was endorsed by Bollywood icon Shah Rukh Khan and actress Kareena Kapoor to build brand recall. Magic prepaid service was promoted with taglines: 'You can do the Magic' and '*Magic hai to mumkin hai*' (If there is Magic, it is possible). The popularity of these stars allowed the brand to connect with the lower affordability sections of the market who dreamt of using mobile services with just about Rs 300. In the early 2000s brand communication changed from 'touch tomorrow' to 'live every moment'. Although this campaign strategy stuck with celebrities the difference here was that for the first time music maestro A.R. Rahman was roped in to promote the brand. He composed exclusive symphonies for Airtel one of which went on to become the most downloaded ring tone.

Armed with network capability and instant awareness the brand could have been left stuck at the lower rung of value hierarchy. Surely a mobile service provider allows two people to communicate and talk but then this is what other brands also allow you to do. Here the brand hits parity with other players with nothing significant left to differentiate itself from others in the pack. But with time Airtel explored and added newer, higher order meaning to the brand's core to find a deeper connect with its customers. The brand has seen its progression from being a literal communication network to acquiring higher meaning for customers. The challenges at this level move the brand to a higher altar and give it a role in its customer's life that allows him or her to realise more meaningful goals. The idea is to push up the brand's delivery to service higher order needs. The brand must find new ways to resonate and bond with its customers. The commoditisation of the market space calls for the cultivation of an emotional angle essential for forging customer relationship. Is there a way to connect the brand's functional proposition of communication with inner and deeper concerns of people? Can the brand forge emotional links and intersect with 'heart matters' beyond 'mind matters'?

Express Yourself to Breaking Barriers

The quest for a greater meaning and emotional connection led the brand to look for ways to defining brand identity beyond the communication network which by now stood commoditised. In one of the advertisement campaigns Airtel exhibited how ordinary communication can create extraordinary effects. The idea was to surround the brand with emotions that struck a deeper emotional chord with people. Here the brand's communication diverged from the often repeated and clichéd ideas used for marketing cell services. The brand's business is seen to evolve from communication to expression. Communication is passé. Everybody communicates, it is mechanical and at times communication is nothing more than hollow transfer of verbal symbols without meaning. Actual communication is when words move mountains and create impact. One of the brand campaigns showed the following images:

- Ad begins with a clip from Quit India Movement; caption 'Two words can bring down an empire.'
- Martin Luther King, Jr's 'I have a dream' speech; caption 'One dream can change the world.'
- David Shepherd's declaration of Sachin Tendulkar out; caption 'One raised finger can break a billion hearts.'
- Winston Churchill addressing a huge congregation of people during war caption '... and two can win a war!'
- Dalai Lama; caption 'Whisper can inspire hope ...'
- Mother Teresa; caption 'One can instill faith.'
- Lata Mangeshkar; caption 'Some voices can move a nation.'
- Nusrat Fateh Ali Khan; caption 'Yet some others can dissolve boundaries.'
- Demolition of the Berlin Wall; caption 'One act of defiance can spark a revolution.'
- A large number of people holding candles; caption 'One hundred thousand candles can end a war...'
- The background score is composed by A.R. Rahman followed by the sign-off 'That is the power of human expression'.

This campaign takes a break away from the clichéd product-centric approach to brand building by incorporating texture and depth to brand meaning. When we think of it in reality communication is not itself an end. It is rather a means to express an inner idea. And here the brand is evolved as the facilitator of expression. Airtel in its ongoing journey to move further up in forging even a deeper connect released a new campaign 'Barriers break when people talk'. Presently the world is passing through a tough phase. The earth has become a divided planet not because it was meant to be this way but people inhabiting it have etched boundaries on its surface. This division and differences have led to battles and wars causing great loss of human lives. The planet could become better if people could talk and resolve their conflicts. The barriers of humanity are artificial and they would dissolve because beneath apparent differences of religion, language, colour, and so on, at the core we are just the same. The brand seeks to develop resonance by attending to the masked and hidden craving to have a world of peace and harmony. The television commercial goes like this:

- The ad begins with a little boy eating at home who looks across the window to discover a ball falling outside his home. As he moves out curiously to look for the ball he discovers another boy across the fence asking him to pass the ball over to him. He initially hesitates and looks around to verify if he is being watched for he is talking to the enemy, then he kicks the ball across. Upon receiving the ball the other boy invites him to play with him. This invitation makes him forget about the enemy and boundary and he sneaks through the fence to play. Now in their natural self, both boys begin to play and enjoy. At this point the voiceover announces '*Deewarein gir jaati hain, faasle mit jaate hain, jahan do baatein ho jaati hain*' (Walls fall down, distances are erased, where two words are spoken [barriers break when people talk]).

Figure 5.4 exhibits the journey of Airtel of how a brand must continuously strive to break boundaries in search of new meaning. This search should mark a progression in customer–brand relationship from mundane to significance. This progression must mark a progression of value. Market crowding and commoditisation are two of the many scary realities of the present day marketing environment. Value embedded in the product element of brand soon gets common across all participants in an industry. This leaves the marketer with a serious challenge of crafting brand identity with richer and deeper meaning.

Figure 5.4: Brand Development Trajectory

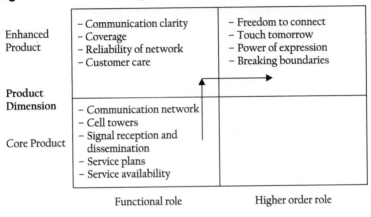

	Functional role	Higher order role
Enhanced Product	– Communication clarity – Coverage – Reliability of network – Customer care	– Freedom to connect – Touch tomorrow – Power of expression – Breaking boundaries
Product Dimension Core Product	– Communication network – Cell towers – Signal reception and dissemination – Service plans – Service availability	

Brand's consumer context

Source: Author.

CONCLUDING REMARKS

Effective branding is transformational. With branding a brand can break away from the low value commodity spiral to move up in the higher value orbit. Brands can develop intersection points of higher value delivery. The connection and bonding so created is difficult for other brands to copy and neutralise. Products permit easy reengineering and copying in order to be tangibles but brands being intangible entities are difficult to copy. The first impression appropriated by a brand becomes the benchmark to process all future communications. And a copy brand in such cases reinforces the previous image of the original brand held in the prospects' minds instead of diluting the brand. The business of the product carried by Surf or Airtel is not much different from other products in the category. But the brand ideas set these brands apart and they connect with the higher order concerns of the target consumers. The Surf brand provides freedom to children to reach their fullest potential. The brand affords parents an opportunity to be good parents and not being obstructionists in the child's growth. This way the brand now assumes a more important role in consumers' lives. For effective stain free wash 'Surf Excel *hai na*'. That is the reason why the brand claims 'don't worry about stains they are good'. Behind every stain there is a lesson learnt. Every stain has its own story. In case of Airtel the core promise of the brand has moved beyond communication to expression to a much bigger role that communication can play in making this world a better place.

6

Pressing Hot Buttons in Consumer Value Space

What is the truth behind the top brands—global or national or local? Although the expanse of their vicinity may vary in scope and size, one common factor that characterises all of these is their capacity to press some hot buttons in consumers that create outcomes every marketer dreams of. What are these dreamt of outcomes? Some of these internally relevant metrics include surpluses or profits that the firm generates for its shareholders. But these metrics depend on externally driven responses that the firm manages to elicit from its customers. The most desired end state for a marketer is brand loyalty and commitment. Check what your customer does if the brand that you market is not available to him or her:

- Does she/he bother to begin with?
- How quick does she/he find a substitute brand?
- Does she/he resist the substitute brand on account of performance differences?
- Does she/he resist the substitute brand for psychological reasons—emotions?

- Does she/he resist the substitute brand for both psychological and functional differences?
- Does she/he resist the substitute brand for reasons that can't be articulated?

BRANDING DISCRIMINATION

Branding is an exercise in reductionism. A brand is designed by definition to achieve power at the expense of other brands. Power brands become unequal among equals. However competition promotes equality. Competition is essential for efficient and effective allocation of economic resources. It is for this reason law favours competition. It leads to an overall well being of customers. Competition is the vehicle for ensuring better value delivery by facilitating free flow of resources and eliminating supernormal surpluses related to monopolies. If competition promotes well being in society in general and for consumers in specific on the one hand it robs the marketer of its powers on the other hand. It is in this context that the marketer is left looking for ways and means to reverse the effects of competition without violating the competition laws.

Branding allows marketers to 'eliminate' or 'kill' competition. With branding a marketer can stage a bloodless coup. Competition is demolished when rival brands are pushed outside the consideration set of consumers. Brands are about building resistance. Brands succeed when customers resist to lures and temptations of competitive brands. Successful brands build barriers to switching. The mountains so created act to insulate and buffer from competitive assaults. Why would the buyer of a Nokia mobile phone resist accepting rival brands like Sony Erickson or LG or Samsung? Or why would a customer of Maggi noodles refuse to buy Top Ramen? The answer may lay hidden in the unique value links that brands like Nokia and Maggi have forged which are not shared by other brands.

In any product category usually a number of brands compete for customers' purchase vote. For instance in bottled drinking water market the brands include:

- Aquafina,
- Kinley,
- Bisleri,
- Paras,
- Bailey,
- Hello,
- Himalyan and many others.

For a given set of target customers a brand achieves success when it is able to reduce a customer's choice set of brands that are considered acceptable. The mark of ultimate supremacy is when a brand is the sole resident of the consumer's evoked set. So what do brand leaders like Colgate, Nike, Usha fans, HP, Bisleri, LG, Mercedes, Dettol antiseptic and J&J baby soap have in common? These brands consistently manage to knock out their rivals from the consideration of their target customers. They break the perception of equality by delivering superior results on the dimensions considered important by the customers.

So when, for example, if Kinley is not available and the customer cannot do without water how difficult is it for this customer to reach out to a substitute brand would determine the power that Kinley enjoys. Brand power has a direct connection with the perceived difficulty or discomfort that it develops in consumers' minds in substituting rival brands. What defines commodity status in this context? It is the absence of this discomfort or difficulty involved in switching. In some product categories prima facie many brands compete with one another. The truth hidden beneath the apparent façade of branding can only be learnt when the surface is scratched. Mere use of attractive brand names, advertising, glossy packaging, and so on, does not create brands. Actually these may be nothing more than commodities in the packaged form with their unique names. The acid test of branding success is when a brand is successfully able to build customer resistance towards substitutes. Dettol leads the pack of antiseptic liquid category because the brand has successfully dug deep perceived trenches around it which prevent customers from making a jump over to the other substitute brands. Does this trenching in the consumer's mind explain power forever brands? The answer is definitely positive. Figure 6.1 shows that effective brand building requires building switching barriers from one brand to another.

Figure 6.1: Branding Builds Switching Barriers

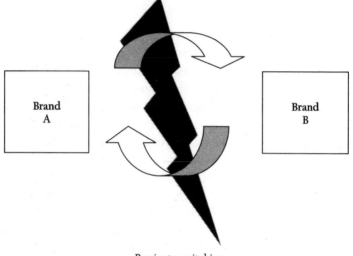

Barrier to switching

Source: Author.

Brands teach consumers to discriminate among available alternatives. Every single rupee that a marketer invests in business must contribute to building discrimination. So for a brand like Kinley to be successful it must elicit a consumer's discrimination response. And why must the consumer discriminate in favour of Kinley at the cost of other brands? Branding in this way is not a speculative exercise. Discovery of hooks that would break consumer difference is the key to successful branding. And successful brands dig the truth beyond the obvious to transform customers into being intensely choosy about what they pick from a plethora of competitors vying for their attention and favour. Brands often deploy product as a prime vehicle of value delivery and thereby achieve positive performance related discrimination at the point of purchase.

The whole process of brand reductionism discussed in this section is summarised in Figure 6.2:

Figure 6.2: Branding: A Process of Reductionism

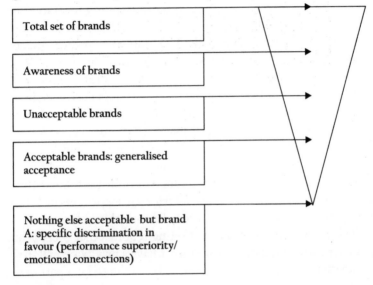

Total set of brands

Awareness of brands

Unacceptable brands

Acceptable brands: generalised acceptance

Nothing else acceptable but brand A: specific discrimination in favour (performance superiority/ emotional connections)

Source: Author.

The descending product parity in various categories is rendering the product component of brands near similar and thereby making the product driven hooks less effective. The diminished product differences often fail to create defensible customer resistance. The challenge for brand building now goes beyond developing a superior product alone. A brand must press a hot button changing the customer to completely swing in its favour. Excellent brands take the marketing battle beyond product functionality into the realm of emotions. Strong functionality coupled with emotional value delivery sows the seeds of affective blindness necessary to drive rivals out of the consideration of customers. But the issue is what these buttons could be and where are they located?

CHARGE OF THE NON-REASON

There are things and persons that people avoid and so some brands are also avoided. Yet at the same time there are things and persons that create pull towards them and we are happy to move towards them. At the core of this avoidance behaviour lays friction or disturbance. And consumers except in a few rare times seek balance and poise. Friction being a negative state is avoided. No one would like to be in a negative state of existence. As most discomforting things and people are avoided probably brands are also dealt with in similar fashion. Power brands draw their power from the pull that they create for the target customer. Brand Dettol is pulled by customers from the supermarket shelves for the promise and delivery that it makes to its customers. A buyer of Rolex watch avoids Timex not because it does not keep correct time or is unreliable but for some kind of perceived friction that it would create. The rival brands of both Dettol and Rolex may not suffer on account of inferior antiseptic germ killing liquid or poor quality watch. It may be something else.

The entry to modern day marketing requires that every brand in order to be in the race must at least have a product equal to the competition. This is the minimum table stake to be a part of the game. This is an essential condition but not sufficient. This only marks the beginning of the journey. Effective branding requires transcending this competitive threshold and going beyond in value delivery terms. Good product provides good reasons to buy but this is becoming insufficient. The branding journey begins with the product and culminates into something of greater value than functionality implied in the product. Product is an alibi and may not be the reason for brand patronage. Ask the following questions and probe whether the consumers really provide correct answers:

- Why does one buy Nike over others?
- Why is Marlboro the preferred smoke?
- Why does one buy Waterman?
- Why is Levis the best buy?

- Why is Tata salt good?
- Why is Dabur honey preferred?

This kind of exercise engages a customer consciously and the answers are conditioned by awareness. However this kind of probing is limiting and ill equipped to gauge inner customer reality. One of the greatest victims of this kind of probing was Coca Cola Company. It suffered over 600 million US dollars loss when it launched New Coke and withdrew the old one just because its market research found that people preferred Pepsi on account of superior taste. Basing product development on consumer feedback it developed a better-tasting drink with the mission to outdo Pepsi in the market by attracting its customers with a new better-tasting drink. But the actual marketplace results were quite shocking when those very customers who preferred the new drink in the taste refused to patronise it in its avatar as New Coke. The research failed to discover how the brand intersected with customers beneath the act of buying and drinking a cola. The hidden interface which in fact bonded the customers with the brand was never discovered and handled by the marketing research.

Consumption is not a visible phenomenon only. The meaning of things and brands is not usually visible to naked eyes. The actual value exchange is often hidden from the eyes like the submerged portion of the iceberg. Merely scratching the surface is hardly revealing and insightful. Directly seeking reasons for one's behaviour is hardly insightful and revealing. In the above cases the list of reasons is likely to be predominantly product centric. And the real cause may go undetected. A brand's intersection may go beyond the product to encompass obvious value dimensions. For instance Nike to the eyes is nothing more than a sports shoe but its meaning not visible to the eyes is about an attitude cherished by certain class of customers. And Waterman is much more than a fine piece of writing instrument. The people who only see a writing pen with the name 'Waterman' written on it totally miss the point.

Some of the commodities or products typically operate in structurally constraining conditions. These are held at the lower end of the value spectrum by people because of their role. For instance a toilet cleaner or a headache remedy. In these situations the marketer is left with not much freedom but to pursue a pro-duct centric approach to brand building. The product centric value path is pursued not because of choice but because of compulsion. These product categories are typically perceived to be less significant for they do not hold much value beyond problem avoidance. The brand in such categories is sought as a means to get rid of the negative state that a consumer may be in. In such cases the brand idea is confined to product. Salt is sought for its saltiness. A product like Nycil or Borosoft draws its legitimacy from its ability to provide relief from prickly heat. Despite this a careful examination of product–customer interaction may reveal the presence of hidden buttons that can provide opportunities for brand building at a higher level of value exchange.

Power brands develop and create intersections at a much deeper level to produce asymmetrical value delivery. The hot buttons embedded in consumer physiology and psychology need to be identified and pressed. Brand Nike presses the hot button of product superiority but then so do other brands that compete with this iconic brand. Customers all over the world have mad like following for Nike that none other competitor is able to garner. That means that the brand does press some other hot buttons that charge customers like the 'march of the light brigade' driven by something beyond that resides outside the domain of reason.

HOT BUTTONS

Products are 'manufactured' in factories but brands are created in customers' minds. The transition from something perceived to be lower in value to something of higher value requires pressing hot buttons in consumer value space. A storage trunk may draw its relevance from its use in storing valuables. But to see only a trunk in a brand like Louis Vuitton (LV) is to completely miss the core branding idea. Actually a brand like LV draws its strength from displacing the trunk or hand bag out of its category held to be less valuable and placing it into a category considered more important and valuable. A sales person in a LV showroom can be seen selling a bag or trunk but what actually gets bought may be radically different from visible reality.

The brand intersects with customers in a complex fashion to create value. It would be a mistake to narrowly seek explanation of LV brand's fierce command over its customers solely in its product quality. The idea of product quality rarely touches the customer's thought process in the LV showroom. It is taken for granted. The brand has graduated from its first stage of developing brand conviction a long time back. Rather its showroom environment and brand communication are carefully constructed to deflect customers from thinking to affective orientation. The branding at LV is aimed at casting a spell over its prospects and sending them into a trance like condition. Brands in order to be successful must 'possess' their prospects like a spirit. It is only then that coveted branding outcomes can be reached. Top brands aim to make a jump over the thinking brain to the limbic brain to create affective blindness. It is only then that these become 'uncontestable' in contest space.

A brand must chart out its course for cultivating meaningfulness in the customer's life by identifying the value buttons. Values are central to our existence. These are the end states of existence that one strives to achieve. The variations in values across customers, time and space present a mosaic of branding opportunities. Customers are essentially seekers of values. And it is these values that provide the landscape for brand building. Brands in a product category are bound by their product definition to offer similar product functionality yet connecting with different customer segments is possible by choosing to invest customer relevant values in the brand.

Branding success can come by easily in the early stages of product life cycle by focusing on the functional core of the product. And it is possible because of category creation benefits that automatically flow to newly introduced products. Uniqueness is inherent in the introductory stage of the product life cycle. But as the product category matures and other players arrive space gets shared. The commonality of functionality embedded in other brands joining the market gradually pushes the category to the throes of commoditisation. The brand at this juncture must 'move up' beyond product centric perspective to pressing other value buttons to strike a chord with its customers. Customers get accustomed to expecting some functions or attributes or features as their interaction grows with the product category. For instance when CFL arrived in the lamps market a different category came into existence. Compact florescent lamps brought electricity savings proposition to the market and created differentiation. Later the CFL category met its *fait accompli*. The category is now crowded with tens of brands that adorn shelves with identical shapes, names and communication. It is here that the branding challenge begins. The brand must achieve newer more meaningful customer intersections to leverage the value delivery in its favour. Figure 6.3 shows how a brand must push buttons to maintain differentiation.

Figure 6.3:   Product Life Cycle and Differentiation

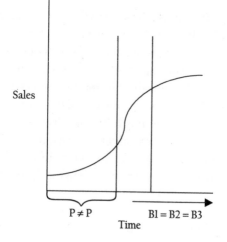

Source: Author.
Note: B = Brand, P = Product.

Consider the toothpaste brands available in the market:

- Colgate
- Pepsodent
- Close-Up
- Babool
- Anchor

Do these brands press different value buttons to attract customers in their target group? The answer is positive. When one is confronted with these brands at the conscious level of brand–customer interface—the negotiated category is toothpaste. But when hooks are lowered below the conscious a different picture unfolds. Most of these brands make entry into the market with toothpaste—chemical composition packed in a tube form used to maintain oral hygiene. The hidden imprints these brands have created are different. And these hidden below the conscious connections create a charge pulling the consumer to the brand. Colgate pulls the security and safety button for decay prevention in children and Pepsodent pulls the button for taking worries off the mothers' heads about the decay causing germs that begin to work when something is eaten. Close-Up is a confidence building device in situations involving proximity with the opposite sex. It provides assurance against potential rejection in a social situation especially vis-à-vis the opposite sex. Babool allows a rupee to stretch farther and thereby become a generator of family happiness. Anchor allows vegetarians to carry on with their beliefs with conviction in a new area of their life. It in a way allows realisation of sacrosanct beliefs.

For customers their values provide the contextual frame of reference for all their behaviours including buying and brand patronage. Brands inherently have no meaning for customers. Customers have allegiance to their values not to brands unless otherwise created. Brands acquire relevant meaning by connecting with the values appropriate to their context. Consider the following brands:

- As mentioned in Chapter 5, Airtel, the mobile service provider brand, could continue to boast about its network superiority and connectivity to forge links with its target customers. Yet the brand's recent communication takes the brand interface to a new higher level of value bonding. The children playing football across barbed wire fencing dividing the two countries takes the mobile service provider brand to a much more important and relevant level (communication can break boundaries). Airtel brand is much more than about a talking service, rather it is about elimination of divisions that mar present society.

- On similar lines Tata tea's new brand communication 'wake up' (*jaago*) uses the term in figurative sense to distinguish between waking up and awakening. The brand connects with the need to awaken to the problems and malaise that surround society (youth awakening). The brand sets itself apart from the cliché communications that many tea brands use to highlight the tea quality and packaging.

- Daikin air conditioner sought to establish the brand on the differentiating platform of silence. Air conditioners cool well but often this cooling is accompanied by disturbing noise. The earlier brand communications highlighted that Daikin air conditioners are so silent that one could hear the noise produced by the dropping of a paper pin or movement of ants in a room. But silence is a product related virtue. The issue is how does this attribute relate with consumer benefits and values? Consumers respond to values not to the products. Products or brands that are not in sync with values suffer from meaning disconnect. This requires elaboration of the brand's meaning in consumer benefit terms. The latest brand communication has evolved the concept of silence operation of the machine (product feature) to calm (customer relevant value) of the senses and thereby promotes peace of mind.

THE TURF

The purpose of branding is to elicit a favourable customer response. The brand must charge the customer to act in its favour amongst the cacophony of rival brands. Eliciting favourable response is not a matter of the deployment of brute force in favourable behaviour extraction. To be in its mission the brand must appeal to the senses and sensibilities of its prospects. Meaning is not inherent in a brand. It has to be cultivated and created. The values must be invested. The pulling power of a brand is determined by its ability to deliver results perceived to be desired and valued by the prospects. What is Good Knight? A brand like this one has an opportunity to operate at two levels: the defensive and offensive.

At the defensive level the brand draws its relevance from defending customer existence. A mosquito repellent acquires its role and relevance in a customer's life by providing protection against mosquito bites. This meaning is purely product centric. It could prove to be limited when other brands arrive in the market and adopt product focused views. The uniqueness of the brand has a danger of becoming generic in the wake of similar functions offered by other brands. Therefore meaning extension can come by if the brand is connected with offensive level concerns of the consumers. The brand can build its capital as a devise that is less about 'prevention of a negative state' but as an aid in achieving 'more positive' states of existence. For instance mothers (performing the buyer's role) can move up on motherhood (higher nurturance and care) or a good night's sleep for kids (happy existence) by discriminating in favour of Good Knight. It all depends upon how the brand seeks to build customer value intersections. Unless a product suffers from category limitation—generally insignificant categories—strategies can explore higher value buttons embedded in the totality of consumer reality. Product centrism locks the brand into concrete and rationalistic orientation which later could pose encumbrances in sentimental connections with the brand.

The winning brands activate purchase motives in consumers' minds. A brand in order to win the marketing race must identify specific purchase motives in the target consumers. There are five portals that provide platforms for building winning brands (Buccholz and Wördemann 2000): benefits and promises; norms and values; perceptions and programmes; identity and self expression and emotions and love.

Benefits and Promises

Brands can succeed by creating a compelling virtual benefit. What is in the brand for me? Here consumer benefits can be of two types: real or factual and virtual or subjective. Consumers perceive objective reality through perceptual filters. Hence brands that are technically superior are not necessarily held higher by the market. Perception of superiority carefully cultivated moves the luxury brands which need not be the best in the product class. Consumers buy into a proposition rather than a sum of objectively assessed product benefits.

Consumers buy into the notion of quality not actual objective quality. It is difficult for consumers to tell the difference between brands. So is BMW better than Mercedes? Is Coke better than Pepsi? Is Lenovo better than HP? Although New Coke won over Coke in taste tests, American consumers rejected New Coke. With competition intensified in most product categories brands seem to be becoming similar. Finding the differences in quality is an expert's job. Yet some brands score over others by leaps and bounds although they may not top in quality. In such a situation the perception of quality or superiority comes in handy for the consumer to solve a buying problem.

Norms and Values

In this context the brand can motivate consumers because of its role as inner conflict solver or conflict avoider. Values are central to human existence. Values are widely held beliefs that set apart the desirable from the undesirable. Values guide behaviours by providing benchmarks to decide the acceptable from the unacceptable. Values define the concept of right and wrong. Something that is considered legitimate in one culture may be highly objectionable in another. For instance FTV has often been criticised in India for obscenity, whereas people in the Western world find nothing wrong with its programming. Indian culture traditionally emphasises abstinence rather than sensual gratification.

- The first way brand can leverage norms and values into building a compelling consumer motivation is by positioning the brand as a guilt eliminator. Guilt is felt when an implicit norm is broken—unable to give a good lunch to your child in school; unable to pamper your life partner. A brand can allow consumers to wash off their guilty consciences. For instance many diamond brands build compelling motivation as surrogate love (expensive diamonds compensate for the guilt of ignoring one's partner).
- Second, we all take pride in certain beliefs that we hold and abide by. For instance, I am modern and not old fashioned. I am a sport. I am not clumsy. By challenging or satisfying pride a brand can press the winning button (remember *Jo Jeeta Wohi Sikandar?*). Rexona deo challenges consumer pride when foul body odour prevents people from coming close.
- Third, a brand can pull triggers by highlighting consumer inconsistencies (discrepant behaviour) and positioning itself as a means to resolve them. Krack Cream leveraged this by their campaign *'Oopar se raj rani, par neeche se naukrani'* (A queen from above, but a maid from below) thereby bringing the contradiction of spending much on cosmetics but ignoring the toes.

Identity and Self-expression

Brands often draw their relevance from their capacity to do the talking without using words for the consumer. The identity, personality and character are invisible constructs and these are expressed through a variety of symbols. Suppose you happen to stop at a red light and right next to you three cars also stop: an Ambassador, Mercedes and Maruti 800. Can you guess who is inside the car? The first one is a bureaucrat or politician, second one is an established, rich person and the third one is a middle-class person making an entry into the world of decent living. Shoe brands like Woodland and Nike signify two different wearer identities—outdoors and adventurous for Woodland and aggressive and fiercely competitive for Nike. Brands are a very powerful means of non-verbal communication. It is this ability of brands to position and define a person in a social frame that pulls consumers.

Why are jeans labels patched outside instead of inside? It is because these small leather patches metamorphose more or less identical denims into highly differentiated identity expression devices. Levis signifies a cool, free, rebel, hip, original and all-American character, whereas Wrangler conjures up images of rugged, and tough sports like rodeo. Brands derive their value by developing images that consumers would like to wear. Brand image is not consistent with self perception or the images that consumers would like to project become cases of rejection. A consumer may prefer to drive a Jaguar instead of a Toyota Corolla to a special meeting because he wants to wear (to be seen as) the stereotypical profile of a Jaguar user.

Brands that identity profile can be developed by answering questions for consumers like: How do I view myself? (Confident.) How would I like to see myself? (More confident.) How do others see me? (Unattractive.) And how would I like to be seen by others? (Attractive.) These are self and social dimensions. Pull is generated when brands are invested with images that match with the existing and idealised desired states of the consumers (Fair and Handsome promises how the brand can transform the prospect from a dissonant existing state—rejection, dislike, unconfident—to the desired state). Brand can serve the identity and self expression function in a number of ways:

- Expression of invisible internal character or trait (Dunhill signifies sophistication and Bata symbolises maturity, down to earthiness).
- Expression of consumer ideologies (never cracks under pressure—Tag Heuer ('What are you made of?') or Adidas ('Impossible is nothing').
- Entitlement to a group's membership (a Rolls Royce car gains a prospect entry into nobility, Khadi once stood for a group seeking self-reliance, Louis Vuitton bags and trunks signify rich and well-heeled members of society).

- Expression of personal message—brands can not only convey messages but they can also become messages (expensive chocolate and diamonds stand for love).

Love and Emotions

A brand's role in a consumer's life may go beyond provision of functional performance. Product quality and functionality can get the brand to win the rational mind but equality achieved by competitors pushes the consumer into the non-committal zone. Steady relationships are based on true love. The withdrawal of Coke enraged consumers because the company had withdrawn not just the product from the market but a relationship that people loved and cherished. Coke to them was much more than a product. It was a loved companion with whom Americans grew. Great brands develop emotional bonding by tapping into the emotional reservoir of their consumers. Successful brands jump over the rational mind to connect directly with the emotional side. Emotional bonding provides the best insulation against the competitive assaults thereby making the brand less contestable.

Brands like Calvin Klein, Armani and BMW leverage the power of emotions in the human interface even with inanimate objects like perfumes, suits and cars. Brand strategy based on emotional leverage can use different paths:

- Brand as friend: in this mode the brand forges emotional linkages with its prospects by demonstrating solidarity on an emotional issue (conflict) denied or not understood by others. Whisper demonstrates its commitment to the issue of women empowerment (girl child education) in society plagued by biases and prejudices.
- Tap into emotions: love, fear, anger, excitement, joy, sadness, shame, serenity, anxiety, depression, and so on, are emotions embedded in our minds. Brands connect and bond with their customers by developing links with specific emotions. Amul ice cream taps into happiness and joy, Airtel reduced

roaming plans and leveraged the love emotion (how many times would you call?); Enamor brand of lingerie pulls the wishful or desire buttons; Master Card ('Seeing your parents enjoy like kids—priceless. There are some things money can't buy. For everything else, there's Master Card'). Many brands connect with prospects as removers of the negative or unpleasant emotional states (Domex, Head & Shoulders, Rexona).

BRAND TURF

The turf for brand development is consumer needs and wants. The justification for a brand as a value package comes from the market. Brand relevance is driven largely by the value provision role it performs in people's lives. The missing link between satisfaction and loyalty must be discovered to innovate on brand delivery. But the question is what do consumers need and what motivates them to behave. The search for answers to these questions led to the discovery of a new kind of motivational framework (Robinette and Brand 2001). Five factors that constitute this framework are: product, money, equity, experience and energy. These consumer motivation factors represent the rational and emotional components. Money and product are rational and equity, experience and energy represent the emotional side.

Money (the price component) and product (features and attributes) are minimum essential requirements to be a part of the marketing game. These comprise entry tickets to the branding stadium. The advantages developed around product features and prices are quickly replicated. Utmost care must be exercised in preventing these dimension from becoming competitive disadvantages for the brand. No amount of emotional connections can make a car win customer patronage if it is disproportionately highly priced and fails in doing the job it is supposed to do. The emotional dimension in branding supplements the rational dimension rather than supplanting it. Solid brands are not created out of high powered communications.

The first of the emotional elements is equity. Equity combines trust and identity. Brands earn trust when customers can rely upon the brands for consistent performance. For instance FedEx has earned a reputation for on time express delivery of packets. Consumers trusted Bajaj for reliable scooter performance. Bata's Naughty Boy shoe brand was a trusted name for shoes for school going kids. HMT watches enjoyed consumer trust for the reliable performance of their watches. But these brands suffered on account of poor emotional connects as time changed. Consumers must be able to relate with the brand in human terms as people relate with other people. HMT's image as a government enterprise, unchanging, static, laid back and old, pushed the brand out of sync with new customers who needed more than a watch. This gap was filled by Titan.

Every intersection point with the brand provides an opportunity to leave a distinct mark on customer experience. Customer experience is the second component of the emotional dimension. Brand experience is made up of various touch points. These touch points include web sites, letters, carry bags, employees, product, communications, endorsements and programmes. Cumulatively these affect consumer attitudes. Every moment of truth presents a potential opportunity for making an emotional connection. Services being interactions oriented brands face the challenge of achieving differentiation by providing unique experiences. The crucial question to ask in this context is what mark you leave when customers come in contact with your system.

Emotional energy is the last component of the emotional dimension. Customers make energy investments by way of time and effort in a product or service. How cumbersome is reaching out for a product or service? Is availability convenient? How time consuming is it? Shifting the ordering of product or service to the Internet offers great energy savings. With Internet banking and ATMs banks have created good amounts of time and effort savings.

Brands trigger consumer motivation by pressing the hot buttons. Relating the brand with a compelling motive or need embedded in the totality of a consumer is the key to developing a successful brand. However not all needs are perceived as compelling or equally important. Needs or motives can be positioned on a continuum of importance. Some influence behaviour more strongly than the others. One such framework (Maddock and Fulton 1996) arranges consumer motives in this order of importance (first being stronger need and the last being the weaker need): spiritual, personal, physical, adaptation, territorial, expectation, sexual, place, time, play and circumstance. Emotions like love, passion, guilt, acceptance, self esteem and self image are connected with spiritual and personal motives and they enjoy greater influence on behaviour. As discussed earlier consumers seek values not products and brands per se. To get into the consumers' buying radar the brand must build correct value connection. It is this value connection that bestows the brand with meaning and relevance from the consumer's perspective as shown in Figures 6.4 and 6.5.

Winning brands charge consumers emotionally by creating a kind of affective blindness by connecting with higher order needs. Products or services in their naked form are nothing more than bundled functionality but by effective brand building strategies these are evolved into something of higher value. Consider the following:

- A diamond (hardened carbon of very little practical use) converted into a symbol of love and self esteem.

Figure 6.4: Brand and Consumer Intersection = Value Delivery

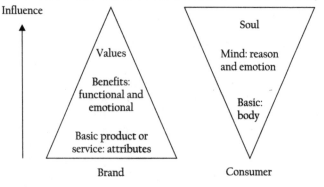

Source: Author.

Figure 6.5: Interrelationship of Brand Package and Consumer Values

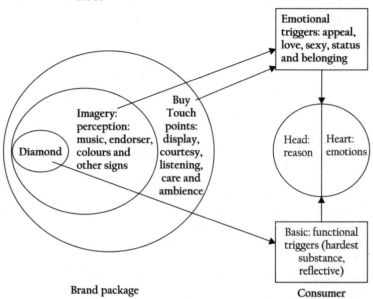

Source: Author.

- A car (a mechanical assembly of parts and components) converted into something highly experiential (sports car) and status symbol.
- A chocolate (a concoction of cocoa beans, milk solids, emulsifiers, and so on) connects with the love and emotion motives.

CONCLUDING REMARKS

Brands are valued because they play a crucial role in driving financial results like profits and returns on investments. Financial metrics in turn depend on marketing outcomes. Top brands enjoy phenomenal customer support and commitment by creating some of the mountains or trenches which prevent switching.

The higher are the barriers the safer is the brand as customers resist substituting it with its rivals in the market. Knocking competition out mentally is the core of all branding exercises. Creation of customer commitment and loyalty is difficult in the current marketing environment because laws promote competition and thereby accelerate the process of commoditisation. The branding agenda precisely attempts to reverse this trend by pressing hot motivational buttons that push up value delivery and thereby create asymmetry. This is often achieved by taking the brand away from its inherent physical product category to place it in the category that holds higher meaning for customers. This requires accomplishment of a perceptual transition. Brands can press hot buttons in the form of benefits and promises; norms and values; perceptions and programmes; identity and self expression and emotions and love. Customers are rarely interested in the products or product category. Central to their lives is the management of life as it continually changes. Brands must explore the totality of customer reality to discover life challenges and develop value links that ultimately help them reach their goals.

7

Internal and External Leveraging of Brand Assets

Think of products like typewriters, tape recorders, video cassette recorders, hand wound watches, black and white televisions, long playing records, kerosene lanterns, scooters and try to figure out something common that runs across these. It is not very difficult to guess that some of these have either vanished or are on the threshold of vanishing from the marketplace. The market is not a static concept. The forces that make up the so called 'market' are dynamic. The competitors change, consumer needs and wants shift, technology evolves and government policies and pressure groups' concerns change. The consequent reality of this transformation is the concept of product life cycle. The life cycle concept proposes that products like human beings also pass through different stages of existence on their way to ultimate extinction.

The life cycle of a product is broken down in four stages: introduction, growth, maturity and decline. Each of these stages has its unique characteristics in terms of buyer response, competitors' behaviour and resulting strategy challenges. The fact of life in organisations is that products have limited life. The forces of time make these irrelevant and undesired leaving no market for them. Reliance exclusively on a product for marketing success can seriously jeopardise the future of an organisation. This calls for developing mechanisms to burst the operation of life cycle and thereby obtain perpetuity in the life of a business organisation.

LIFE CYCLE

Developing an optimum portfolio of products is a serious managerial challenge. The product assortment of an organisation should ideally be geared to ensure current survival and future growth. If there is a need for current bread winners there is also a pressing concern to develop babies who would be future bread winners and caretakers of the present bread winners. One good example of a company bursting the effect of product life cycle is ITC. From being an exclusive tobacco company a decade back it has evolved into diversified players with participation in markets that would ensure success in future. Two strategies can be discerned from ITC's case:

- First, at the macro level the company has aligned its product or business portfolio by expanding its operations into new businesses like confectionary, ready to eat food (Kitchens of India), ready to wear apparel (Wills Lifestyle and John Players), shampoo (Superia, Vivel and Fiama de Wills), biscuits (Sunfeast), stationery (Hallmark), consumer staples (Aashirwad) and snacks (Bingo), hospitality (Maurya and Fortune). These products signify the directional change of the company into non-tobacco businesses. Moving into these businesses makes strategic sense because these markets would compensate for business loss due to the declining cigarette market.
- Second, at the micro level one of its most prominent and successful cigarette brands have been branched into non-cigarette product categories. 'Wills' started as a cigarette brand—Navy Cut popularised by the famous ad campaign 'Made for each other' is branched into the lifestyle segment. Now the company markets ready made apparels, fragrances

and shampoos (Essenza de Wills) under the Wills Lifestyle name. Wills Lifestyle has emerged as one of the top five players in the branded apparel industry.

Reading the signals of ensuing change much before they develop into an overwhelming force is what allows a firm to develop coping mechanism proactively. It is like taking charge with horns and turning the forces of change from threats to advantages. Any failure in this regard can send even the mightiest of the mighty firms into oblivion. The fit between the firm and the market cannot be taken for granted for ever. The dynamism in the market forces fills the job of the brand manager with stimulation and challenge. Developing defences against the life cycle effect on the one hand and seizing opportunities unleashed by environmental dynamism on the other hand sets the agenda and excitement to the job of managing the brand.

LEVERAGE WITHIN

One of the top most brands in the Indian market place is Colgate. The product portfolio of the Colgate brand makes an interesting case of growth strategy available for a company. The Colgate brand markets the following toothpastes under its umbrella:

- Colgate Dental Cream
- Colgate Herbal
- Colgate Fresh Stripes
- Colgate Salt
- Colgate Tartar
- Colgate Total
- Colgate for Kids

What does this kind of growth strategy imply? Over time Colgate brand which started as Colgate Dental Cream has evolved into a line or various toothpaste variants. Although each of the variations of Colgate sticks to the original product category (the toothpaste), it is differentiated in its own right. There are two angles to this kind of growth:

1. Market
2. Company

The strategy here does not call for deviating either from the currently served market or the company competencies and strengths. Rather the strategy leverages both to seek greater participation and sales volume. It is a low risk option to achieve growth. In the above case the brand used is the same with some modifier to explain the difference in the product. For instance, 'salt' differentiates this variation from others. However, in some cases firms choose to use different brand names to signify variations of the same product. These cases involve employing a multi-branding strategy. Use of individual brand names often is desired to create sharper image and minimise brand confusion. Consider the soaps portfolio of Unilever:

- Lux
- Hamam
- Lifebuoy
- Dove
- Breeze
- Pears
- Rexona

Introducing product variations does not call for any significant changes in the production or technical competencies of the company. With little change in the operations the firm can increase its participation in the market by creating product variations. For instance in the above cases Colgate continues to leverage its toothpaste making skills and competencies to launch different types of toothpastes and HUL has managed to create a complete line of soaps. The lesser the deviation the lesser is the risk implied. The strategy is based on the skills and competency of the internal system—primarily manufacturing and operations. The systems are flexed to extend multiple marketplace responses. Over time every firm develops mastery in certain internal operations related skills and processes. The idea that acts as a catalyst for this kind of increased market participation is to leverage the internally accumulated strengths. The internal strengths and capabilities of the system are leveraged to plug holes in the market. In this kind of strategy when a firm moves to increase its participation in a given market by launching product variations the marketing competencies developed over time are leveraged. Consider the following:

- Nokia leverages its mobile-manufacturing skills and resources.
- Hyundai leverages its car-making skills and resources.
- Titan leverages its wrist-watch-making resources and skills.
- Bata leverages its shoe-making resources and skills.
- JCB leverages its excavator-making resources and skills.
- Siemens leverages its switchgear-making resources and skills.
- HP leverages its printer-making resources and skills.
- L&T leverages its engineering and construction resources and skills.

All of the above firms offer wide variations of products. This kind of strategy leads to the creation and launch of a product (within the product class) and then to tapping the market horizontally or vertically or both. Serving the customer requires development of channels, sales force, distribution network, displays and other communication linkages. When a new introduction does not cross over the market boundary previously cultivated marketing competencies can be leveraged to achieve desired customer service levels. For instance nothing radically different is involved in the distribution, displays, channel movement and communication functions for new market entries.

The strategy of product variations is akin to carpet bombing warfare strategy. Figure 7.1 shows that a market usually is made up of several segments. Often firms start their operations by targeting one of the most lucrative segments. Marketing strategy commands that the market be segmented and depending upon

Figure 7.1:   Leveraging Manufacturing Competencies to Tap Segments

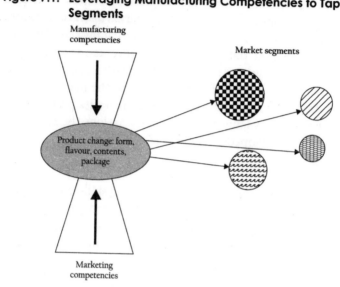

Source: Author.

the attractiveness the segments be targeted. This kind of precise focus obviously excludes simultaneous focus on all segments to begin with. It is risky to spread efforts on a wider space in the beginning. Thus effectiveness and efficiency considerations demand that firms start their operations with a single segment. Consider the following:

- Maruti started with its focus on the entry-level car segment.
- Titan's initial focus had been on value-for-money, appearance-conscious segment.
- Nirma's target has been the economy consumer.
- Hero Honda began with an economy bike (CD 100).
- Maggi focused on the in-house, ready-to-eat quick-food segment.
- Pepsi's target has been young, rebellious and anti-establishment youth.
- Aaj Tak news channel focused on the Hindi uncomplicated news segment.

Once Maruti developed its competencies in car making in India its car range expanded to cover other segments. Its range now includes B segment (Zen), C segment (Swift, Swift Dzire) and D segment (SX4). Titan after consolidating its manufacturing and marketing launch expanded its line of watches to cover up other segments like watches for women (Raga), youth (Fastrack), office wear (Steel Collection), economy (Sonata), technology (chronograph series), innovation (Edge) and expensive Swiss brand (Xylys). The growth trajectory of Hero Honda, the leader in motorcycles has been similar. It started with Hero Honda CD 100 targeting the economy segment ('Fill it, shut it, forget it'). Later Hero Honda expanded its targeting to include other segments with Splendor, Passion, CBZ, Hunk, Karizma, Pleasure, Achiever and CD Dawn. There are two ways a marketer can bank upon its existing set of competencies to achieve greater participation: horizontal line extension and vertical line extension.

1. **Horizontal extension of line:** This strategy involves making additions to the line by changing the peripheral aspects of the current product without altering the price point. The peripheral changes may involve colour, fragrance, packaging, and so on. For instance shampoo marketers often change fragrance, colour and ingredients. A chocolate may come in different variations—white, dark and bitter. Horizontal line extensions are usually common in the fast moving consumer goods market. The key idea behind this strategy is to extract more business out of the current market segment by multiplying consumption. Product variety at times acts to add frequency to consumption. Band switching is often common in low involvement situations where the risk perceived by the consumer tends to be lower. Product variety offered in such circumstances allows a firm to:

    • increase turnover (Maggi's variety may induce customers to eat Maggi more number of times);

- prevent losing customers (variants allow customers to switching and yet remain within the firm's portfolio, for instance a large number of Colgate variants allow switching customers to be within the company's net. Variants allow customers to cope with boredom);
- attract new customers (some of the non-buyers may be induced to buy the product, for example a mint flavour ketchup may attract non-sauce customers, who are interested in mint, to the category) and
- protect customer base from being lost to rivals (line extensions launched by a rival firm can induce customers to switch over to the competition. For instance the launch of jasmine Arial detergent by P&G necessitated the launch of fragrant Surf Excel by HUL so that the latter's customers base was protected).

2. **Vertical extension of line:** Important to vertical line extension is variation in the price points. The vertical movement of line may see additions either at the lower or higher price points or both. For instance Maruti's addition of SX4 is upward line extension. LG's Sampoorna brand exclusively meant for rural price-sensitive market is downward line extension. Tata Motors's product portfolio has witnessed both upward line extension (Indigo) and downward line extension (Nano). Vertical extensions are useful because:

- This way the firm is able to cover up the entire segment spectrum. Coverage achieved in this fashion does not leave any flanks to remain open for competitive assault by aggressors. For instance Japanese car makers quietly made inroads in the American car market by entering into the lower end of the market, the flank which was not covered by American car makers.
- Presence in all price points allows the firm to develop a perception of dominance in the market. The ubiquity so created lends the firm an aura of category dominance.

BARRIERS TO ACCEPTANCE

Two questions are important in the context of strategy involving the launch of product variations:

1. When a market entity is hugely successful in a given market why must the variations be created?
2. What prevents the current product to capture customers in the adjacent segments?

Two words are critical in the above questions. In the first question it is 'successful' and in the second it is 'prevents'. Most of the firms enter the market by carefully crafting marketing strategy. Three cornerstones of marketing strategy are: segmentation, targeting and positioning. The core idea governing marketing strategy is that the market is not made up of one homogeneous set of consumers. Consumers differ in their demographics and psychology. This results in formation of numerous permutations and combinations of consumer groups each enjoying different degrees of similarity on various dimensions. A cursory glance at the toothpaste market would reveal divisions in the market as:

- economy conscious
- seekers of natural product
- people with sensitive teeth
- freshness seekers
- whitening benefit
- concerned about cavities
- longer protection
- ingredient conscious (clove or salt)
- sensory stimulation oriented

These divisions in the market imply presence of barriers trenched among various islands of consumers. The presence of these barriers gives the market a fragmented or divided structure. Absence of these divisions creates a homogeneous market. From the marketing perspective divided structure is pro consumer whereas homogeneous structure is pro marketer. It becomes imperative for the marketer to identify these consumer groups and then as a second step choose one or more as the target(s) of its marketing effort. Effectiveness of marketing demands that each group is offered satisfaction unique to its demands. This automatically leads to the development of focused offering directed to satisfying a specific group. The segment focus of marketing strategy is not choice but a compulsion in the present day environment. However in the past marketers did not pay much attention to customer differences and offered one single satisfaction aimed at all groups. This is best embodied in the classic statement made by Ford: 'Any customer can have a car painted any color that he wants so long as it is black.'

The pursuit of risk minimisation leads companies to begin their operations with a limited focus. Accordingly the attractive segment becomes the target of marketing efforts. A product or service designed specifically to meet the unique demands of a customer group seeks to achieve depth in customer satisfaction. The competitive environment is raising the satisfaction bar. The generalised satisfactions are therefore giving way to more focused offerings. For instance the market now does not need a toothpaste to offer a generalised solution to oral hygiene problems. Rather customers now demand specific satisfactions in the form of more focused offerings. It is not possible for firms to devise 'one size fits all solution'. Thus focus comes at the cost of sacrifice. A product that appeals to one segment or usage by design distances itself from the other segments or usage. Suitability to one segment simultaneously costs the product unsuitability to the other.

Operating in the toothpaste market provided Colgate with operations know-how and expertise in the given domain. The same is true of Hero Honda, Maruti Suzuki, Hindustan Unilever, Titan, Tata and others. Tapping the potential of the adjacent customer groups of the same larger market requires overcoming the barriers of the acceptance of the product in the new group. This strategy of volume and revenue growth leverages the manufacturing or operational strengths in creating product variations to tap into the market potential. The new entries in this context are not brand dependent (do not leverage brand), rather they are internal manufacturing and operations dependent. It is much easier to launch variations by minor tinkering with the production systems rather than moving into a different new product space.

The firm sticks to its knitting—the technology, operations and manufacturing domain—yet leverages these to dish out the same basic product incorporating variations of different kinds to expand its market appeal in the untapped groups or applications. The focus in this strategy is on the physical part of the brand—that is, the product. There are many ways to create product variations to expand appeal: ingredient or contents change, form modification, packaging change, colour variations and manufacturing process differences.

- Ingredient: computers with different types of micro processors; cornflakes with bran, chocolate, fruits, rice, wheat; sugar free ice cream.
- Form: powder, bar, flakes, liquid, granules (many detergent and soap companies employ these).
- Size: various weights or grammage (cooking oils come in different litre containers, sachets and tetra packs; one-bite chocolates).
- Colour: green, yellow, red, blue (notional differences to multiply usage).
- Flavours: different flavours to provide new stimulations and use-frequency enhancement (orange, lime, rose).
- Packaging: variations in aesthetics (gift packages).
- Application or usage (the suggested application—watch for gift).

The shampoo sachets (packaging variation) allowed firms to target consumers at the lower end of the market by overcoming the price barrier which hindered bottled shampoo to penetrate this market segment. Bisleri bottled water made its way to the institutional market by launching water dispensers. High water consumption and cost in institutional settings acted to hinder acceptance of bottles in this group. Maggi Cuppa Mania aims to capture the on the go market. In all these instances the product part of the brand is tinkered with or changed to overcome the barrier to acceptance in the adjacent segment (use and applications included) of the same market. Hindustan Unilever's tea line includes Brooke Bond Red Label, Lipton Yellow, Lipton Green Label, Brooke Bond Taj Mahal, Brooke Bond Taaza, Brooke Bond Thanda and Connoisseur Himalyan.

This strategy involving leverage of manufacturing systems and process leads to the extension of a product line. These products owe their birth to a number of overlaps. These include:

- functionality (similar functions performed—different variations of televisions or cameras);
- target consumers (same consumer or adjacent consumer groups of the same market);
- price-points proximity (ultra economy, economy, mid-price, premium, super premium—cigarettes, soaps);
- channel of distribution (for example, conventional channels);
- application and usage (breakfast cereals for in-between meal hunger) and
- manufacturing process (manufacturing process of a car or detergent making).

These overlaps make this strategy of growth involve considerably less risk. Choose any business firm for verifying this hypothesis. Most of the firms begin with building competencies in a technology domain and later move on to flexing it to achieve greater coverage in the current market. In essence the line extension strategy seeks to enhance revenue stream without hopping over the product category and market domain. Essentially line extension is a strategy of intra product category and the market moves to seek growth with minimum risks. The strategy of seeking growth from the current market with current products is labelled as market penetration by Ansoff (1984).

There are many lures why managers are drawn into line extension strategy (Quelch and Kenney 1994). These are as follows:

- Line extensions provide a firm a low cost and low risk opportunity to meet the needs of the various consumer segments in the market.
- With line extensions consumers can be provided with something different to cater to their need for experiencing something new. This is one of the easy ways to keep the consumer within the marketer's fold.
- With line extensions the upper and lower price points can be covered providing the firm with greater pricing breadth.
- With minor product changes and modifications excess capacity could be put to use.
- Line extensions present an easy and quick way to gain sales increases without requiring a long drawn expensive new product development process.
- A firm can get greater control over highly priced and competitive contested shelf space and thereby gain more visibility at the point of sale.
- This strategy allows a firm to satisfy the channel's demand for broad and varied product line.

EXTERNAL LEVERAGE

The strategy discussed above rested on flexing the manufacturing or technology domain of the firm into creating and launching product variations to achieve greater market coverage. Hence the firm's market entries enjoyed great commonness with each other. And it is this commonness that acted to minimise risk for the firm. Deviations imply risk and uncertainty. Breaking away from the known and established prevents application of stereotypical responses. For instance a company like Harley Davidson specialises in heavy motorcycle space and Bata is expert in shoe manufacturing and marketing. Any venture that pushes these firms outside their established domains would call of meeting new set marketing challenges. Therefore in the light of this constraint the strategy mentioned in the previous section makes sense. If there is an easy way out to achieve growth why should the difficult path be treaded upon? The logic is simple. For instance a technology company like

LG may find it difficult to branch into a technologically unrelated area like ready to wear or shoe manufacturing. The incompatibility of technology and production systems in a way forces the firms to stick to their domain of expertise. It is for this reason that diversifying into unrelated fields has not been a recommended strategy in the industrial era.

The new business paradigm seems to put this assumption to a serious test. Sticking to the known turf makes sense and many firms do stick to their turf. But a newer parallel reality is also true. The product portfolios of many firms do include entries from unrelated product classes. Can a firm achieve marketing success even if this involves transgressing the historical competency domain or knitting?

Consider a company like Gillette and consider its market entries. It markets four different products:

1. Gillette razors (these come in different variations).
2. Gillette after shave lotions.
3. Gillette shaving foams.
4. Gillette shaving gel.

What is common across these products in terms of manufacturing technology? Razors as a product category is different from after shave lotions; and shaving foams have little in common with razors. Consider another very well established company in the name of Caterpillar. Caterpillar is a well-established brand of heavy earth-moving equipments and yet it markets rugged boots and clothes under its banner. Titan's brand Fastrack originated as a watch brand and now it adorns a range of sun glasses and accessories. A brand like Mont Blanc covers a diversified product portfolio including pens, watches, perfumes, and so on. Nike has moved beyond high performance sports shoes to include sports equipment and apparel into its product portfolio. Harley Davidson brand is found on products as diverse as motor bikes, cigarettes, perfumes, jackets and beer. The expansion here involves jumping over the manufacturing or technology domain to an unrelated field.

All these examples involve two significant things: constant brand name and varying product domain. That is, the brand used across the market entries remains the same whereas the product categories make a jump. For instance:

- Mont Blanc jumped outside the pen category over to watches, jewellery and perfumes.
- Park Avenue jumped from the ready-to-wear line to include soaps, after shaves, deodorants, belts and shoes.
- Godrej runs across diversified product categories like almirahs, furniture, refrigerators, air conditioners and appliances.
- Dettol now adorns categories like talc, shaving cream, soap and medicated bands.

The above strategy involving a jump over the product domain is very commonly pursued by firms that seek growth. But this move somewhat runs counter to the logic that distancing from the knitting exposes the firm to risk and uncertainty. Prima facie a firm that has cultivated skills and competencies in the field of ready to wear clothes (designing, procurement, logistics, distribution, stitching, and so on) seems highly incompatible with a field like personal grooming products—soaps, deodorants and accessories. Yet this is a commonly pursued path that started in the late 20th century.

The dismantling of boundaries and liberal ideology to trade now permits easy flow of goods, ideas and information across borders. The age old model in which manufacturing was the precondition for marketing has given way to a new alternate conceptualisation. Now a firm need not manufacture its marketed products and services. These can be outsourced and the firm can exclusively focus its efforts on brand building. A new kind of segregation is emerging. There are firms that are given to back end operations efficiency and effectiveness. These firms specialise in product domains working intensively on the technology and manufacturing side. These are their assets. On the other hand there are firms that work closer to the markets tracking consumer demands and changes.

They command marketing prowess and develop competencies in serving consumers and commanding their trust, loyalty and bonding. Brands are their assets. So when a brand like Mont Blanc crosses over to market a new product under its brand (for example a watch) it need not manufacture it. It can be outsourced. However the product quality must be ensured to match the brand image. An exclusive arrangement can be chalked out with an authentic Swiss watch manufacturer which can design and develop watches that match the identity of the brand. Similarly jewellery can be outsourced to a design house in France. The key task of brand custodians here is to ensure the correct choice of products and quality matching.

THE CONCEPT

The strategy when growth is pursued by marketing a new product from a different domain or class under a common brand name is called 'brand extension'. Here the product makes a jump but the brand name remains constant. How is this strategy different from line extension strategy? And how does it exploit the external leverage? What makes this strategy click? What critical success factors does it bank upon to solicit customer response? These questions can be answered by paying attention to the initial point of reference or the starting consideration that determines the choice of the product for extension. Just answer the following questions:

- Is the choice of new entry dictated by the internal systems (production and technology considerations)?
- Is the choice of the new entry governed by the brand (image installed in consumers' minds)?
- Is the choice of new market entry made independent of both of the above two considerations?

No firm can afford to be radical and reckless. Every decision has to be tested on its merits and risk considerations. The environment around the business unit spins both opportunities and threats. The presence of opportunities does not imply that they could be easily realised and converted into business gains. A business unit is not an endless bundle of strengths and competencies. Constraints are inextricably related to decision processes. So how can identification of a product that is to be added to the portfolio be devoid of any kind of risk assessment? When a brand hangs on products belonging to several product classes and succeeds it may draw its victory from a latent source. The brand name itself may act to trigger consumer response.

In the line extension strategy the choice of the product which generally is in the form of the variation of the existing product is dictated by the current production systems. It is for this reason that the line extensions arrive in the form of the current product's variations. Any addition of a product from a different category or class can generally not be produced by a system which is meant for a different product. A television factory can make different variations of televisions or at best different types of technologically similar electronic devices. These systems cannot be flexed into producing soaps and detergents or ready to wear apparels. Here technology and systems act as constraints and therefore provide flexibility within a narrow sphere for launching variations to tap the market potential. Similarly a watch manufacturing facility can never be leveraged into the making of leather accessories.

Brand extension strategy in a way is based on the freedom bestowed on a firm by its ability to market (not necessarily manufacture) a different product from its current product domain. The marketer need not be the producer. A firm can forge some kind of procurement arrangement and market a product under its current brand. The essential question that now arises is: can the firm branch into marketing any product or does the choice have to be made within the context of some constraint? The answer is that a firm can not branch into marketing of any product without any regard of the constraints.

In brand extension strategy the brand acts both as source of leverage and constraint. The choice is dictated by the brand's image installed in the consumers' minds. Brand image is 'the' driver of the extension opportunity space. Production inconsistencies and incompatibilities are overcome by outsourcing or by developing some kind of in-house production arrangements. However, the presence of external inconsistencies and incompatibilities can thwart marketing success. Only those products should become candidates for brand extensions which can successful leverage the brand's strengths and minimise the crossover of its weaknesses. Therefore the product selection process begins with the brand which is held in the consumer's mind. The relationship between brand extension and line extension is displayed in Figure 7.2.

Figure 7.2: Brand Extension and Line Extension: The Starting Point

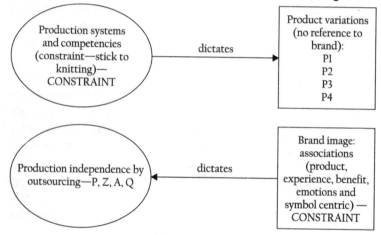

Source: Author.

OPPORTUNITIES

Brand extensions strategy is heavily dependent on the brand's strengths (strengths of recall and associations) and structure (type or brand schema or associative network). What is stored in the brand container in consumers' minds serves as the starting point for finding extension opportunities. The brand strength determines whether a brand will contribute favourably to the extension candidate. The weaker the person, the lesser is the support and protection potential. In a similar vein weaker brand names if attached to a new product category would probably contribute weakly to its success. By associating with a strong brand a new product can get the ruboff of the brand's strengths and gain positive consumer response. The structural dimension of the brand dictates the extension space of the brand. Some brands have narrow extension space. That is they can stretch into close proximity of the product space. Some brands can be stretched into highly dissimilar product categories and enjoy wider extension space.

Leveraging the brand involves selecting the products to which the brands would be extended. Suppose Cadbury intends to extend its hugely successful milk beverage brand Bournvita to a new product category, what category should it be? Or if Titan wants to leverage its brand into a new product category which categories should it lend its name to? If the hugely successful butter brand Amul wants to venture into new product categories which one should it be branched into? Using an established name to market new products belonging to other categories is not as easy as it may appear. For instance when the Ponds brand went on to promote toothpaste the result was disastrous. People did not see any value added in apparels marketed by Bata under its Ambassador brand. There is very little sense in seeing a popular ceiling fan brand Polar on a product like a water purifier. It may be quite discomforting to see Hyundai, primarily known in India as a car brand, on electronic products like televisions.

Inappropriate brand extensions can prove to be dangerous. Wrongly created brand extensions can be harmful in the following ways (Aaker 1991):

- Failure to contribute to success to extension: the reason why a brand name is added to the extension candidate is the assumption that it would add value (by way of brand awareness, associations and attitude) and contribute to its success. When this does not happen as for instance when the addition of the Pepsi name did not add value to Urban Wear brand (clothing), the question is what is Pepsi contributing to Urban Wear? Nothing except the name.
- Negative contribution to extension: sometimes use of an established name in a new category makes a negative contribution instead of making a positive one. The product value gets diminished by brand usage. Nirma's extension into

toothpaste created dissonance. How can something soapy and applied on dirty clothes be put into one's mouth?

- Hurting parent brand: the last category of brand extension disasters is when an extension hurts the parent brand by transferring undesirable associations. Finding Pierre Cardin name on inexpensive pens contributes to the dilution of exclusivity of its ready to wear line.

Finding extension candidates presents a serious challenge for the marketer. Any reckless move can not only lead to extension failure but also may end up inflicting damage to the parent brand. It is for this reason that it is imperative that right candidates for brand extensions are found. The rightness of extension candidates is in this context dictated by consistency and fit. When a brand name (Liril) is added to a product from a different category (mouthwash) two individual constructs (the brand and the product) are merged into one. The consumer's response to this merger (cognitive, affective and co-native) determines the success of the extension. The above case in which the Liril brand is extended into the mouthwash category may lead to a dissonant state in consumers and hence may fail to elicit positive response. The challenge therefore is to find extension product categories that fit well with the concept of brand because the brand is leveraged to lend success to the extension.

The starting process for discovering extension opportunities is to find out what the brand stands for in consumers' minds. The brand being a perceptual entity inhabits in the consumer's mind. Therefore the brand association must be determined. In order to get a complete blow up of brand associations a variety of tools could be applied from simple word association tests to complicated projective techniques. The associations so gathered would reveal the brand reality held in the mind. Can a brand which enjoys neither brand awareness nor associations be leveraged into promoting a new brand? Probably not, because the brand though in existence is not present in the consumer's mind. The question of brand leverage does not arise in this situation. Presence of a brand is the first condition for its leverage.

Once the brand structure (associations) has been discovered then the second task is to identify product classes where these are deemed appropriate and desirable. For instance suppose Liril is young, vivacious, girly and freshness then what product categories need to be like this? If Dettol is antiseptic then in what product categories antiseptic is desirable? If Dove is mild then in what product categories mildness or gentleness is desired? If Louis Philippe is luxury then in what categories luxury connotation is wanted? This process of developing the list of products wherein the brand characteristics are considered desirable is likely to generate a long list of extension categories. Now this list needs to be narrowed down to a limited set of products on the basis of the extent of fit.

The third stage of extension candidate selection calls for evaluation of the product categories identified in the previous stage. For instance if Liril's attributes lead to talcum powder, deodorant, perfume, detergent, lingerie, mouth wash, face wash, body lotion; then each of these alternatives must be presented in the concept form to the prospective buyer for testing. Two-pronged criteria can be applied: fit testing and advantage or distinctive-ness testing. Consider your response to a concept—Liril freshness lime drink. This kind of concept probably creates friction in the mind—the response can be gathered from facial expressions which may raise eyebrows, invite frown or simple laughter. This means the brand does not go well with the product category in question. A simple scale could be employed to record the perceptual category fit (how likely or unlikely is this brand to launch this product).

Once the list is further narrowed down to a set where the brand and category fit is higher, the analysis should turn to the outside category reality. It is not necessary that a product category that fits well with the brand would assuredly create success. The issue is whether the brand contributes something distinctive to the extension in the product category context. How does the brand extension compare with other brands in the extension category—in terms of distinctiveness and superiority?

- Distinctiveness: difference from others in the pack (competition focus).
- Superiority: better on the buyer value sought compared to other brands in the category (consumer focus).

Dove's extension into the shampoo category appears to satisfy these criteria. The Dove brand enjoyed strong association of 'mildness and softness'. Now when brand Dove is extended into the shampoo category how does Dove shampoo score on the criteria of distinctiveness and superiority? First, there was no powerful brand present in the shampoo market that positioned itself as a mild shampoo (except for J&J's No Tears, which has very limited appeal). Second, does the product benefit of mildness make the product superior from the consumer's perspective? Shampoo consumers do look for mild but effective products because this way the harmful effect on hair can be minimised.

In a nutshell brand leverage opportunities could be identified by seeking answers of the four questions:

1. What does the brand stand for in the minds of the people?
2. Given the set of associations how do these stack up in terms of their strengths—associations could be rated on the scale of strength.
3. What are the product categories where these associations are relevant?
4. When the brand name is lent to the relevant product category does the brand stand to become distinct (different from others in the category) and relevant (customer benefit)?

LEVERAGE SCOPE

A related question concerning leverage is how far can a brand be leveraged from its original product category? For instance a brand like Tata hangs on highly diversified product categories including software, cars, trucks, salt, construction steel, heavy machinery, watches and retailing. This is true for other brands like Godrej which lends its signature to dissimilar products like locks, office furniture, soaps, office equipments, real estate, chicken, refrigerators, electronics, security systems and farm implements. Other brands appear to follow a restrictive approach. This is especially true for many companies from the US and the European Union. The question that arises is why do some brands cut across product categories while others do not? For instance Robin is a blue fabric whitener, Cherry is a shoe polish and Nokia is the name of a mobile phone. The critical issue is why do the brands that are so restrictive in their approach wed to only one product?

A brand's capacity to transfer value across its parent product domain depends on the nature of the brand. What is the predominant thought or essential belief held as its core in the prospect's mind? Prima facie those brands that appear on a number of dissimilar product categories have to be elastic and flexible. The restrictive brands are hard and inflexible. What do we mean by brand elasticity or inelasticity? Elasticity of brand implies when a brand's core associations are atypical of a product category and they can be generalised across product categories. On the other hand a brand's leverage space becomes limited when its core associations are typical to a product category. Consider brands like Tata and Sony. Tata stands for trust and bankability and Sony signifies expertise (innovation and quality) in the electronics domain. These two brands differ in their leverage scope. Trust is something that is needed across all kinds of product categories but Sony is a little restrictive in the sense that it can apply to products within the electronics space. Further, consider brands like Colgate and Dettol. These brands have even narrower images related to the product domain—toothpaste and antiseptic.

Product centricity of associations limits the leverage scope while abstract or customer image centric associations free a brand to cross over its original product domain. Armani stands for style and luxury, something atypical to a product category. Similarly Big Bazaar stands for economy. Both luxury and economy are abstract concepts and therefore enjoy greater scope to lend their equity to a variety of products. Nike stands for an attitude and Calvin Klein signifies iconoclasm and sexiness. All these brands appropriate an abstract idea.

As Figure 7.3 shows, many product categories' route to success lies in giving the brand a product centric mission. Here the brand builds its success on the strength of appropriation of a unique product expertise or formula. This route to brand building is necessitated by customer considerations. This may happen when the potential buyers look for reasons for making a purchase. Brands like Moov and Burnol signify their expertise in a narrow area—backache pain management and treatment for burns. Colgate is positioned as an expert in oral hygiene. Vim competes in the area of dishwashing. Carrier is an expert in air conditioner technology. These brands may find it very hard to move across their product or expertise domain. The very competence that makes them look like an expert also creates strong value propositions that make these brands less appealing in the other categories. In the shoe category Bata is too much of a shoe oriented brand and because of this narrow focus it manages to garner a high share in the shoe market but its name becomes restrictive in giving fillip to products in the non-shoe categories. Nike on the other hand is a life style or attitude centric brand therefore it easily manages to cross over to non-shoe product categories like apparel, watches, perfumes and fitness equipments.

A brand has two sides, one is product and the other is the core idea or belief. One represents the factory and the other relates to

Figure 7.3: Brand Meaning and Extension Spread

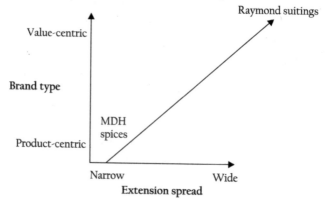

Source: Author.

the consumer. A pen is a mechanical device used to write. A brand built on a pen centric concept (such as Add Gel—looks, functions, durability, reliability, price and colours) is likely to enjoy a narrow extension space. A brand of pen, on the other hand which is constructed on consumer oriented concepts (Mont Blanc—esteem, luxury, independence, free will and class) is likely to enjoy a wide extension space. Before embarking upon a programme of brand extensions it is essential to appraise the brand's limitations. Repercussions of a reckless extension often go beyond failed extension to inflicting damage to the parent brand.

CONCLUDING REMARKS

Product life cycle is an important facet of marketing. Product categories come into existence and vanish. Developing strategic responses to meet the challenges unleashed by the change is a crucial determinant of success. The product portfolio therefore has to be reached and researched from time to time in order to make it in sync with the emergent business realities. There are two strategies that firms often use to manage business growth. The first involves leveraging the strengths and competencies that have evolved over time and are embedded in internal business systems. Leveraging assets and competencies found within the systems leads to line extension strategies. Line extensions involve launching variations of a given product class. This promises a less risky approach to business development. Product variations do not involve crossing over the given competency domain. The second strategy involves leveraging an asset externally held in consumers' minds. In brand extensions, products from different product categories are launched under a given brand name. This involves using an established brand name to promote a product belonging to a different class. The choice of extension candidate should not be made recklessly. A wrong extension move can not only create extension failure but can also hurt the parent brand. Brands differ in their extension scope depending upon their core association structure. Product centric brands usually have narrow extension scope compared to value centric brands.

8

Decoding Branding Strategy

Take a random pick of companies and list the brands in their portfolio. Mosaics of patterns are likely to emerge. Lack of one single pattern implies that firms face different hidden realities and challenges. Firms adopt several ways to cope with these challenges. If we assume that branding is a strategic issue and requires serious contemplation and deliberation then it may be possible to uncover a hidden pattern beneath these mosaics. This hidden pattern can throw insights into the strategy that firms follow to meet their survival and growth aspirations. The portfolio of brands marketed by a firm in the true sense is branding strategy actualised. An appreciation of branding strategy is crucial for an effective brand stewardship. The logic and rationale guiding branding must be culled out from an apparently chaotic and patternless assembly of brands marketed by a firm.

DECODING PATTERNS

There is no one universal branding strategy that business firms follow. Branding approaches come in a bewildering variety. A superficial examination in this context usually does not lead to any meaningful insights. Consider the following:

- Some of the Japanese and Korean firms like LG (electronics to refrigerators to consumer toiletries), Honda (cars to gen sets or lawnmowers) and Hyundai (cars to ships to electronics) use a single brand name for all of their products regardless of their product domain.
- Some of the companies use different brand names for their different points in the product line—for instance HUL's detergent line: Surf (premium), Rin (mid-price) and Wheel (economy).
- In many cases of category differences firms use different names to suggest category differences like Future group's Food Bazaar (food retailing), Big Bazaar (hyper market), Central (lifestyle retailing) and Pantaloon (apparel).
- Some of the companies combine their corporate names with another name to signify a category domain like Sony Handycam, Sony Cyber Shot, Sony Bravia, Sony Micro Vault, Sony Playstation, Sony Walkman, Sony Vaio and Sony Discman.
- Some companies use different brand names for the same products in the same class like Hindustan Unilever: Lux, Dove, Rexona, Lifebuoy, Liril and Breeze.
- Some companies use one single brand name for different but complementary products like Denim and Gillette.
- Some companies use dictionary names for branding while others use semantically coined words such as Exxon and Xerox.
- In many cases a brand name that originates in one category like Dettol (antiseptic liquid) is used later for marketing products in other product categories (shaving cream and bathing soap).

ONE TO MANY

An attempt to decode pattern in the brand portfolio must be preceded by an understanding as to why a firm multiplies its market entries. Why do firms evolve from one product and one brand status to a complex multi-product and multi-brand structure?

Many times brand portfolios grow into a highly unwieldy and complex structure consisting of hundreds of brands like Hindustan Unilever's brand structure once upon a time. This kind of expansion is plagued by redundancies that seriously impact profitability. Hindustan Unilever eventually had to reduce their brands portfolio to a valuable set of 30 brands defined as power brands. Restrictions to add new additions when a strong market justification exists can cause a firm to miss a promising opportunity.

The lure of growth draws companies to increase their market participation. Depending upon market opportunities, internal resource and competencies, firms multiply their market entries. The justification for product portfolio expansion stems from market conditions. Be it market potential or competitive compulsions the firm ends up with an array of products and services. Consider the case of Marico, initially known for two powerful brands Parachute hair oil and Saffola heart-friendly cooking oil, which has now the following market entries in its portfolio:

- Saffola
- Parachute
- Kaya Skin Clinic
- Sudari luxury Ayurvedic skin-care products
- Saffola salt
- Mediker
- Hair & Care
- Revive
- Sweekar
- Silk-n-Shine
- Nihar Naturals
- Shanti Badam Amla
- Manjal
- Oil of Malabar

The same is true for Nirma which revolutionised the detergent market by making a detergent powder accessible to the economy consumer. Nirma's product portfolio underwent expansion sequentially from detergent powder to other products in a systematic manner. Nirma's product portfolio includes the following:

- Nirma washing powder
- Nirma Super washing power
- Nirma detergent cake
- Nirma Popular
- Nirma Popular detergent cake
- Super Nirma detergent cake
- Nirma Bath
- Nirma Beauty
- Nirma Clean Dishwash bar
- Nirma Bartan Bar
- Nirma Shudh Salt
- Nirma industrial products (LAB, AOS, Sulfuric acid, Glycerin, Soda ash, Pure salt, SSP and Sodium Silicate)

A careful observation of the product portfolio of these two companies throws up an interesting insight. In the case of Marico the company name is not at all linked with the brand names and secondly there is little overlapping use of a brand name. Each brand seems to confine itself to one product. That is, a brand is not shared across products. The Nirma name in the other case appears on almost all products. Now the issue is why do companies employ different branding strategies? There is no short cut answer to this question. The branding strategy followed by a firm depends upon the relationship between the product category and the brand. In any given market condition three key considerations drive the branding approach:

1. The company name—existing image or equity in prospects' minds.
2. The competition—extent of differentiation.
3. The customer needs and wants—specificity of demand.

The above three dimensions set the context for branding decisions. Should the firm use an existing brand to provide boost to a new entry directly or must it lend its support in an indirect manner or avoid any connection whatsoever with it? The answers to these questions are key influences on branding strategy.

SINGLE BRAND

Many companies are exponents of this kind of branding strategy. Branding in this case is employed simplistically by which all the marketing entities are christened by one single name. And these are not small companies but big ones. Consider the following:

- Philips
- Canon
- Virgin
- Hewlett Packard
- DCM
- Nike
- GE
- Oberoi
- Taj Hotel
- LIC

The strategy of using a single corporate name in a way could mean an ad hoc or unplanned approach to branding. A marketer may prefer to put one single name across all the products without applying his/her mind. This could happen in markets plagued by shortages where demand far exceeds supply. Concern for mere product availability may push the role of branding out of consideration of consumers. Branding in such a scenario is diminished to an act of putting a name on the product. This is particularly true for seller-oriented markets. The automatic pull of the market created by shortages and strong demand does not push managers into using branding as a competitive weapon. For instance until the beginning of the 1990s most of the markets were regulated and products and services were in short supply. Mere availability of products and services would make customers happy. In such cases many marketers employed their own names or family names to mark their products and services. Cases like these include Bajaj, Godrej, Tata and Birla. These names appeared on a very diverse set of products and services irrespective of branding logic and considerations. For instance a common brand for products like locks, toilet soaps, electronics, chicken, typewriter and furniture may not be a good idea in a competitive marketplace.

However some firms may use a single brand as a deliberate strategy because of its appropriateness and advantages. The internal reality is a true indicator of whether a single brand approach is employed as a deliberate strategy or it is absence of a strategy. From the perspective of the marketer single or umbrella branding offers a number of advantages. First of all it is a simple brand structure and does away with the need to search and evaluate brand names. Second, promoting a single brand name works out to be far less expensive than the promotion of different brands. The simplicity and economy considerations are two pro manager internal pulls. How about the effect this branding approach has on the consumer?

Higher exposures could be achieved when a firm has only one brand. High frequency of brand exposures could play a critical role in building strong recall and recognition compared to a situation when the budget has to be allocated on a number of brands. Further the brand meaning and values are easily and clearly transferred across different product contexts. For instance the values that brand Siemens stands for get installed in all the product domains which bear this brand. This kind of umbrella branding permits easy leverage of brand success from one product domain to the other. Use of the Reliance name could give great mileage to businesses like communication, insurance and energy. Reliance Energy's issue was hugely oversubscribed primarily on the strength of the brand name. South Korean giants like LG, Samsung and Hyundai have managed to successfully leverage their umbrella brands in diverse product category domains.

Are there some flip sides of umbrella or single brand strategy? One of the important limitations of this strategy stems from the law of focus. Breadth may come at the cost of focus. Umbrella strategy may not work when the products in the portfolio belong to a diverse set of technology or customer domains. When the products are categorised differently in the perception of customers' use a single name may become a burden instead of becoming an asset. Dichotomies in the values coveted in different product categories may make the use of a single brand name inappropriate. For instance Nirma name's equity could work when within the detergent and soaps domain but it could become a burden in ready to wear or automobile domains. Even in related product categories which enjoy a lot of technological similarities like computers and televisions use of a name established in one category like LG in televisions may fail to work wonders in computers. The appropriateness of umbrella branding hinges on the fact as to how products are classified or categorised in the perceptual system of the customer. When dividing lines between the product categories are harder they would obstruct the use of one name for all.

Umbrella brands usually operate at a higher level of meaning. LG and Samsung signify domain specific mastery and excellence. Tata stands for trust. Bata is the economical solution to footwear needs. A common value link holds the product portfolio together by a single name. It is only then that the brand meaning is generalised across different products. The umbrella name transfers values and meaning that is often sufficient to move the market. But in a state of fragmented and specialised market structures the ability of umbrella branding in focusing on specialised consumer groups is severely constrained. When customers demand a specific and highly differentiated value then generalised values embedded in a corporate name may prove to be insufficient. In such situations consumers expect differentiation rather than generalisation. For instance, Toyota's umbrella values could not be taken over to the high end luxury market therefore Lexus was created.

INDIVIDUAL BRANDS

Look at the brand portfolio of Paras Pharmaceuticals:

- After Bath — freshness cream
- Bathfresh — 'just bathed' freshness cream
- Borosoft — non-sticky antiseptic cream
- D'Cold — cough and cold remedy
- Dermicool — prickly heat powder
- Dermicool soap — freshness soap for summer
- Krack — cream for cracked heels
- Livon — for detangled hair
- Livon Silkyhue — detangles and restores shine, smoothness and softness of coloured hair
- Moov — backache specialist
- Mrs Marino — after shampoo hair rinse softener
- Numes — hair coat for glossy hair
- Recova — skin repair cream
- Ring Guard — treatment for ringworm
- Setwet — styling gel
- Stopache — headache remedy

In this case each of the brands is standalone with its unique identity and selling proposition. Many firms employ this kind of branding strategy such as P&G, Reckitt Benckiser and Hindustan Unilever. Here each of the brands appropriates a distinct value proposition in a pioneering manner and achieves category dominance. For instance Krack represents the product category of creams for cracked heels and Livon hogs the category of hair detangling solution. Hindustan Unilever's toilet soap brands like Lux, Lifebuoy, Pears, Dove and Liril though belonging to one category are so vividly positioned that there is no confusion about the target consumer and the value proposition. Lux stands for beauty and appeals to middle class women who identify with cine stars. Liril on the other hand is aimed for young vivacious girls who look for freshness in their bathing experience.

The commonness of brands creates an image ruboff between the product category associations and brand associations. As long as the products belong to a similar or malleable category one name does the job. For instance the image of excellence in televisions may prove to be good for other electronics products like audio equipments. But if the market entries belong to categories perceived dissimilar by the consumers then the use of one name can cause friction and dissonance. Another strategic consideration is that the marketed products although may belong to one category yet using one name may not be a good idea if the market is fragmented and divided. The image transferred by a common name may become a burden rather than an advantage, in which case the use of an independent name is recommended. For instance LG now uses a different name for its top end washing machines (Tromm). Moving up the segment usually demands cre-ation of a distinct name and strict control of its meaning. Raymond uses Manzoni brand for the ultra premium readymade apparels. The exclusiveness and class needed to cater to this highly focused consumer segment demanded creation of a separate brand from Park Avenue.

Individual branding becomes a compulsion when the divisions in the market are etched out well. These divisions could be based on consumer characteristics, applications, usage or time, and so on. For instance suppose there are two prime usages of shampoo: a fashionable look and dandruff solution. There are three strategic options that are available to a marketer:

1. One shampoo for both the needs.
2. One brand with two variants.
3. Two brands, each meant for a specific use.

The internal pro-simplicity and efficiency-oriented logic would command the marketer to choose either of the first two options. But these two needs are separate compartments in the cognitive structure separated by a divider in consumers' minds. When consumers look for an 'acceptable' solution then a two in one brand would be sufficient. If the need rises slightly upwards in the hierarchy of specificity then two variations could do the job. Further if the consumer is highly demanding and considers these two needs as distinct and specialised applications, in that case two separate brands would be essential. Two birds cannot be killed with one stone. As markets become sophisticated one brand may not be a good idea to cater to diversified consumer needs.

- Which one would you pick if you suffer from a dandruff problem: Pantene dandruff variant or Clinic All Clear?
- If you want to buy a luxury car which one would you settle for: high end Toyota or entry Mercedes?
- If you want to buy freshness toothpaste which one would you buy: Colgate Gel or Close-Up?

Some consumers may see an overlap between the two brands in question whereas others may find very little of it. Depending upon consumer sophistication and specificity the interpretation of the brands would be different. For sophisticated consumers the core of the brand and consumer need would govern the choice. For instance Pantene is for hair vitality ('hair that shine') not dandruff; Toyota is a good reliable car not a luxury car and Close-Up is the toothpaste for freshness not Colgate Gel.

HYBRID

The strategies in Figure 8.1 present two extreme ends of branding. Many firms instead of sticking on to these extremes seek to combine the two and employ hybrid branding structure. Consider the following:

- Ortem fans (reverse the spelling and it becomes Metro known for tyres)
- Nestle Kitkat
- Lux ('A quality product from Hindustan Unilever Ltd')
- Tudor (available at official Rolex showrooms)
- Passion by Calvin Klein

- Pizza McPuff
- Tata Indica
- IBM Thinkpad
- Toyota Corolla
- Bear by Polar

Figure 8.1: Brand Strategy: Divergent Pull

One Brand (Virgin) Internal logic: simple and economical and strong corporate identity but diminished focus. External logic: diffused meaning, lack of differentiation.	⬌	Individual brands (P&G) Internal logic: expensive and low synergy but specific targeting and category dominance. External logic: vivid meaning, clear brand image.

Source: Author.

In the individual brand strategy the brand stands on its own merit. It does not bank upon the strength or heritage of the corporate name. For instance very few people would know that Whisper and Ariel are P&G products or Lizol and Mortien are Reckitt Benckiser brands. The reason why these brands do not signify any connection with the parent company is because they are innovative breakthrough products which can sustain on their own. Also these brands seek to create highly focused brand images. On the extreme are market entries which have names no different from their corporate names like Reliance, HP and Bata. In these cases what a corporate brand stands for gets transferred on to the product in question. But sometimes the choice does not seem so direct and mutually exclusive. That is, individual branding does not appear to be the correct choice because a complete image transfer would rob the market entry of its individuality. And the brand if completely dissociated with the corporate brand may fail to elicit customer response. Hence the solution is sought in somehow combining the two extremes.

Creatively combining the two ends opens a plethora of branding structures which could be used depending upon the market conditions. The brand and corporate brand link can range from direct to subtle. A brand can be linked directly to a corporate name like Maruti Zen. It is self evident that Zen is Maruti's product.

On the other hand linking the brand with the corporate name is necessary but linking it directly may not be a good idea. This is done for achieving selective transfer of parent brand associations. For instance Lexus is a standalone brand in its own right and its linkages with the Toyota name were never directly revealed. Yet it is widely known that it is Toyota's brand. The decisions to this effect require serious contemplation about the rules of the game in achieving marketing success. And success in this context means moving the consumer into making a purchase decision in favour of the said brand.

DIRECT ENDORSEMENT

Endorsement means support to a claim. Sometimes a corporate brand is used to lend credibility and assurance to a brand. This way corporate credibility and assurance is passed on to the new brand. This generally is conveyed when a company makes statements like 'a quality product from' or 'X brand by ABC'. This kind of proclamations made in the mass media seek to convey the brand's pedigree and reputation. This way a brand wins over the scepticism and uncertainty that consumers often have regarding a brand when it is not associated with a known corporate name. The idea is to build brand acceptance by deriving strength and support from the corporate name.

- Westside outlets display a sign that reads 'Tata Enterprise'
- Sonata by Tata
- Flotter from the house of Action
- Courtyard by Marriott
- Borolene presents Suthol antiseptic liquid
- Hindustan Unilever presents Pureit
- Godrej presents Cartini knives and scissors

Any new brand first of all has to win a battle in the minds of its prospects. Any new offering in order to be successful must establish its credentials that it would deliver the promised performance. This could be a time consuming process. Newness implies absence of knowledge and unavailability of ready to use pre-established attitudes. The marketer tries to short cut this process by the employing endorsements to lend support to a new brand. Endorsements rely upon the belief that existing knowledge and attitude would get transferred to the new brand. Credibility and reputation of the corporate lends new substance to the claims made by the new brand. The use of an established corporate name in a way conveys 'don't worry the brand is new but we assure you of its performance'.

The critical question here is what kind of perceptions the brand creates without an endorser. A brand may seem to be on shaky grounds in developing consumer confidence on its own. The inadequacy of pulling the consumer into buying the product necessitates plugging into an existing reservoir of strength. How would you rate 'Celebrations' chocolate brand if it were not to have any link with Cadbury? The Cadbury endorsement bestows the brand instant acceptability and buyer confidence. In this kind of endorsement the endorser assumes a direct and influential role in driving consumer behaviour.

LINKING NAME

Unlike the previous strategy involving a direct endorsement statement ('Polo by Ralph Lauren') sometimes the marketer wants the connections to be a little subtle and indirect. This indirect linking permits the brand to achieve some control over its identity. Pidilite is one of the companies that adopts this linking name strategy. Consider its brands:

- Fevicol
- Fevicryl
- Fevibond
- Feviquick
- Fevitite
- Fevistick
- Feviwetseal

Shahnaz Husain, maker of premium herbal cosmetics employs the linking name strategy. Though the link is not direct, consumers can easily make out that these brands belong to Shahanaz Hussain:

- Shalife
- Shaclear
- Shapearl
- Shagold
- Shabutter

Similarly, the Amul (expertise in milk processing) name is linked to a variety of brands like Amulya, Amulspray, Nutramul and Amul Kool. The letters from the word 'Amul' in some form are combined with others to create brand names. These letters signal the brand's connection with the corporate brand and thereby allow it to draw on its strengths. Understanding this link is not as direct and explicit as it was in the previous case but it is not also very difficult. The phonetics and other brand elements act as linking agents to get a positive equity rub of the corporate name.

As the link between the brand and corporate name becomes indirect the brand acquires space for carving out its own identity and image. The brands so created are bound together by a common element considered relevant in the brand's area of operation. For instance connecting with the Amul name the brands exploit the expertise in milk processing. But the important condition here is that the endorsed brand's application area must be consistent with the parent brand's area of expertise. Linking the brands in this manner creates a family of brands bound together by some commonality.

TOKEN SUPPORT

In some cases the endorsed brand relies upon the master brand or corporate name for a token support. Unlike the previous approaches when the involvement of the master brand is more obvious here the endorser assumes a less prominent role in driving consumer buying. Token support is gained when the endorsed brand discloses its connection with the corporate name such as 'brand owned by Coca Cola Company', or the Godrej signature, or a symbol (Apple) or a statement ('Future Group Idea').

What compels a brand to use endorser support but in a very minor way? What harm would the direct associations bring to the endorsed brand? The reasons behind extreme selectivity in acquiring support are two-fold. First, when the endorser brand delves into different product market contexts its direct involvement can add diffusion and confusion to the endorser's image. However a token endorsement can add some basic credibility and assurance to the endorsed brand ('oh yes this company does exist' rather than 'I have no idea who is the maker of this brand').

Activating pre-existing familiarity with the corporate name in a very oblique manner pushes the buyer's confidence and makes him or her more comfortable than with a brand with no familiarity. Second, the endorsed brand may want to keep the endorser at a distance because direct connection may bring undesirable associations. For instance suppose Pepsi comes about to launching a natural drink. A direct endorsement in all probability is likely to harm the brand because of its 'synthetic' associations. However a token endorsement can lend assurance and credibility to the endorsed brand as linked to an established and well known multinational company, a known manufacturer of a wide variety of beverages.

SUB-BRANDING

Consider the branding strategy of Sony. Sony is an innovative company and it leverages its core competence to create products that are highly differentiated. Accordingly Sony employs the strategy of combining the corporate name with a new name to signify the product innovation:

- Sony Walkman
- Sony Discman

- Sony Handycam
- Sony Cybershot
- Sony Bravia
- Sony Trinitron
- Sony Microvault
- Sony Vaio

Another company known for its expertise, the razor making Gillette follows the same approach. Its razor portfolio includes the following brands:

- Gillette Sensor
- Gillette Vector
- Gillette Sensor Excel
- Gillette Presto
- Gillette Mach III

What if Sony used descriptive names along with the corporate name? The structure in that case would have been like umbrella branding and the core aspect of innovation and differentiation embodied in each of the products would have been lost. The sub-brands like Trinitron or Discman or Cybershot play an equal role in driving consumer buying. Along the same line Gillette sub-brands indicate the product type and target customer. Sensor is a higher end razor for the discerning consumer whereas Vector aims at the lower end economy conscious market. The Presto brand is a throw away razor meant for the convenience conscious consumer. In both of the above cases the associations implied in master brands like Sony and Gillette are expanded by adding a sub-brand. So 'Handycam' adds a new set of associations (functional or emotional or both) to the Sony brand to make it more appealing to consumers. Gillette's campaign of Sensor Excel ('The best a man can get') instils an emotional context to an otherwise unromantic razor technology associations appropriated by the Gillette name.

Let us explore the role played by different components of sub-brands. Consider the following brands:

- Maruti 800
- Honda City
- Ford Fiesta
- Compaq Presario
- HP Laserjet
- Dell Inspiron

Which of the two parts—the corporate name or the later part—plays a dominant role in activating consumer purchase? We respond favourably to the later part because of its association with the first part of the brand. The sub-brand acts in a secondary role. City car is valued for it is related to Honda, and 800 is desired for its connection with Maruti brand. When a consumer buys Dell Inspiron what drives his or her purchase—Dell or Inspiron? Probably both, but more of Dell than Inspiron. Relatively speaking the sub-brand plays a minor role and the master brand a major role in driving consumer purchases. Here the master brand is in the driving position. In some cases a sub-brand may gain equal importance because of some compelling value proposition. In such situations the sub-brand becomes an equal partner in activating consumer purchase. Consider the following brands:

- Intel Centrino
- Gillette Mach III
- DuPont Lycra
- Sony Trinitron

No doubt in all of the above cases the corporate brand brings credibility but the sub-brand also offers a major rallying point to consumers. The later components of brands like Centrino, Mach III, Lycra and Trinitron signify technological advancements and innovations. For a safety razor buyer Mach III is as important as Gillette. The sub-brand here brings its own equally important innovative consumer relevant proposition.

THE CHOICE

Making a choice about branding strategy requires careful consideration of factors driving brand success. The two ends of the branding choice continuum represent different kinds of strategic paths to negotiate the marketing environment. Easy generalisation as to which particular brand structure is the best is not possible. The most crucial issue here is to base the choice on the basis of the critical determinant of success in the given context. Brands succeed when consumers reward them by positive-purchase responses. The factors driving consumer buying in a particular product market context affect the choice of branding structure.

An established corporate brand (Xerox, Nirma, Videocon, HCL and HP) or a product brand (Dettol, Lifebuoy, Wills) is a great reservoir of associations, trust, credibility, visibility and source of communication efficiencies. A new market offering can tap into these pre-existing strengths as a short cut path to marketing success. So the issue is if the given brand can make a positive contribution to the new offering then the pull of branding is towards the umbrella brand structure. Using an existing brand makes sense when its association makes the new offer's value proposition more appealing—the master brand's associations being relevant (the Tata name brings honesty and ethical associations to Ginger hotels, Dettol brings antiseptic associations to the bathing soap context '100 per cent bath'); credible (the Onida name contributed to the credibility of its air conditioners, ThinkPad became a credible player in notebooks because of its IBM linkages) and allows it to gain visibility in trade and consumers' minds (the Colgate name gives instant visibility to its new toothpaste variants and toothbrushes) in an inexpensive way. The brand does not have to start from scratch. It can ride piggy back on the existing brand. Thus when an existing corporate or product brand can contribute significantly to the new offering then there is no reason why a new brand should be created.

Can there be forceful reasons for not using the existing brand name? The answer is going to be positive in those cases in which a given brand's strengths become weaknesses in the new context. An established brand provides an easy and quick access to a set of associations, credibility, trust and visibility. However in certain circumstances these very things may hurt the prospects of a new offering. This happens when brand associations rob the value from the product itself instead of enhancing perceived value. When is this likely? Consider Tata Motors's plans to get into an ultra luxury car segment. Tata associations in this segment are likely to be more of a burden than a benefit. The buyer in the luxury segment is likely to steer away from Tata because of its value segment associations. Madura Garments employs multiple brands to cater to different segments: Louis Philippe (Luxury), Van Heusen (power dressing), Allen Solly (Friday dressing) and Peter England (value for money). Titan's foray into the high end Swiss market segment avoids direct connection with Titan. Its new range is called Xylys, independent of Titan (Indian mid-price brand).

Often markets are segmented along functionality. For instance toothpaste consumers seek a variety of benefits or functionalities like herbal formulation, teeth whiteness, sensory pleasure, gum care, economy benefits, ego defence and cavity protection. Hindustan Unilever in a bid to dominate the ego defence functionality created Close-Up (for close ups). Taking Close-Up to the cavity protection (kids) would not have been effective, therefore the brand Pepsodent (*dishum-dishum*, keeps fighting germs even after brushing) was born and pre-empted this proposition. When the mission is to pre-empt and dominate a functional proposition then standing under the shade of an existing brand is not a good idea. It is preferable to seize the proposition exclusively under a distinct name.

A product may embody breakthrough advancement. Look at the cars around, they all look the same. Imagine a company has created a hydrogen car. This innovative departure from the norm has to be signalled to the market. Here creating a new brand is a far better option than putting it under an existing umbrella. LG created Viewty brand for its high megapixel mobile camera.

Apple creates breakthrough products and launches them under distinct brand identities like iMac, iPhone, iPod, Macintosh and Mac Air. Old brand associations may cross over to the new idea that may end up creating a confused image.

CONCLUDING REMARKS

An observation of the market entries by different companies would reveal a mosaic of branding strategies followed by these companies. A brand is much more than a simple name. At its most basic level it identifies the marketer behind a branded commodity. Taken passively, branding strategy would mean employing one single corporate name across all the products and services offered by a firm. However customer and competitive considerations may seriously challenge the application of this kind of monolithic branding structure. The other extreme form that branding strategy could take is when each product of the firm is given individual identity without any overt connection with the company or other offerings of the firm. Individual branding allows promises of benefits of category dominance if the product is a new innovative idea and signals vivid brand promise. Somewhere in between these two extremes lie many branding approaches which seek to draw benefits of the given two ends of 'one brand for all' and 'one brand one product' strategy. These strategies seek to tap into the asset reservoir of an existing name yet at the same time try to achieve differentiation advantages. Accordingly, hybrid strategies include explicit endorsements where established brands give direct support to a new entry and implicit endorsements where the established brand supports indirectly. This way new brands seek to tap into brand equity selectively.

Shifting Brand Gears to Stay Connected

One brand survey shortlisted 18 brands that stood the test of time (Shukla 2008). These brands managed to stay in business consistently over a long period spanning over a century in some cases. The icons that defied the whirlwind of change and successfully managed to stay afloat include:

- Horlicks – 1873
- Bata – 1894
- Lifebuoy – 1895
- Raymond – 1925
- Lux – 1929
- Dettol – 1930
- Parle-G – 1939
- Amul – 1946
- Fevicol – 1959
- Ambassador – 1957
- Amitabh Bachchan – 1969
- Sholay – 1975
- Thums Up – 1977
- Hajmola – 1978

- Fair & Lovely – 1978
- Onida – 1981
- Maruti 800 – 1983

Like any other living being, brands are also subject to vagaries of time. The dynamism of the factors and actors that make up the external reality of the brands perpetually spin to upset the strategic fit. Brands being inanimate do not age the way living beings do. But their constancy amidst rapidly volatile environment exposes them to the risks of being obsolete and irrelevant for the target audience. Navigating a brand over time requires shifting brand levers to stay connected with their consumers who they seek to serve. Otherwise the marketing streets are littered with corpses of brands that were once darlings of the market but now have gone into oblivion.

INTO OBLIVION

In marketing once successful does not imply successful forever. Brands are intermediate entities that reside in the minds of people. Brands derive their value from the command over consumer buying. The consumer side of the equation generally is in a state of flux constantly changing and evolving. However the marketer's side has a tendency to remain in a sate of inertia if the brand achieves a certain degree of success. The successful formula or concept embedded in a brand pulls managers to seek constancy. Managers get possessed by the success formula and consequently the managerial focus shifts on the brand's maintenance. The resonance which forms the basis of brand success often gets ignored. The brand must strive for the external connection that it owes its success to. Effective brand management over time necessitates that the brand is revitalised and enthused with fresh energy as time passes by. Apple receives silver bullets by launching new exciting products. Xerox and IBM are no longer the same brands as when they first arrived. The story is the same for Philips. The brand evolved from being a lighting company to a diversified electronics conglomerate and its communication now focuses on the 'sense and simplicity' of its products when things in electronics are being complicated with features aimed to achieve differentiation.

Staying afloat in the water requires perpetual paddling. The prime force behind any brand success is consumers and their values, beliefs, lifestyle and demographic traits undergo transformation with each passing moment. An out of sync brand promise causes consumers to abandon it and look for something new. It is here that opportunities are created for innovators to build new brands. Inability to maintain a fit with target consumer needs and aspirations results in a brand getting abandoned. Consider the following brands that have either gone into oblivion or lost the iconic status that they once enjoyed:

- Dalda and Rath — *vanaspati*
- DCM, Binny and Mafatlal — fabrics
- Jawa, Rajdoot, Enfield — motor cycles
- Lambretta, Vijay Super — scooters
- HMT, Allwyn — wrist watches
- BPL, Bush, Televista, JK, Dyanora, Uptron, Beltek — televisions
- Bush, Murphy — radios
- Carona — shoes
- Afghan Snow — face cream
- Halo — shampoo
- Fiat, Standard, Ambassador — cars
- Modella, Lal Imli Dhariwal — blankets
- Singer, Luxmi — sewing machines
- Jai, Moti — toilet soaps
- Dalmia — biscuits
- Wings, Avis, Fu's — jeans wear
- Gem, Allwyn, Mac, Leonard — refrigerators
- Anacin, Saridon — headache remedy

A brand falls out of favour with its target consumer when it suffers from erosion in the basis of its bonding. At the very fundamental level a brand embodies functional benefits. Functionality is embedded in its product component. Change may render a product obsolete. New better products can render the existing ones inferior. For instance brands like Rath and Dalda have lost the grip over cooking medium market because now people favour refined oils. Refined oils are supposed to be better in terms of health benefits compared to *ghee* made of vegetable oils. The health conscious customer who is sensitive about the type of 'fat' constituting the cooking medium finds a better solution in refined oils. Newer technologies create new products which often radically alter functionality and offer better solutions to customer needs. For instance word processors made typewriters inferior and compact disc players cut the life of video cassette players short.

Brands derive their relevance from the value propositions that they make to their customers. Besides functionality the other basis of brand bonding could include emotions, self expression and values consistency. Change can even make these value propositions irrelevant. Brands suffer when the associations cease to excite the consumer. HMT brand once firmly established as a durable and reliable watch suffered on account of its image. The brand did not gel with the imagery that post liberalisation consumers identified with. A wrist watch now meant much more to the new consumer than a time keeping mechanical devise. In the new context the watch is looked at for more reasons than functionality embedded in its 'movement'. For some it is a device of self expression and earning esteem. The brand suffered for the want of an appropriate symbolism. Menswear brand Vivaldi of Bombay Dyeing was once being endorsed by Karan Kapoor (son of famous Indian actor Shashi Kapoor). Though the brand endorser enjoyed the pedigree of the first family of Bollywood and great looks, he could never establish himself as a star. The new generation of youth who identified with values like success and achievement would find the brand devoid of meaning. Such image inconsistencies often become the root cause of brand disenchantment.

BRAND ENVIRONMENT

Brands do not operate in a vacuum. A brand is defined in a variety of ways including love mark, trust mark, a sign or symbol. The final measure of success is what kind of relationship a brand enjoys with its target consumer. Brands succeed when they have followers in the market. There has to be some basis of bonding between the consumer and brand. However any disconnect between the value embedded in the brand and the needs and wants of consumers is liable to create cracks in the consumer's love or trust or satisfaction. Brands that fall out of consumers' favour must have enjoyed consumer preference and liking. Environmental changes could put a brand into serious jeopardy if the brand steward fails to anticipate and develop counter mechanisms. Change sometimes dawns without much noise and signal and often it arrives with a bang. For instance:

- Coke brand suffered great market share loss when an environment protection watch group alleged pesticide contamination in cola.
- Cadbury brand suffered a setback on account of the worm controversy.
- Shoe brand Nike got a dent in its image by sweatshop disclosures.
- McDonald's brand got sucked into controversy involving beef tallow in fries.
- KFC's use of monosodium glutamate (MSG) in its products.
- Reliance mobiles were charged for getting heated.
- Faulty batteries in Nokia mobile phones.

Controversies like the above have a potential of affecting the brand permanently by seriously denting its trust. This requires careful handling of the situation. One such example of how a brand can be steered clear though a controversy by the able handling of a situation is Tylenol by Johnson & Johnson. In 1982 several people died by taking cyanide-laced Tylenol. The company instead of getting into a denial mode and blame-shifting immediately recalled stock at the cost of 100 million US dollars. By owning the responsibility for the tampering and deft handling of the entire episode, Johnson & Johnson regained public support and trust.

The best way is not to get dragged into any controversy in the first place. Yet it happens for unanticipated reasons that the brand has a risk of serious image dilution. A brand being a set of meaning and associations inscribed on the mind if it gets negatively affected can linger forever denting its performance for all times to come. Effecting a change in something physical is much easier but memories and impressions are difficult to change. So a contaminated drink or worms in the chocolate could easily be removed by enforcing stricter quality control. But if brand image is dented once it may be near impossible to resurrect it to its previous glory. Brand acts as a perceptual anchor that is used to judge external reality. So if a brand's image is spoilt then image correcting messages are likely to be discounted or discarded leading to lack of inertia in imagery. Once image pollution is accepted by consumers then messages aimed to bring about changes are likely to be filtered, rejected and distorted to avoid any kind of cognitive inconsistency from setting in. Once a notion is accepted all inconsistent stimuli have a danger of being rejected and left unprocessed.

At the heart of a brand's success lies consumer connection or resonance. Depending upon the brand belief and identity each brand is guided by its strategy to forge consumer links. For instance some brands follow the functional route (Lizol toilet cleaner) while others take up experiential (PVR or Disney) or value expression (Woodland or Louis Philippe) paths. Consumers respond to a brand positively when its associations and installed imagery represents what it is supposed to. Brand image studies or audits are essential in this regard to discover how exactly the brand is perceived by the consumer. Some of the questions in this regard are useful:

- What comes to your mind when you think of brand X?
- What is the first word that comes to your mind when you think of brand X?
- What words would you associate with brand X from a given list of words?
- If brand X were to be an animal which one would it be?
- If brand X were to be a person, describe that person?

- What objects would you associate with brand X?
- What feelings are engendered when you think of brand X?
- What kind of relationship do you have with brand X?

The inventory so developed after this exercise would provide a blow up as to how a given brand is perceived by its consumers. Depending upon the strategy the brand manager would have a vision of the brand's intended image. The answers to two questions could lend insight and set up the brand management agenda: how should the brand be perceived (idealised perception) and how is the brand actually perceived? Discrepancies between the intended image and actual image may call for an image correction programme. It is for this reason brands often embark upon image correction programmes.

The competitive angle of the brand cannot be ignored. It is not only a question as to how a brand relates with its consumers. Competitive relativity calls for building brand superiority on the consumer relevant criteria in comparison to the competition. For instance on all of the above dimensions a brand like Whirlpool may score on all desirable responses but this may not translate into affirmative consumer response. It is quite possible that other brands like Samsung and LG may score better on these very parameters. An absolute brand image audit is only partially useful. Development of an insightful strategy development calls for a comparative assessment. The following questions prove to be useful:

- What does the customer look for (the basic dimension of brand delivery)?
- How is the brand perceived on those dimensions?
- How are other competing brands perceived on those dimensions?
- How can the brand develop competitive differentiation?
- How does this differentiation relate with consumer value?

Change in the environmental factors like the following can upset a brand's resonance with consumers. It is important for the brand manager to scan environmental factors on an ongoing basis and shift gears to maintain its value link as things evolve and change. Attention must be paid to the following:

- Government policies
  – Energy efficiency (energy star ratings), pollution (Euro standards for automobiles), trade mark infringement (counterfeit brands or similar brand elements), import and export restrictions (reduced customs or free imports).

- Technology
  – Watch for continuous and discontinuous change (manual type writers, electric, electronic and computer).

- Competition
  – Competitive attack and value parity.

- Consumer evolution
  – Demographic and psychographic shifts (from future orientation to immediate gratification; from collectivist to individualistic orientation).

- Economic advancement
  – Affluence (brands move up in price continuum LG Tromm, Sony Bravia, Nokia Vertu), inflation (value for money stores and brands).

Brand success does not solely depend upon its intended customers although this appears to be the most obvious target. Many other constituencies play a vital role determining a brand's performance. A service brand like Kingfisher airline or Oberoi hotel would miserably fail at the point of experience creation if company employees are not committed and enthusiastic in living the brand promise. Channel support is of crucial importance if a brand has to succeed in the highly contested market faced by FMCG marketers. Firms that employ the outsourcing model can never achieve desired results in the absence of partner support. It is therefore essential to periodically monitor the brand perception held by different stakeholders and carry out course correction if needed. The constituencies to watch out for include the following:

- Employees (their attitude, commitment and enthusiasm level).
- Potential consumers (awareness, attitude, emotions).
- Channel partners (rate of return, company support, partnership level, conflict resolution, cooperation and competence advancement).
- Stock holders (corporate governance, wealth generation).
- Government (public relations and image building).
- Consumer protection and other watch groups (social, ethical and environmentally consistent practices).

IDENTITY CHANGE

The change in the Indian economy and socio–psychological mind space has been discontinuous. The forces of change unleashed by liberalisation have drastically altered not only the shape of industry in India but also the socio-cultural transformation has been knee jerk. The post 1980s generation especially in urban India has grown in an environment that is closer to some of the Western countries rather than to the immediate past from which it evolved into its present form. The beliefs and values of the modern consuming class are at so much of a departure that old and established brands find it hard to connect with them. Brands like Godrej, Ceat, Videocon, Britannia, Parle, BPL, Tata, Aditya Birla, Bank of Baroda and Canara Bank have had to embark upon identity transformation processes. Philips, one of the top giants in electronics underwent a similar exercise in 2004 when it abandoned its corporate slogan 'Let's make things better' for 'Sense and simplicity'.

Some of the Indian brands that embarked upon programmes in contemporising their corporate identities include the following (Singh and Biwalkar 2008). Historical presence of these brands on the one hand allows for awareness and recognition advantage but on the other hand it also brings burden of image inconsistencies. The history and heritage call for repackaging in such a way that a continuity and evolution is signalled. An unchanging brand may be misinterpreted as stagnating, old and archaic.

- Ceat Tyres – Ceat name and symbol of Rhino represented the brand for over 25 years. The brand signed off as 'Born Tough'. Now the brand appears in a new avatar without the Rhino and sign off. The letter 'E' has been crafted as three bars in orange colour to represent energy and upward movement. The logo is intended to signal a more youthful image. Rhino has gone because now the claim of toughness in a tyre brand is no longer relevant but the new consumer wants performance and youthful image.

- Shoppers' Stop – The old circular signage of the brand has been abandoned in favour of straight line structure in with letters appear in white against a black rectangular bar. Black colour connotes upscale and luxury image. A subtle change in the name has been made from 'Shoppers' Stop' to 'Shopper Stop'. The apostrophe has gone from the name. The idea of driving the new identity is to move the brand up in the value chain from being perceived as premium to luxury. Now the company stocks international luxury brands to cater to new young consumers who want nothing less than global brands. The brand touch points like the displays, trial rooms, employees and atmospherics have been recast accordingly to create an experience of luxury for its customers. The new brand identity is supported by the tag line 'Start something new' from the earlier 'Shopping and beyond'.

• Godrej   – The house of Godrej is highly diversified with stakes in areas that range from real estate to office furniture to processed chicken. The brand has been identified with a lower case signature in black colour that spelled the word 'Godrej'. The company is driven into the rebranding mode to connect with new young consumers who are exposed to a wider set of brands including foreign ones. The brand in its new form has a new redesigned colourful logo (the name and signature has been kept in its earlier form) with ruby, green and red hues. Ruby is added to signify energy, green stands for innovation and red represents growth.

• VLCC   – The trigger to re-brand the company in this case came from the need to reflect the evolving product portfolio. Starting as fitness and slimming centre the company expanded to include the personal care range which initially sold at their own centres. The company wanted to take to the general trade channels. Although the brand enjoyed recall and recognition in a limited way the company faced the challenge to convey its new evolved format as a natural product company that offered products for skin, hair and other beauty related applications. The new logo retains the 'VLCC' intact but the colour and symbol has undergone a change. The logo sports a new sign off changing from 'slimming beauty fitness' to 'natural sciences'. A green plant leaf is included to represent Ayurveda and herbal formulations.

• Philips
— Now all brand communications of Philips products sign off with a new line 'Sense and Simplicity' instead of the earlier 'Lets Make Things Better'. This signifies the shift of the focus of the company from being a technology powerhouse to lifestyle business. Instead of focusing on the 'tech and spec' game the brand seeks to provide its customers with great experience through design. The brand seeks to build differentiation by something called the 'Philips experience' at every touch point instead of the role of making things better that has been taken over by Chinese companies.

The fluidity in the environmental forces often create disconnect with the brand necessitating brand alignment. Kentucky Fried Chicken had to shorten its brand to KFC to deemphasise the fried part with the rise of health consciousness. International Business Machines become IBM as the brand evolved from being hardware business to services business. Grasim's acquisition of L&T's cement business created considerable duplication as it already had Birla Plus brand. Grasim branded L&T as Ultratech Cement ('The engineer's choice') and now seeks to migrate Birla Plus's customers on to one single brand. UTI bank became Axis bank because the bank could not use the name any longer. Bajaj created more stylised and tech looking logo to convey its evolution from being a scooter-centric to being a motorcycle company. The new logo intended to signal the transition from being an old and static company to a vibrant and technologically evolving one.

Dabur abandoned its banyan tree in favour of a new modern looking one. The company wanted its brand to encompass an expanding business portfolio from earlier being perceived as an Ayurvedic formulation company.

LOSING RELEVANCE

Brands like Ambassador cars, Bata shoes, Murphy radios, DCM fabrics, HMT watches, Hamam bath soaps, Bajaj scooters, Godrej refrigerators, Televista televisions, Gola shoes, Det detergent and Tinopal fabric whitener were once shining stars in their markets. Many of these brands now seem to be in their twilight zone. The fall in some cases is drastic while in others it is somewhat slow but steady. In the end if a brand exhibits signs of slowdown the corporate monitoring system must immediately capture these brands and set in motion strategies to put them back into business. At the heart of a brand's decline is the loss of its appeal and relevance to the target consumers. A brand could suffer on account of three reasons:

1. Erosion in the value of its product.
2. Irrelevance of imagery, values and emotions.
3. Shift in the target consumer.

For brands that entirely relied on black and white televisions or radios the decline was inevitable. Fountain pens were outmoded by ball point pens which provided greater convenience. Brands can show signs of ageing because the values and imagery of those brands may go out of sync with its target customers. Fair & Lovely brand of fairness cream was quick to adjust appeal from being primarily focused on enhancing marriage prospects of eligible girls to a confidence and career builder. Refrigerators once tried to woo customers on the basis of technology (PUF or versatile chambers or cooling zones or tropicalised compressors) but now these attributes that were once differentiators are now taken for granted. Refrigerators are now positioned as lifestyle products.

General Motors's Oldsmobile brand lost its appeal because it was perceived to be the car of the older generation—'father's car'. The brand aged as its consumers aged creating a disconnection with the new generation. In India something similar is true for the Fiat brand. The brand conjures up images of the pre-liberalisation era. Inability to fill the void created by shrinking customer base with new ones contributes to the decline. Birla's boxy, sturdy and tough Ambassador car, which was designed to take on the broken potholed Indian roads, lost relevance with the coming of new age cars on the one hand and improved road conditions on the other. Burnol stood generic for creams meant for a handy treatment of burns. The brand lost its relevance as means involved in home cooking and lighting improved from fire wood to usage of coal to kerosene stoves to cooking gas. The incidences of common burns virtually vanished. As a result the brand went off the shopping list of people.

Getting the dirty clothes back into reusable shape needed two mandatory steps. First, washing and then treating it with fabric whitener. Fabric whiteners like Ranipal and then Tinopal were essential for primarily two reasons: first, men wore white shirts (colours being perceived as feminine), with shirts being considered office wear; second, white connotes hygiene and purity in a country like India and finally the then detergent and washing soaps did a poor job of cleaning. As a result it was inevitable for white clothes to acquire some yellowish tinge. Socio-culturally now coloured clothes are no longer a bastion of feminine dressing. With time men have become open to wearing non-whites (red, purple, orange, indigo blue) creating lesser number of whites in their wardrobes. Technologically, detergents and washing bars have become sophisticated. Accordingly twin functionalities of washing and whitening is inbuilt in modern day detergents. The rising standards of living allow people to maintain a particular level of cleanliness and hygiene and the role of whites in signalling this kind of socio cultural segregation has become less pronounced.

Technological discontinuities sometimes are responsible for altering the fortunes of many brands. Consider the photographic equipment industry. Historically brands like Canon, Nikon, Olympus and Kodak fought with each other for supremacy. But if these companies continue to wage war on each other, caught in myopic perceptions of competition, a serious erosion of their market share is imminent. Players outside their technology or product domain are inching to lock horns for consumers. Mobile instrument companies like Nokia, LG, Motorola and Samsung have upgraded their mobile handsets not only in conventional tele-communication functionalities but also there has been a crossover into the digital photography turf. The embedded camera systems in mobile hand sets have over time become sophisticated in resolution comparable to digital cameras. Such convergence may not threaten the hard core professional segment of the camera market but the consumers at the fringes do pose a potential loss.

BECOMING GENERIC

Just take a pause and have a look at the following:

- Thermos
- Linoleum
- Escalator
- Sunmica
- Laser
- Frisbee
- Formica
- Gramophone
- Aspirin
- Dalda
- Colgate
- Xerox
- FedEx
- Scotch tape
- Walkman
- Google
- Nylon

The brand names listed have one thing in common. From being brand names they have either completely become or are in the process of becoming a word that represents the product class or a process. Xerox has become a verb commonly used to suggest photocopying. In many offices the purchase manager places order for a few Canon xerox machines. People refer to any flask as thermos. So consumers have a distinct preference for Milton thermos for its durability. And many consider the paste used for dental hygiene is Colgate which comes by different names and types, so that they ask for Pepsodent colgate at the store. Sometime people advise not to use a certain brand of sunmica for table top but use X brand of sunmica. When you need information on some subject then what do you do? Obviously google it. Many of us enjoy googling during idle time. What do you do when an urgent letter has to be sent? What else you call up your courier and FedEx it.

The category dominance by a brand is initially good. The brand corners a large share and people refer to it by its name. As long as the retail shelves adorn only the brand that has created categories like Colgate or Xerox the pioneer makes the buck. But as competition arrives and retail space gets shared the problem begins to emerge. The link between the brand name and the category becomes so strong over time that consumers cease to differentiate between the name and the category in normal usage. We call all kinds of electric lifts 'escalators'. And that is where the brand loses its identity. As the brand name merges with the category, consumers use the pioneer's name to refer to the category and actually buy some other brand. The entire process operates so subtly that despite high awareness and recall the actual buying of the pioneer brand tends to be very limited.

Xerox Company has been a victim of these phenomenon. To separate the photocopying (process) from Xerox (brand name) it ran an advertisement that urged 'not even a Xerox can Xerox'. You can get something photocopied but not Xeroxed. The sign off warned that 'Xerox is not another word for photocopying'. The challenge here is how to make consumers distinguish between the brand and the category. People must discriminate in favour of the Xerox brand as the pioneer of photocopying. The company now is not limited to photocopiers. It wants to project itself as a total office IT equipment provider of multifunction devices. In order to represent the new expanded business domain beyond photocopies the company has unveiled a new logo—the word 'Xerox' spelled in contoured lower case and two bands forming an 'X' like letter in a globe like shape.

How can a brand avoid the brand name completely merging with the product category or process? This merger is not physical but perceptual. Brand communication must always reinforce a perceptual distinction between the product and the brand. The tendency to use brand name alone must be avoided. So in communication instead of saying 'Xerox' a consumer must be reminded by saying 'Xerox photocopier' or Thermos vacuum flask or Colgate toothpaste or FedEx express delivery service. Simultaneous mention of brand name along the product domain would keep the distinction alive in prospects' minds.

BRAND BACK ON COURSE

Launching a new brand is a costly exercise. A very high failure rate also acts to dampen new brand launch efforts. Maintaining revenue and cash flows requires that brands in the portfolio are carefully analysed. The winds of change often throw even the most successful of brands out of balance and at the same time internal mismanagement sometimes can cause brands to aimlessly drift and die. Brand success means an intersection point of dynamic elements. Brand navigation is needed because of this dynamism. Weak current performance often misleads managers to write off brands prematurely. How a brand performs depends upon the strategy driving it. Poor performance sometimes has more to do with internal flaws rather than with brand viability and potential. Firms can systematically develop strategies to bring weak brands back on course.

Consider the case of a long innings brand like Lifebuoy. The brand was born in 1894 in England and launched in red tablet form a year later and since then it has come a long way, long way indeed. The soap hit the Indian shores when the country was in the grip of the plague epidemic. The brand found favours with the consuming public with its 'powerful germicidal, disinfectant properties and carbolic composition'. Later the brand evolved into a masculine orientation as bath soap with a health proposition. The brand was promoted as soap that promoted health by effective cleaning and germicidal properties ('*Tandurusti kee raksha karta hai Lifebuoy, Lifebuoy hai jahan tandrusti hai wahan*' [Fitness is protected by Lifebuoy, Fitness is where Lifebuoy is]: it washes off the germs effectively). Later the brand further moved up to associating with sports and winning by claiming to be the soap of champions. In the 1970s the toilet soap market was becoming competitive with the arrival of differentiated soaps along the lines of fragrance, gender appeal, price points, deodorant and other benefits. Nirma Bath and Tata's OK brand sought to invade the territory owned by Lifebuoy, but later both brands ceded to the supremacy of Lifebuoy.

The market began to witness a chasm between the rural and urban divide in terms of soap segmentation. And Lifebuoy gradually began to acquire rural lower end connotation. In a bid to connect with the urban chic consumer Lifebuoy Personal was launched. The physical aspect of the soap was changed into pink with contoured shaped cake and the communication did not build on the health or germicidal elements to signify the departure. Lifebuoy Personal bombed in the marketplace. Rival Dettol began to cash in on heath and hygiene consciousness ('Dettol 100 per cent bath') in the post 1980s. While HUL's top selling brand was getting relegated to a lower end of the rural downmarket perceived as a soap for hand wash.

HUL realised the presence of hidden potential as it prepared the brand for a makeover. Post 2000, the brand moved on to appeal to the heath conscious urban consumer by leveraging its equity as health soap. The soap evolved from being hard boxy red to soft pink in bean form. Excessive macho characterisation was given up in favour of family orientation. The brand did cling on to the germicidal core but executed it in a much softer form to provide health benefits to the entire family. Currently the brand stands fortified with a number of variants (Lifebuoy Total, Skin Guard, Lifebuoy Plus, Lifebuoy Clear Skin) and a hand wash.

The Lifebuoy story illustrates how a brand of over 100 years can still be in service and enjoy a big market response. A brand appears to be constant across its life. What is important here is to notice dynamism amidst its constancy—the evolution of product, market, communication and adaptation of promise. Reinventing relevance is the core job in managing brand. A brand must paddle like devil as does the duck, yet appear calm and unruffled.

STRATEGIC PATHS

Putting the brand back on the path of glory requires repairing cracks in the consumer bonds. There are three sources where a brand can plug into for revenue enhancement. Whatever be the source the brand must connect with its target in order to be able to move their buying.

- Current target consumers (both present and exited)
- Competitors' consumers
- Non-category users

This process of winning the customer either by proactively retaining the currently served ones or attracting them from competitors may require alteration in the brand's elements. Fine tuning the brand elements is essential to get the brand on course. In this regard the basis of brand bonding has to be revisited and reinvigorated. These include mainly of the following aspects of brands:

- Product   –   basic functionality
- Beliefs and values –   mission
- Expression   –   signalling
- Emotions   –   feelings engendered
- Experience   –   sensory pleasure

The foundational element of any brand is the product or service which gives it a right to enter in the buying frame. A brand's failure to live up to customer expectation would render the brand hollow. No amount of imagery can save a brand in the absence of a solid product. A brand is not a make up device for the product's deficiency. Two possibilities exist: the product category as a whole ceases in relevance such as colour televisions or tape recorders or type writers or radios. Product centric brands strictly move along the product life cycle (Tinopal). The real question in this regard is can the product be used for some unintended or not originally conceived use? Cessation in the original functionality of the product leaves the brand manager with an option of giving the brand a new mission. For instance a gramophone can move over the music reproduction function to giving opportunity to the owner of a system of self expression. However with clever branding a brand can carve out its life cycle different from the product life cycle.

A brand may lose the market despite the fact that the category continues to thrive. This situation signifies breaking bonding with the target consumer. A large number of sliding brands belong to this type of misfortune. The internal brand management fails to read and respond to the changes in the external factors. Consider the following brands:

- Ponds has come out of its cold cream shell to participate in high-end anti-ageing solutions market.
- Lux has gradually evolved from being a bath soap to a complete beauty brand.
- Dettol is no longer an antiseptic liquid brand.
- Nike has crossed over the sports shoes territory to become a sports equipment brand.
- Cadbury Dairy Milk underwent reverse of segmentation to broaden its appeal.
- L&T revisited and adjusted its core to break away from commoditised businesses to high tech high value engineering services.
- Brand Xerox has evolved from being paper photocopying machines to digital printers, scanners and word processing to a complete 'document company'.
- IBM brand has been witness to continuous adjustments in its identity. The brand has evolved from being a 'computer' company to 'solutions' to a cutting edge high value services company.

- Honda brand has transformed from motorcycles to signifying quality and reliability in products such as cars, lawn mowers, power tools and generators, where the core part is a motor.
- Dabur brand underwent an identity change process to signify its evolution from being a pure Ayurvedic pharmaceutical company to its new avatar as an FMCG company that participates in health care, hair care, oral care, skin care and food segments. The brand logo was changed from old *kalpavriksh* (wish-fulfilling tree) to a new stylised tree logo.

Lux is particularly illustrative of how a brand can maintain steady course amidst choppy waters. Lux essentially is a dream machine. The brand has stuck to its core value of beauty which taps into the emotional deprivation of masses by allowing them to dream of coming closer to the icons of beauty represented by film stars. The brand continues to reinvent the concept of beauty with the correct choice of film stars who stand to endorse the brand. These include Leela Chitnis, Madhubala, Hema Malini and Kareena Kapoor. From the perspective of contained product the brand would have suffered if it had stuck to only the bathing bar. The product component of the brand has evolved to fortify Lux's core in the form of shower gels, liquid soaps and moisturising bars. These products have a revitalisation effect on the brand as they represent a new generation of products innovated in the beauty management domain.

The Ambassador brand on the other hand has remained stuck in history. The car industry has grown by leaps and bounds but the Ambassador brand has declined over time. Neither the product element nor the expression nor emotion kept pace with time. Ambassador underwent little or no transformation over time. While its core customers born in the pre independence era continue to shrink, even the bureaucrats and leaders who once bought the brand for its power and elitist symbolism have jettisoned the brand in favour of a new breed of cars. The void so created could never be filled by attracting a new set of customers. Neither the core product nor the expressive brand elements were fine tuned to the evolving expectations of the market.

REVITALISATION

Brands do not have lives of their own. Life is infused by constantly monitoring and mending brand elements. A brand is what its steward makes it to be. In the absence of dynamism great brands often end up being constants in highly changing environments. There are many brands which have suffered fortunes on account of this pull of inertia and constancy as mentioned earlier. Accordingly the sales trends and consumer responses to the brands need to be continuously monitored. This calls for installation of some kind of brand tracking system by which its differentiation and resonance is tracked on an ongoing basis. As and when some kind of trouble is noticed a corrective exercise must be initiated. In the absence of continuous monitoring and adjustments the brand is likely to drift into oblivion.

It is a great challenge for managers to infuse life into a brand and thereby liberate it from the shackles of life cycles stages. This calls for achieving continuity amidst change. Achieving perpetuity in the brand sales requires a thorough understanding of what actually makes a brand. The source of life and death of a brand resides in its composition. As human beings are made of elements and when one or more of these elements ceases to perform its/their function life comes to an end. In a similar vein elements—both tangible and intangible—make up the brand. Any decline of the brand's performance signifies one or more of the brand elements getting out of favour with its target customer. Accordingly a brand's failure may be caused by its awareness, functionality, attributes, image, experience, emotions, packaging, signage, name and logo. The real challenge thus in navigating a brand over time is to monitor its sales and plug the potential loopholes that might act to hurt its performance.

There are several reasons that may cause a brand to perform poorly. Brand strategy must intervene and introduce corrective measures into the following to make the brand stay afloat despite pressures to the contrary.

Brand Awareness

Awareness is one of the important building blocks of brand power. Often times a brand may suffer on account of awareness extinction or erosion. Awareness is a precondition that a brand would participate in consumer decision processes. No matter how strong a brand is in the mind of its creators if consumers do not know of its presence and miss to incorporate it in their purchase decision processes then the entire brand building is likely to fall flat. Getting the brand to enter in the purchase process begins with its presence in consumers' cognitive systems. Brand awareness is very critical in low involvement situations where mind share often equals market share.

Assume you have been asked to fetch salt on your way back home. Which brand are you likely to ask at the shop? Probably Tata and this is what most of the people are likely to do. The same may hold true for spices like chilli powder. Which brand would you ask for at the store or reach out to at the modern retail format? Probably MDH, both of these brands enjoy huge recall and recognition which is leverage by the marketer in building success. The difficulty in recalling a brand often causes the brand to miss out on potential selling opportunities. Therefore it is essential that marketing efforts must aim to maintain top of the mind recall especially in low involvement buying situations. However in other cases an aided recall could be sufficient.

Sometimes a brand gets locked into an extremely narrow product application domain. For instance consumers may think of coffee to be had only in offices or while entertaining guests but not otherwise. The result would be that Nescafe or Bru would suffer from lower sales. Similarly milk additives like Bournvita or Horlicks are to be given to growing children. A photographic film maker like Kodak or Fuji would lose business opportunity if people associate picture clicking only with special occasions. In such situations a brand can get a big boost by creating breadth of uses to which it could be put to and building awareness about it. Here the key lies in making consumers aware of using the brand in all potential use situations wherever it is possible. The challenge is to connect the brand with all its potential use situations in the consumer's mind such that the brand does not suffer on account of its failure to spring up in an opportune use time.

Brand Usage Increase

In this set of efforts the brand seeks to expand its sales by increasing its usage. A brand's fortunes could be given a boost by adopting right strategies that multiply its use. Consumers' usage of the brand could be achieved by a number of ways. These include strategies like, use without a miss, use more, use frequently, use variety, new uses:

- Consumers can be reminded to use the brand that they often fail or forget to use for a variety of reasons ('did you Cherry blossom your shoes today?').
- Promote regularity of brand usage ('take chavanprash regularly without missing it').
- Increase frequency of use ('brush your teeth twice daily'; 'shampoo your hair daily').
- Expand variety of use ('Dabur honey on top of a toast; with milk; and with lime'; Milkmaid for making sweets).
- Make product use more convenient (Nescafe ready mix to make coffee making easier or Parachute coconut oil with bottle warmer).
- Increase usage by introducing new contexts (Titan watches for different segments of time in a day—morning, office, party, casual; Arrow shirt for office, club, casual, sports, casino and ultra formal).
- Reduce negatives associated with frequent use due to false beliefs and culture values (frequent shampoo use would damage hair or frequent hair colouring would harm scalp or wearing contact lenses would hurt eyes). Here a product could be innovated to meet the challenge such as mild shampoo or moisturised breathing contact lenses.

New Unthought-of Usage or Application

Strategically or accidentally a brand may find its application in a use or uses for which it was never intended for. This way a brand can get a great boost in its sales. For instance aspirin is used by heart patients as blood thinner. One of the old classic cases of new use is provided by Arms & Hammer baking soda which found application in deodorising the refrigerators.

Image Adjustments

Image is a critical component of a brand. It is in the image that a brand's value proposition is embedded. A disconnect therein calls for image improvement and adjustment. Before embarking upon image change it is important to plan and prioritise what aspects of the brand need to be deemphasised and emphasised. At the heart of a brand's image a variety of hot buttons could be hidden which act to pull its consumers. These include product attributes and features, emotions, personality traits and symbols. Brands image adjustments are usually prompted when brand audit throws up reasons for consumer disenchantment rooted in any of the above elements constituting image. Accordingly an image correction exercise becomes mandatory to reestablish resonance or preventing cracks from becoming wider gaps.

For instance when Maruti Wagon R did not get desired market response the car was repositioned from being 'original tall boy' to 'for the smarter race'. Kellogg's cereal abandoned its original positioning of light and healthy breakfast cereal to a creator of alert and brilliant minds. Recently the brand is getting repositioned to expand its appeal to the adult segment. KFC deemphasised its 'fried' association as health consciousness witnessed increase globally. Many times the brand's celebrity endorsers have to be changed to connect with the evolving target customers. For instance Dinesh suiting brand was once endorsed by skipper Sunil Gavaskar whose appeal got diminished with time. Shekhar Kapoor enjoyed association with Digjam brand, but as time passed by, the appeal of the actor director got diminished with the emerging target segment.

At the heart of Pepsi sits the youth imagery to bonds with its target customer. Currently in India the brand's icons like Shah Rukh Khan have moved into their mid-forties and are no longer young. Therefore Pepsi is quick to sign up with emerging youth icons like new stars Deepika Padukone and Ranbir Kapoor to achieve a smooth transition. Sometimes brand image needs refurbishment because of age. Brands that have been around for many decades like Bata, Lifebuoy, Lux, Godrej, HMT and Boroline may with time come to be perceived as old fashioned and lacking modern values and energy. In such situations some of the brand's associations may have to be diluted and removed and other desirable associations have to be infused to make it stay on course.

Change Brand Elements

Various elements that make up brand in the minds of its prospects include colours, signs, symbols, labels, packaging. These work subtly to create brand awareness and imagery which often takes place below the consciousness level. How do these elements actually contribute to a brand's performance may be difficult to establish but their influence cannot be completely ruled out. Change forces brands to convey new directions and energy. And brand elements can effectively communicate renewed vision and mandate. Many brands have adopted green colour in their packaging to signify 'naturalness, herbal and pro nature' associations and suppress 'synthetic' connotations. These include various food and cosmetics brands like Lakme and Sunsilk. Corporate symbols of brands like Tata, Bajaj, Videocon, Britannia, Parle, HUL, and so on have been modified to incorporate new meaning.

From Chocolate to Celebration

Cadbury Dairy Milk began its journey way back in late 1940s. Since then it enjoyed a dominant position in the Indian chocolate market. The brand until the 1990s was focused on the children's market positioned as something with the goodness of two glasses of milk. The brand symbol showing thick milk flowing from two glasses into chocolates was essentially meant to get approval from the buyer and influencers (parents especially mothers). Milk signified the health angle of chocolates to overcome consumer scepticism towards the product category. The brand struck a dead end once the leadership in the children's segment was achieved. This called for brand rejuvenation to create new revenue streams for the brand. The brand systematically renewed and broadened its customer base with the help of the following memorable advertising campaigns:

- The real taste of life campaign: Girl crashing into the cricket field spontaneously on the hitting of a six. The other ads in this series attempted to connect with the child in adults (generally suppressed as a result of social conditioning). These campaigns worked to eliminate guilt from the psyche of a chocolate consuming adult.
- Then in the late 1990s the category expansion was achieved by 'Khanewalon ko kahne ka bahana chaiye' (Dairy Milk lovers just need an excuse to eat it). The campaign communicated that you do not need a reason to eat chocolate. It is reason independent. You can freely indulge yourself any time and anywhere. There is nothing awkward when an adult has a chocolate. These campaigns ended with the line 'Kya swad hai zindagi mein' (What flavour there is in life!).
- Then came 'Pappu pass ho gaya' (Pappu has passed!) campaign which linked chocolate with celebratory moments in life. These campaigns placed chocolates next to laddu (typical Indian spherical sweetmeat distributed to mark celebrations) in the buying criteria. Now the brand shifted its focus from an age segmentation to the use or application segmentation.
- The appeal of the brand was further expanded by 'Kuch meetha ho jaye' (Lets have some sweet dish) campaign. This campaign liberated the chocolate from time, usage and age boundaries.

Brands must evolve with time. Cadbury has another brand in its portfolio which has undergone the process of strategic adjustments with evolving consumer needs and wants on the one hand and competitive pressures on the other. The cocoa malt based drink Bournvita looks similar to what it was decades back. But its timelessness is achieved by shifting gears involving product and value proposition changes during the course of its journey. The following have been the landmarks in its journey:

- In the 1970s the brand's positioning centred around the idea of 'Good upbringing' with Bournvita being an essential building block for children. It attempted to appeal to mothers in their nurturance role.
- In the 1980–82 years it was 'Goodness that grows with you'.
- In the late 1980s by 1987, the brand adopted an aggressive posture and stressed on 'Brought up right, Bournvita bright'.
- Towards the end of the last century the competition amongst children was becoming very intense. And staying ahead was the major concern among school going children. In this context Bournvita provided assurance to stay ahead in the competitive world and it signed off as 'Extra energy to stay ahead'.
- In the 1992/95 period *'Shakti har din ke champion ki'* (Energy for the everyday champion) was its sign off line.
- In 2000, *'Bournvita poshan, sahi poshan'* (Bournvita nutrition, right nutrition) encouraged consumption.
- In the following year *'Confidence kuch kar dikhane ka'* (Confidence to achieve) became the reason to buy. The brand's current campaign now has taken the confidence theme to a new arena—dancing. This highlights the changing aspirations and expectations in society. The child is not only expected to be an achiever in the conventional field of studies but the emphasis is also laid on all round development.
- The current Cadbury Bournvita positioning suggests that it contains specific ingredients (RDA: Recommended Dietary Allowance) that augments stamina and concentration in children.

Brands build around personality face danger of being outmoded as a result of ageing of their endorser. For instance Grasim suiting and shirting for long has been endorsed by then star Nawab Pataudi (nobility and class by inheritance). As he passed his hay days the newer generations did not find much connect with the star of yesteryears. Grasim later signed Salman Khan (competitive, stylish, fashionable, successful) to stand behind the brand ('power of fashion'). The same has been true with Digjam brand which used Shekhar Kapoor as the educated and out of mould film director but as he grew old the value disconnect emerged between the brand and the target customer. Fashion and designer brands which develop their personality as a result of their associations with their designers like Coco Chanel, Armani, Alfred Dunhill and Pierre Cardin face similar challenges of ageing as their creators age. Here marketers must maintain a delicate balance between continuity and change to ensure perpetuity of their brands. The idea of exclusivity and class by birth does not excite the new generation. The new generation sees heroes in Sunil Mittal, Ambani, Shah Rukh Khan and Bill Gates who have made it big on their own.

Functional brands like Dettol, Colgate, Gillette, Horlicks, Bournvita and Surf have sustained through long periods of time. Despite being functional brands where the connect is rational and utilitarian they have managed to steer successfully though time. Functional brands are more prone to clinical evaluation and the foundation of their relationship tends to be less emotional and more rational. But despite the category challenges these brands managed to steer their way through by continuous evolution. Take for instance Dettol antiseptic. Initially the brand established its credibility as an effective antiseptic for wounds and nicks and cuts. Despite being a lone and dominant player in the market and enjoying a monopoly like condition, it went on to evolve its functionality and applications. Brand communication made suggestions about new applications like nappy wash, laundry and after shave disinfectant. This strengthened the brand's relationship with its essence. Later in the next leap the brand evolved further to cross over from its liquid form to newer product categories where antiseptic associations were consistent and added unique value. As a result Dettol soap, Dettol shaving cream and Dettol plaster were born.

CONCLUDING REMARKS

Managing a brand in a continuously changing and evolving environment cannot rest on a single success formula. What makes sense today may not make sense tomorrow. Had the forces of the environment been constant then there would not have been a discipline we call by the name of brand management. Brands that have stood the test of time provide testimony to the art and science of managing brands which only a few use effectively. Otherwise thousands of brands come and vanish without any noise. The brands that have beaten the ravages of time prima-facie appear constants but the reality behind them points to the contrary. Changing environments have to be taken head-on with change in the brand's managing and marketing in order to achieve permanence. Time often acts to upset the connect between the brand and its customers. This calls for brand tracking continuously to discover possible cracks in the basis of bonding. And whenever needed doses of revitalisation have to be administered. These include measures such as building and maintaining awareness and recall, image changes, expanding sales and discovering new product uses and modifications of brand elements. The ultimate challenge for an effective brand manager is how to achieve perpetuity amidst a changing environment.

Power Branding: Unequal among Equals

The rise of branding as an important business decision has not been without reasons. The waves of change hitting every day at the business shores diminish the effectiveness of working formulae. Businesses look for perpetuity amidst change. Although managers assume the mantle of steering a business into endless life by devising appropriate strategies, the ultimate arbitrator of the business's fortune is the consumer. Connecting with the chosen consumer is the hall mark of marketing strategy. Marketers act as a linking pin between the consumers on the one hand and the system supplying value on the other. The business model that evolved in industrialisation has undergone a drastic change. Both the supply and the demand side operate on a different paradigm. In the earlier scheme of things managers laid emphasis on domestication of various activities and functions to create an integrated business system. For instance a company like Ford had its stake in sheep farming to mining to manufacturing cars. The model was to control all value creating activities in house that are required to produce a car. This system of control was triggered by the notions of integrated enterprise. Marketers attempted to manage long and complex value chains.

In this vertically integrated enterprise system the firms sought to cultivate competitive advantage to gain monopolistic powers over the markets by developing a combination of 'conventional assets'. Marketing in this scheme of things was product and production centric. Depending upon the uniqueness of conventional assets firms could create inimitable differentiated products. Now in the new fluid and integrated world historical assets have ceased to be as important as new market based assets. Integrated value chains are now breaking into parts. Marketing success is no longer specific to ownership of historical assets. The outsourcing model allows a firm to free its resources from the activities that are better done outside and concentrate instead on what it does the best. In this new business setting brands and branding rather than product and conventional assets has become the real determinant of success.

THE MODEL

Brand begins as an idea somewhere in the mind of an entrepreneur. It is not a result of a mechanical sight process that takes place through the eyes. Rather branding to begin with is a pure mental activity. It is the vision as to how the market or consumers can be made better off and lifted to a higher level of existence. Lacoste brand began with the idea of making tennis apparel breathable so that the player can concentrate on the game without being distracted by physical discomfort. Ratan Tata's vision of providing a safe means of transportation to families who could not afford a car has led to Nano. Long time back Akio Morita's vision liberating music from a fixed place to making it mobile was responsible for the creation of Sony Walkman. The crucial questions in this process are: What is the business of my brand? Is it any different from the product or service it is manifested through? Virtually the same kind of vision preceded before most of the iconic brands saw the light of the day in their physical form.

Ideas remain and die in the mind unless they are translated into reality. Vision translation requires creation of resource systems and structures for converting ideas into reality. Accordingly an entrepreneur has to make the organisation as the primary vehicle to carry out a dream into a physical form. As mentioned in the previous paragraph organisations now do not have to depend on themselves alone to create a product or service in its entirety. This way business systems are liberated globally to outsource the activities and processes that are best done by outside suppliers. The firm can then concentrate on a limited set of activities and processes that it can do the best. The resultant form of business organisation now is a kind of coalition or network of firms connected to a common nucleus—the brand visionary. For instance a pure simple burger sold at any McDonald's is supplied to the company in its component or parts form by a number of participating partners like Shah Bector, Cremica, Trikaya Agriculure, Ooty Farms, Dynamix Dairy, Kitran Foods and Ferrocon Farms.

Figure 10.1 shows how effective branding provides opportunity to move up the marketing exchange to a higher value level. Often lack of vision causes a brand to get locked into the narrow confines of the product or service it carries. The success of a brand lures hundreds of imitators to jump into the brand wagon. This way the product component of the successful brand is copied and imitated with perfection with the belief that the product is what is responsible for success. But what eludes such marketers is the fact that a brand is much more than the product. The product part is just the manifested and physical side but the brand is the spirit or core of what lies invisible. It is this transformation

Figure 10.1: The Brand Vision Model

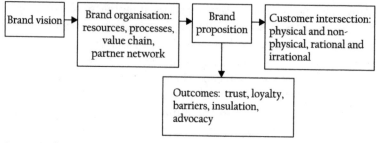

Source: Author.

of something physical and easily discernible into the purely personal and perceptual that allows a brand to develop high order value intersections and push the delivery into a high value orbit.

Nike is much more than various shoe parts—sole, laces, upper, pattern, thread and sole design—sewed together to make a shoe. The people who view Nike as something worn on the feet by its consumers actually miss the essence of branding. Shoe as a product attached to the brand is physical and actually stands as an alibi for buying the brand. It is here that the reason why the brand is bought lies. Nike is as much a mental construct as it is a physical entity that inhabits in the real physical world. The values that make Nike prised are created by the brand's intersections with the body, heart, mind and soul space of its consumers. Branding activity is purely transformational. It is about transcendence of value. Competitors can easily break down the strong brand's product into its tiniest parts and reassemble the similar parts to creating the product as a product. But the meta-physical elements defy dissection and decoding them allows strong brands to be what they are despite proliferation of imitations. There is a number of payoffs that successful marketers get with this process of branding.

ELASTICITY

Broadly there are two important ways to winning in a market. Depending upon the market structure—the number of players in the market, possibility of differentiation, entry and exit barriers—a marketer can adopt two approaches to revenue and surplus generation: by influencing the value perceptions and thereby achieving greater control over the price charged. For instance branded pressure cookers like Hawkins and Prestige are priced much higher (20 to 30 per cent more) than the local or regional brands. Second, the path that many marketers may follow to surplus generation is to create a brand that seeks to build sales volume by attracting a greater number of customers. For instance in the biscuits market Priya Gold brand played the way Nirma had once done by expanding the number of customers at a given price. The firm compensated the low price charged by achieving cost reduction internally by leveraging economies of scale and experience curve effects.

Profit or surplus = number of customers × price − cost of goods sold

Brand building can influence the customer demand function in two fundamental ways: by making the demand curve upwards or by making it inelastic (Figure 10.2a). Second, it can do so by shifting the demand curve to the right side (Figure 10.2b).

Figure 10.2: Brand Building and Shifts in Demand Curve

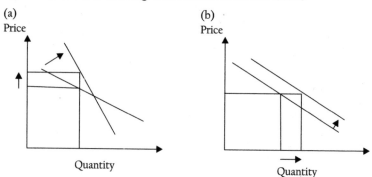

Source: Author.

There are two paths to revenue generation. First, the brand building efforts can be directed into intensifying preference. This way brands make their demand inelastic. High price brands like Armani, Bentley cars, Jimmy Choo shoes, Mont Blanc pens, Cartier watches, Tiffany jewellery, General air conditioners, Bose audio systems, Vertu mobile phones, Hermes scarves and Hilton and Oberoi hotels are some visible followers of this approach. In consumer goods the market is often fragmented into a number of segments with varying demand elasticity propensities. In such cases a marketer can drive the demand curve upward to command higher price. Italian designers and Swiss watch makers command fierce fan following in select consumer groups and outdo their rivals in price a number of times.

The other approach is to develop preference for the brand among a greater number of customers. The brand seeks to expand its appeal within the user and non-user segments. A marketer operating in an industry like cement or industrial gases, where the scale affects the cost structures in profound ways, may deploy branding to achieve volume growth. Japanese car manufacturers created volume brands initially and beat the competition on efficiency in car making. Some of the followers of this approach include Nirma detergent, Babool toothpaste, Maruti, Action shoes, Relaxo Hawaii slippers, Reliance telecommunication, Big Bazaar, Zenith and Apana computers, Cello pens, Ruf and Tuf jeans wears, Tata Salt and Sonata watches.

TRUST

The most important outcome of branding is the creation of trust. Trust is particularly important in the current time when there has been a general erosion of feeling of trust in society. The fundamental pillars of civil society have taken a severe beating with regard to people's trust. There has been a general decline of trust in politicians responsible for governance, police maintainers of law and order and judiciary custodians of equity and justice. This feeling has also seeped into commercial institutions. Brands in this regard are emerging saviours whom one can bank upon for some specific problems. Within the broad domain of the expression 'trust' the following words are often used to signify its import:

- Integrity
- Character
- Care
- Confidence
- Reliance
- Bankability
- Belief
- Character
- Faith

Do these words not describe the essence of branding? In fact each of these words implies the essence of branding. Branding fails if consumers do not use these words when they talk about a brand. The importance of branding stems from the fact that consumers seek certainty and trust in their relationships to brands. The confidence and assurance subsumed under a name like IBM or Tata allows consumers to relax and be sure that now a particular problem is no longer his or her worry. Trust is not where branding terminates but it marks a beginning of a mutually fruitful relationship.

The Economic Times (2008) in the development of its list of the most trusted brands evaluates brands on a number of dimensions. These include relatedness (evoking feeling of warmth and friendliness); perceived popularity (awareness and recognition of brand); quality connotation (what does it stand for in the quality of the product); distinctiveness (uniqueness of brand); value for money (does it strike a chord with consumers) and repurchase intent. The top 10 most trusted brands in the year 2008 were: Nokia, Colgate, Tata Salt, Pepsodent, Ponds, Lux, Britannia, Dettol, Lifebuoy and Vicks. And the 10 top service brands in the list were: LIC, Airtel, State Bank of India, Reliance Mobile, BSNL, Tata Indicom, Indian Oil, Vodafone, ICICI Bank and Bank of India. Brands become prime drivers of business success when they evolve to becoming articles of faith. Emotionally charged belief in a brand throws it out of bounds of competitive wrangling thereby granting it some degree of invincibility.

LOYALTY

In *Gone with the Wind*, Rhett Butler said, 'I don't give a damn'. In the present hugely competitive context the importance of this dialogue stems from the fact that consumers now don't give a damn to marketers. Marketers like Scarlett keep trying to woo and bond with the consumers but at the end they often are rewarded with the typical sentiment that Rhett Butler had for Scarlett. Now too many brands clutter the consumer mind space and shelf space to find favours with consumers. Increased product parity adds further to the woes of the marketers. In the new open and connected world no secrets can be held for long. Product differentiation vanishes soon and product advantages are copied. It is in this scheme of things that brands pay off their creators by providing additional connectors with which consumer bonding could be created.

Brands transform something purely physical into a perceptual entity. Both physical and perceptual dimensions enhance the scope for achieving value transformation. Product on the one hand is a physical concept which is produced or manufactured whereas brand on the other hand is a conceptual or a perceptual idea. Product is a bundle of specifications whereas brand defies specifications. Product embodies performance or functions but brand takes value delivery to an altogether different realm of emotions, self expressions and realisation. The intersections achieved beyond functionality act as additional threads to creating bonding and commitment. Marlboro or Rolex or Johnson & Johnson have transcended the product element to create brand mythology with which consumers bond to get what they wish and cherish.

It is well established that attracting a new customer costs considerably higher than customer retention. Brands help reducing customer defection by creating a psychological buy in. When brands are given psychologically comforting and consistent imagery and personality, prospects of loyalty building are enhanced. An appealing brand identity humanises and personifies the product, which makes it easier for consumers to form an emotional bond with the brand (Ranazzo 1994). This assumes particular importance since in many product categories product differences stand diminished. By turning marketing into something psychological brands shift consumers from thinking to the loving mode. Brands are bought not only for what they 'do' for the consumer but also for what they 'mean' to consumers. The humanisation of a product which is purely inanimate and functional metamorphoses a brand into something capable of having relationships with consumers like partners or friends.

ENTRY BARRIERS

Brands are effective means of creating differentiation aimed to achieve divisions in consumer buying. Differentiation saves the marketer the undesirable effects of commodity markets. Commoditisation implies openness of a buyer to all suppliers. This lack of preference and commitment to a specific supplier makes it easier for a new firm to get established in the market. However successful brands have divided the consumers by polarising their preferences. This poses a significant entry barrier for new players for whom to get a satisfied or committed buyer to shift buying in their favour is a Herculean task. Substantial efforts and investments have to be made in marketing to shake a consumer out of his or her present inertia or loyalty and achieve a state of trial of the new brand. High initial investment required to get a toe hold often defers the payback period by pushing up the break even point. A deferred break even point acts to deter new entry in the market.

Entry barriers created by product differentiation are perhaps the most important in baby care products, OTC drugs and cosmetics. Differentiation acts to deter entry by creating barriers by compelling an entry seeker to spend heavily to overcome existing customer loyalties (Porter 1980). There are a number of products which are easier to manufacture and do not require substantial factory set up costs, yet in these industries only a countable few brands dominate the entire market. Near monopoly like conditions are created by established players by brand building. The intial marketing investments to make presence felt in these markets are so high that only a few firms with substantial financial muscle are able to enter. Even a company like Colgate failed in getting their brand of Optima shampoo establish in the highly differentiated shampoo market. Presently established brands are incumbent players who enjoy monopoly like situations. Strong brands like Intel in micro processors, IBM and Accenture in e-business solutions and Ferrari in sports cars enjoy monopoly like situations in consumers' minds although on paper these industries are fully competitive.

ADVOCACY

Among various characteristics power brands are differentiated on the basis of something called 'emotional capital' (Temporal 2002). These brands create emotional capital on the basis of: creating personal relevance; evoking powerful emotions; developing immense trust; engendering loyalty and friendship and providing great experience. An emotionally satisfying experience then becomes a talking point for the consumer. Great brands do not follow a defensive approach in their marketing. The guiding light for their marketing does not aim at merely satisfying consumers but aims to upgrade customer experience to higher levels. Achieving customer satisfaction toward extremely satisfied or totally satisfied levels converts consumers into brand advocates. Brand advocates feel enthusiastic and spread the good word about the brand. These highly satisfied customers are called 'apostles' who act like unpaid sales people for the business. Apostles tend to be happy to talk about their experiences with others and thereby fulfil the twin roles of communicating about the brand and simultaneously make personal recommendations.

Brands like Zippo lighter, Apple, Beetle and Harley have their committed cult followers who just cannot avoid but bring these brands into their conversations. A pleasant journey on Virgin Atlantic or Kingfisher is shared in social circles. When consumers assume this kind of unpaid for salesmanship the brand stands to gain that which no amount of commercially paid communications can achieve. Word of mouth is more trusted especially if it comes from a friend or somebody close. The role of word of mouth assumes particular importance in the current time of diminished trust. Advice rather than advertising scores high in winning customer conviction. People do not talk without reasons. The themes of conversations normally revolve around central life interests. Super brands go on to become pillars of central life interest. Many luxury brands like Armani and Chanel have brilliantly leveraged the power of word of mouth. It is not rare to see people bring these brands to either confirm or express their identities.

INSULATION

Marketing by nature involves competition. Companies mount attacks on their competitors in order to snatch customers from each other. Consider the following: Colgate was attacked by Pepsodent and a host of other brands; Britannia historically fought a battle with Parle in biscuits but now it is assaulted by Priya Gold; Iodex was surprised by Moov and HMT was taken by surprise by Titan and now a plethora of brands vie for a share of the wrist watch market. Marketers lose when their customers shift buying to some other brand.

Brands can provide effective insulation against competitive attacks by pulling customers out of decision making. Brands help customers form habits and resort to routine based buying. This way customer openness to competitive information is significantly reduced. A committed and loyal consumer whose brand relationships are based on emotional and value identification does not entertain contradictory information that extols virtues of a rival brand. Brand loyalty based especially on psychological anchors acts to discard information that challenges the existing notions and beliefs. This way the buyer is locked in a close loop where only confirmatory information is sought and received which further strengthens the brand beliefs and commitment. Rational appeals to disrupt emotional commitment tend to be futile because consumer filters do not allow communications to move further up in the perceptual process. And it is difficult to compare and contrast emotions on their value. So if a buyer likes blue colour it is not possible to revise his or her liking for some other colour because the choice is not based on hard concrete reason. Brands transform and make market entities into something not easily contested.

SUBSTITUTION

Marketing is an endless battle for gaining control over the market. The competition policies promulgated by government tend to strip marketers of monopolistic gains available to incumbent players in structurally blocked entry conditions. Marketers are now forced to tread on a slippery path. As competitors gain entry and their offerings achieve parity the markets degenerate into commodity like status. The absence of differentiation eventually sends the inter-firm rivalry to a paradigm dog-eat-dog situation. The only meaningful way to differentiate offerings gets down to price. Excessive price focus can force firms to operate at wafer thin margins that often lead to collapse.

Consider the television industry. Most of the players now offer almost identical product functionality. Yet the market is prevented from degenerating into a commodity like status. So is true for many other industries. The pressures of commoditisation can be resisted by effective brand building. The onset of product similarity leading to price elastic demand can be blocked by building brand differentiation based on non-product dimensions. Branding is not about product differentiation only. Product is only a part of the brand. The finer contours of brand development revolve around leveraging differentiation possibilities that exist in potential consumers. The consumer triggered differentiation does not happen through product specifications and manufacturing technology. Brands seek to provide very unique and personalised experiences which defy quantification. The psychic overtones of branding transform a commodity like product into a non-physical entity.

Customer resistance to switching and inelasticity has more to do with psycho–social aversion than an un-preferred brand creates although it may perform adequate on the functionality dimension. Often consumers speak of their brand as 'my kind of brand'. Or brand is spoken of as 'friend and companion'. This is where a brand acquires an unequal status from others who struggle to create equality. Inequality built around self expression, identification and emotions pulls a brand outside the boundary of comparison. An incomparability so achieved contributes to the rigidities in consumer demand that works in favour of a brand builder. Great brands are abstractions created around a product which makes them incomparable and un-substitutable, thereby allowing the marketer a greater grip over its consumers.

BRAND ASSET

Brands are no longer ghosts and invisible entities which defy valuation and trading. During the later part of the 20th century businesses have come to realise that a carefully crafted brand like any other conventional asset is both valuable and can be traded in the market. A strong brand is probably the ultimate asset that a business would like to possess. In this regard the observation of John Stuart is most compelling. He once said, 'If this business were split I would give you the land and bricks and mortar and I would take the brands and trade marks, and I would fare better than you' (John Stuart quoted in Pelissier 2009).

In most businesses good companies enjoy a great discrepancy between the book value of their assets and the market value these command. And the market value out does the book value a number of times. This discrepancy is created by the role of intangibles including the brand that the business commands. How much is the contribution made by brand in creating shareholders' value? One such study done by Interbrand and JP Morgan reached the conclusion that on average a brand's contribution to shareholder value exceeds more than one-third of the total value. Some of the world's top company's market capitalisation got a boost from their brand power as high as 70 per cent. For instance the higher end of brand contribution to market capitalisation was estimated to be 71 per cent for McDonald's, 68 per cent for Disney and 51 per cent for Coca Cola; Mercedes Benz was at 47 per cent and IBM at 39 per cent. Brands like any other commodity can be traded among parties willing to sell and buy them. And some brands command astronomical valuations. Consider the valuations of some of the top brands which run into billions of dollars. Brands like Coke, Microsoft, IBM, GE, Intel and Nokia were valued at 69.6, 64.1, 51.2, 41.3, 30.9 and 30 billion US dollars respectively (*The Business Week* 2002).

OTHER CONTRIBUTIONS

Brands have multi-dimensional effects on business besides direct effects on customers and competition. Brands can impact legislators, watch groups, employees and other business partners. Strong brands are less likely to behave in a socially irresponsible manner. This socially consistent behaviour may be prompted by the sheer amount of trust the brand enjoys with its public. An unknown brand does not have much at stake and therefore may be prompted to employ practices for self aggrandisement and short-term gains. As a brand gains iconic status its responsibility towards all stake holders rises. Brands often become victims of excessive scrutiny and surveillance. Stray cases of corporate mis-behaviour are blown out of proportion for their newsworthiness. Strong brands are built on trust and any and very high expectations are imposed on them by various groups. Any deviation therefore is likely to attract high media attention. It is for these pressures that top brands have to maintain high standards of social, ethical and ecologically consistent behaviour.

Branding facilitates business functioning in a number of ways. For instance Infosys is one of the companies that rank very high for potential candidates for making a career for the values that this brand stands for. Infosys ranks among the top most respected companies in India along with corporate brands such as Reliance Industries, Wipro, Hindustan Lever, Maruti Udyog and Dr Reddy's Lab (Ahmed 2008). Corporate respect and reputation acts as a great source of talent and competence attraction in all spheres of business activity. Different corporate brands provide opportun-ities for flowering different kinds of talents. 3M is cherished for innovative culture and Pepsi is known for youthfulness and icono-clasm. Business partners like bankers, suppliers and retailers welcome being part of known brands than the unknown ones. Partners get rewarded economically, socially and psychologically by being associated with a known brand rather than an unknown figure. Japanese companies are valued for their partnership model instead of an arm's length approach. They believe in a win–win game instead of a win–lose game. The partnership model practiced by these companies is driven by collective interest and gain instead of enrichment at others' expense.

A brand's contribution often extends beyond financial wealth. Some brands make active contributions to societal welfare by performance of several corporate social welfare activities. Henry Ford in this context once said, 'the purpose of corporation is to do as much good as we can, everywhere for everybody concerned ... and incidentally to make money' (White 2005: 5). There are various areas where good brands make contributions like environment and ecology, health and wellbeing of people, diversity and human rights and community services. Godfrey Philips is associated with bravery awards initiative which is given to recognise and honour the uncommon spirit of the common man. ONGC's PURA schemes promote, sponsor, manage, construct and assist in any programme given to providing amenities to rural areas in a number of activities. Toothpaste brand Colgate is associated with promotion of oral hygiene so that children have healthy teeth. P&G's Whisper brand is associated with the welfare of the girl child. Dove has an esteem academy which promotes the concept of real beauty. Brand Tata is synonymous with community welfare. Long time back when the concept of social contribution was not known in industry Tata Steel focused on community welfare and its brand communication claimed 'We also make steel'. Thus brand building on the one hand acts as a tool to gain power over the marketplace forces as a means to achieving superlative top line and bottom line performance and on the other hand it also involves attending to the distributive and welfare concerns of society. Accordingly many brands are beginning to lay emphasis on their societal role as the very part of their identity and essence.

CONCLUDING REMARKS

Brand building if done strategically and effectively must culminate into the creation of power brands. Power in the context of branding implies gaining control over the marketplace forces towards furthering the ends of wealth generation. Brands and branding is all about creating monopoly by destroying competition in the minds of consumers. Brands are useful for consumers for their choice simplification role and risk reduction potential. For marketers brands are important for their value addition role. Specifically with effective branding the marketer can alter demand–price relationship, create entry barriers to the potential entrants, command pricing freedom, create customer bonding based on trust and develop insulation from competitive threats. Besides all this brands in their own right have now come to be recognised as tradable assets with specific monetary value. Brands make significant contribution to market capitalisation which far exceeds the book value of the firm. Finally top brands play an important role in contributing to non-business causes to promote welfare in society.

References

Aaker, D. 1991. *Managing Brand Equity*. New York: The Free Press.

Achrol, R. 1997. 'Changes in the Theory of Inter-organizational Relations in Marketing: toward a Network Paradigm', *Journal of Academy of Marketing Science*, 25(9): 9.

Ahmed, Feroz. 2008. 'A Matter of Respect.' Available online at http://www. businessworld.in/index.php/A-Matter-of-Respect.html (downloaded on 06.11.2009).

Anderson, J. 1980. *Cognitive Psychology and Its Implications*. San Francisco: W.H. Freeman.

Ansoff, I. 1965. *Corporate Strategy*. Harmondsworth: Penguin.

Ashkenas, R., T. Ulrich, and S. Herr. 1998. *The Boundaryless Organisation: Breaking the Chains of Organizational Structure*. San Francisco: Jossey-Bass.

Baker, S. and M. Bass. 2003. *New Consumer: Managing a Living System*. West Sussex: John Wiley.

Bettman, J. 1979. *Information Processing Theory of Consumer Choice*. Reading, MA: Addison-Wesley.

Borden, N. 1964. 'The Concept of the Marketing Mix', *Journal of Advertising Research* (June): 2–7.

Business Week/Interbrand. 2005. 'The World's Best Brands.' Available online at http://www.businessweek.com/magazine/toc/06_32/B399606globalbrands. htm (downloaded on 15.09.2009).

Campbell, A., M. Devine, and D. Young. 1990. *A Sense of Mission*. London: The Economist Books.

Chiaravalle, B. and B.F. Schenck. 2006. *Branding for Dummies*. New Jersey: John Wiley.

Colvin, G. 2007. 'Selling P&G', *Fortune*, 17 (September): 75–81.

Confederation of Indian Industry. 2006. 'Theme Paper', The Marketing Summit, New Delhi, 17–18 August.

Culliton, J. 1948. *The Management of Marketing Costs*. Boston, MA: Division of Research, Harvard University.

Damasio, A. 1994. *Descartes' Error: Emotion, Reason, and the Human Brain*. New York: Grosset/Putnam.

Das, P. 2008. 'Nano Man's Car', *Times of India*, 11 January, p. 1.

Davis, S. and C. Meyers. 1998. *Blur: The Speed of Change in the Connected Economy*. New York: Warner Books.

Day, G. 2002. 'Marketing and the CEO's Growth Imperative', Speech delivered to the Marketing Science Institute, Boston, MA, 25 April.

Dick, A. and K. Basu. 1994. 'Customer Loyalty: Toward an Integrated Conceptual Framework', *Journal of the Academy of Marketing Sciences* (Spring): 99–113.

Drawbaugh, K. 2001. *Brands in Balance: Meeting the Challenges to Commercial Identity.* New Delhi: Reuters.

Drucker, P. 1973. *Management: Tasks, Responsibilities, Practices.* New York: Harper and Row, pp. 64–65.

Edward, Helen and Derek Day. 2005. *Creating Passion Brands: Getting to the Heart of Branding.* Pentonville Road, London: Kogan Page.

Edwards, P. 1998. 'The Age of the Trust Brand', *Market Leader* (Winter): 15–19.

Gardner, B.B. and Sidney J. Levy. 1955. 'The Product and the Brand', *Harvard Business Review* (March–April): 55.

Gascoigne, B. 1967. *The Twentieth-century Drama.* London: Hutchinson & Co.

Giddens, A. 1991. *Modernity and Self Identity: Self and Society in the Late Modern Age.* Cambridge, UK: Polity Press.

Gordon. W. and S. Ford-Hutchinson. 2002. 'Brains and Brands: Rethinking the Consumer', *Admap*, 37(1): 47–50.

Gutman, J. 1982. 'A Means–End Chain Model Based on Consumer Categorization Processes', *Journal of Marketing*, 46(2): 60–72.

Holbrook, M. and E. Hirchman. 1982. 'The Experiential Aspects of Consumption: Consumer Fantasies, Feelings and Fun', *Journal of Consumer Behavior*, 9(September): 132–40.

Howard, J. and J. Sheth. 1961. *The Theory of Buyer Behavior.* New York: John Wiley. Available online at http://www.businessworld.in/index.php/A-Matter-of-Respect.html (downloaded on 30.09.2009).

Izard, C. 1977. *Human Emotions.* New York: Plenum Press.

James, W. 1890. *The Principles of Psychology*, Volume 1. Henry Holt.

Jones, J. 1998. *What's in a Brand?* New Delhi: Tata McGraw Hill.

Jones, T. and W. Sasser Jr. 1995. 'Why Satisfied Customers Defect', *Harvard Business Review* (November–December): 88–99.

King, S. 1973. *Developing New Brands.* London: Pitman.

Kukday, K. and N. Mahajan. 2006. 'Romancing the Phone: Nokia's Designer Adds Human Character to Mobile', *The Times of India*, 26 August, p. 17.

Lecture by Archbishop of Sydney, Dr George Pell, at the launch of 'Meaninglessness: The Solutions of Nietzsche, Freud and Rorty' by Michael Casy in the Crypt of St Mary's Cathedral on 4 December 2001.

Levitt, T. 1960.'Marketing Myopia', *Harvard Business Review* (April–May): 45–46.

Levy, S. 1959. 'Symbols for Sale', *Harvard Business Review*, 37(July–August): 117–24.

Maitra, S. 2001. *The Philosophy of Sri Aurobindo.* Pondicherry: Sri Aurobindo Ashram Publication.

Martineau, P. 1957. *Motivation in Advertising*. New York: McGraw Hill.

Maslow, A. 1970. *Motivation and Personality*. New York: Harper & Row.

McCarthy, J. 1996. *Basic Marketing: A Managerial Approach*. Homewood, IL: Irwin.

McCracken, G. 2005. *Culture and Consumption II: Markets, Meanings, and Brand Management*. Bloomington, IN: Indiana University Press.

Merriam-Webster. 2009. *Merriam-Webster Dictionary*. Available online at http://www.merriam-webster.com/dictionary (downloaded on 30.09.2009).

Mitchell, A. 2003. 'Beyond Brand Narcissism', in Nicholas Ind (ed.), *Beyond Branding: How the New Values of Transparency and Integrity Are Changing the World of Brands*, pp. 36–55. London: Kogan Page.

Oxford University Press. *A Dictionary of Finance and Business*. 1997. New Delhi: Oxford University Press.

Pelissier, Joe. 2009. 'Why Branding Is so Important.' Available online at http://ezinearticles.com/?Why-Branding-is-So-Important&id=2058028 (downloaded on 28.08.2009).

Porter, M. 1980. *The Competitive Strategy*. New York: The Free Press.

Quelch, J. and D. Kenny. 1994. 'Extend Profits, Not Product Lines', *Harvard Business Review* (September–October): 153–54.

Ranazzo, S. 1994. *Mythmaking on Madison Avenue*. Chicago, IL: Brobus Publication.

Random House. 2006. *Random House Unabridged Dictionary*. New York: Random House.

Reichheld, F. and W. Sasser Jr. 1990. 'Zero Defections: Quality Comes to Services', *Harvard Business Review* (September–October): 106.

Riezebos, R., B. Kist, and G. Kootstra. 2003. *Brand Management: A Theoretical and Practical Approach*. Harlow, England: Pearson Education.

Sawhney, M. 2006. 'Networking a Growing Planet', *The Economic Times*, 10 August, p. 10.

Schmitt, B. 1999. *Experiential Marketing*. New York: The Free Press.

Selfknowledge.com. 2009. 'Definition of Sight'. Available online at http://www.selfknowledge.com/88281.htm (downloaded on 30.09.2009).

Settle, R. and P. Alreck. 1989. 'Reducing Buyers' Sense of Risk', *Marketing Communications* (January): 34–40.

Shridharan, R. 1999. 'The Car that Changed the Corporation', *Business Today*, 7 February, pp. 60–74.

Shukla, A. 2008. 'In Consumer Custody', *Mint*, 9 June, Campaign 1–Campaign 8.

Singh, P. and M. Biwalkar. 2008. 'Makeover Magic', *Business World*, 26 May, pp. 64–68.

Sloan, P. 1985. 'Klein's Sultry Avedon Ads for Obsession Hit TV', *Advertising Age*, 25 (March): 104.

Streufert, S. and M. Driver. 1971. *The General Incongruity Adaptation Level (GIAL)*, Technical Report 32, Homewood, IL: Dorsey Press.

Taylor, D. 2006. *Brand Vision*. Chichester, England: John Wiley.

Temporal, P. 2002. *Advanced Brand Management: From Vision to Valuation*. Singapore: John Wiley.

The Business Line. 2004. 'P&G Drops Prices of Detergent Brands Ariel, Tide', 03 March 2004. Available online at http://www.thehindubusinessline. com/2004/03/03/stories/2004030300690600.htm (downloaded on 30.09.2009).

The Business Week. 2002. 'The Best Global Brands', 6 August, pp. 95–98.

The Economic Times. 2006. 'Colgate: Brand Equity's Trusted Brand', Brand Equity, 15 February, Mumbai, pp. 1–4.

The Economic Times. 2008. 'Brand Equity', 11 June, pp. 1–4.

The Economist. 1993. 'Shoot out at the Check-Out', 5 June, pp. 69–72.

The Reader's Digest. 2008. 'Trusted Brands 2008: The Ultimate Seal of Consumer Approval', *The Reader's Digest*, May, pp. 134–204.

The Week. 2008. 'Love all Trust Few', *The Week*, 18 May, p. 12.

Tuan, Y. 1980. 'The Significance of the Artifact', *Geographical Review*, 70(4): 462–72.

Valentine, V. and G. Gordon. 2000. 'The 21st Century Consumer: A New Model of Thinking', *Journal of Marketing Research*, 42(2): 185–206.

Watson, T. 1963. *A Business and Its Beliefs*. New York: McGraw Hill.

White, Allen L. 2005. 'Fade, Integrate or Transform:The Future of CSR.' Available online at http://www.jussemper.org/Newsletters/Resources/BSR_Allen-White.pdf (downloaded on 30.09.2009).

Zaltman, G. 2003. *How Customers Think*. Cambridge, MA: Harvard Business Press.

About the Author

Harsh V. Verma is Associate Professor at the Faculty of Management Studies (FMS), University of Delhi, where he teaches courses like Marketing Management, Consumer Behaviour, Marketing of Services and Brand Management. He has taught Services Marketing elective at the Indian Institute of Management Lucknow for several years. He is actively involved in training executives of both Indian companies and MNCs in the marketing area. Some of the companies for which he has conducted training include Nestle, BSNL, Siemens, GAIL, State Bank of India, Indian Oil Corporation, Taj Hotels and TATA Motors. His article 'Packaging: A Magic Tool for the Marketer' was reprinted in the *World's Executive Digest* as one of the best management articles worldwide. He has published books like *Brand Management* and *Marketing of Services: Strategies for Success*. His book *Marketing of Services: Strategies for Success* was among the first few in the area of services marketing and it won the DMA Escorts Book of the Year Award in 1993.